BRITISH GEOLOGICAL SURVEY

I H FORSYTH
I H S HALL and
A A McMILLAN

Geology of the Airdrie district

CONTRIBUTORS
Geophysics
M J Arthur
Palaeontology
P J Brand
D K Graham
Hydrogeology
N S Robins

Memoir for 1:50 000 Geological Sheet 31W (Scotland)

LONDON: HMSO 1996

First published 1996

ISBN 0 11 884508 X

Bibliographical reference

FORSYTH, I H, HALL, I H S, and McMILLAN, A A. 1996. Geology of the Airdrie district. *Memoir of the British Geological Survey*, Sheet 31W (Scotland).

Authors

I H Forsyth, BSc
I H S Hall, BSc
A A McMillan, BSc
British Geological Survey, Edinburgh

Contributors

M J Arthur, MSc, DIC
P J Brand, BSc
D K Graham, BA
British Geological Survey, Edinburgh

N S Robins, MSc
British Geological Survey, Wallingford

Printed in the UK for HMSO

Dd 301319 C8 4/96

Other publications of the Survey dealing with this and adjoining districts

BOOKS

British Regional Geology
The Midland Valley of Scotland, 3rd edition, 1985

Memoirs
The economic geology of the Central Coalfield of Scotland, Area I, 1937, Area II, 1917, Area V, 1926 and Area VII, 1920
The geology of the Glasgow district (Sheet 30E), in preparation

BGS Reports
Lithostratigraphy of the late Devonian and early Carboniferous rocks in the Midland Valley of Scotland, Vol. 18, No. 3, 1986

MAPS

1:625 000
Geological (North) 1979
Quaternary (North) 1977
Aeromagnetic (North) 1972
Bouguer Gravity anomaly (North) 1981

1:250 000
Argyll, Solid, 1987, Aeromagnetic, 1981, Bouguer Gravity, 1979
Clyde, Solid, 1985, Aeromagnetic, 1980, Bouguer Gravity, 1985
Tay-Forth, Solid, 1986, Aeromagnetic, 1981, Bouguer Gravity, 1979
Borders, Solid, 1986, Aeromagnetic, 1980, Bouguer Gravity, 1981

1:50 000
Sheet 23W (Hamilton) Solid, 1995; Drift, 1995
Sheet 30E (Glasgow) Solid, 1994; Drift, 1995
Sheet 31W (Airdrie) Solid, 1992; Drift, 1993
Sheet 31E (Falkirk) Solid, 1995; Solid & Drift, 1995
Sheet 39W (Stirling) Solid, 1974; Drift, 1974

Geology of the Airdrie district

The district described in this memoir lies at the heart of the Midland Valley and includes the eastern part of Glasgow and the large conurbations of Airdrie, Coatbridge, Cumbernauld, Kilsyth, Kirkintilloch and the northern part of Motherwell, together forming one of the most densely populated areas in Scotland. By contrast, the Kilsyth Hills, which occupy more than 100 sq km in the north of the district, are sparsely populated and mostly given over to hill farming and forestry.

The oldest rocks that crop out in the district were deposited on the coastal floodplain of a major river system during the early Carboniferous. Marginal marine conditions became established for a time prior to recommencement of fluvial sedimentation as uplift took place in the Highlands. In mid-Dinantian times, a major break in sedimentation occurred along the southern margin of the Kilsyth Hills which was probably related to the uprise of the South Campsie Linear Vent System. This and a series of other linear vent systems, all with a Caledonoid trend, became the sources of a major episode of vulcanicity. These vents remained active till the later stages of vulcanism when eruption was confined to a large central volcano. This thick sequence of mainly alkaline basaltic lavas is typical of that which occurs in continental rift systems throughout the world. After the cessation of vulcanicity in the late mid-Dinantian, cyclothemic sequences accumulated in fluviodeltaic and fluvial environments, punctuated by frequent short-lived marine transgressions, throughout most of the Carboniferous. During the deposition of the Limestone Coal Formation and the Coal Measures, deltaic conditions prevailed allowing frequent and sometimes prolonged colonisation of the delta-top by plants which were subsequently preserved as coal. The Carboniferous rocks were then invaded by two groups of igneous intrusions. The earlier group comprises late Carboniferous–early Permian quartz-dolerite sills and dykes, which occur extensively in the district. The later group is a complex of olivine-dolerite sills of mid-Permian age which only occurs in the south-west of the district.

The final chapter in the geological history of the district was the repeated glaciations during the Quaternary, the effects of which are clearly displayed in the present landscape.

Tephra cone developed on early lavas of the Clyde Plateau Volcanic Formation, Meikle Bin [665 825] (D4863).

CONTENTS

FIGURES

PLATES

TABLES

PREFACE

This memoir provides the first general account since 1879 of the geology of the area which includes eastern Glasgow and extends from the Kilsyth Hills in the north to the Cathkin Braes in the south and beyond Cumbernauld and Airdrie in the east. Despite the fact that the southern part of the area is one of the most densely populated and industrialised parts in Scotland, the northern area is sparsely populated, has pleasant scenery and many features of considerable interest and importance in understanding the geological development of the Midland Valley. The central and southern parts are rich in industrial archaeology, the coals, ironstones and fireclays of Carboniferous age having supported a thriving mining industry during the 19th and early part of the 20th centuries. Mining reserves became uneconomical in recent times although there is potential for further opencast mining of coal and fireclay. Hard rock aggregate is currently being utilised and there are viable resources of sand and gravel.

A comprehensive description of the stratigraphy is given here. The locations of old mine workings are essential in the land-use planning necessary to facilitate the transition from heavy to light industry which is currently taking place and therefore they too are described.

Peter J Cook, DSc, CGeol, FGS
Director

British Geological Survey
Kingsley Dunham Centre
Keyworth
Nottingham NG12 5GG

March 1996

ACKNOWLEDGEMENTS

The memoir was written mainly by Mr I H Forsyth and Mr I H S Hall. The Quaternary chapter was written by Mr A A McMillan. It was compiled by Mr I H S Hall and edited by Drs D J Fettes and G C Clark.

The section on the Clyde Plateau Volcanic Formation is largely based on notes and data from thin sections and analyses provided by Dr P M Craig. The Carboniferous macrofauna were revised by Mr P J Brand and Dr R B Wilson, and the Carboniferous miospores were identified by Dr B Owens. The Quaternary macrofauna were identified by Mr D K Graham and the microfauna by Miss D M Gregory and Dr I P Wilkinson. Photographs were mainly taken by Mr T Bain and Mr F I MacTaggart.

The cores and samples from boreholes, drilled by the Geological Survey in 1975–78 to examine the Carboniferous succession and in 1986 to investigate the stratigraphy of the Quaternary sediments, were examined by Dr P M Craig, Mr M A E Browne, Mr I H Forsyth, Mr I H S Hall, Mr K I G Lawrie and Mr A A McMillan. The cores from boreholes drilled by civil engineering contractors to investigate foundation conditions and exploratory boreholes drilled by British Coal were examined by Mr M A E Browne, Mr J M Dean, Mr I H Forsyth, Mr D N Halley, Mrs S M Jones and Mr K I G Lawrie.

NOTES

Throughout the memoir the word 'district' refers to the area covered by the 1:50 000 Airdrie (31W) Sheet.

Boreholes listed in Appendix 1 are held by the British Geological Survey, Murchison House, West Mains Road, Edinburgh EH9 3LA.

National Grid references are given in square brackets; all lie within the 100 km square NS.

HISTORY OF THE SURVEY OF THE AIRDRIE SHEET

The Airdrie district is covered by Sheet 31W of the geological map of Scotland which was originally surveyed by J Geikie, E Hull, R L Jack and B N Peach and published in Solid and Drift versions at a scale of one inch to one mile in 1875. The area was resurveyed between 1904 and 1919 by C B Crampton, L W Hinxman, B N Peach, E B Bailey, C T Clough, J S G Wilson, E M Anderson, R G Carruthers and W B Wright and revised editions of the Solid and Drift maps were published in 1924. The western half of the Airdrie district was published in 1911 as part of the Glasgow District Special Sheet. A second edition of the Special Sheet, which included additional information, was published in 1931 as separate Solid and Drift maps. Resurvey of the district was commenced in 1953, the Solid geology being completed in 1986 and the Drift in 1990. The work was financed in part by the Department of the Environment between 1982 and 1989 during land-use-for-planning studies in Glasgow, Airdrie–Coatbridge and Motherwell. The survey was carried out by Mr I H Forsyth, Mr A A McMillan, Dr P M Craig, Dr W A Read, Mr I B Cameron and Mr M A E Browne, with contributions by Mr D N Halley, Mr A M Aitken, Mrs S M Jones, Mr I H S Hall and Mr J I Chisholm under the supervision of Messrs J Knox, T R M Lawrie, E G Poole and J I Chisholm. Separate Solid and Drift editions of the Airdrie Sheet have been published at the scale of 1:50 000.

The first survey was accompanied by a Sheet Explanation published in 1879, and the part which lies on the Glasgow Special Sheet was described in a special memoir of the Glasgow District, the 1st edition being published in 1911 and a 2nd edition in 1925. The memoirs describing the economic geology of the Central Coalfield of Scotland, Areas I, II, V and VII, also refer to the Airdrie district, though the most recent of these was published in 1937.

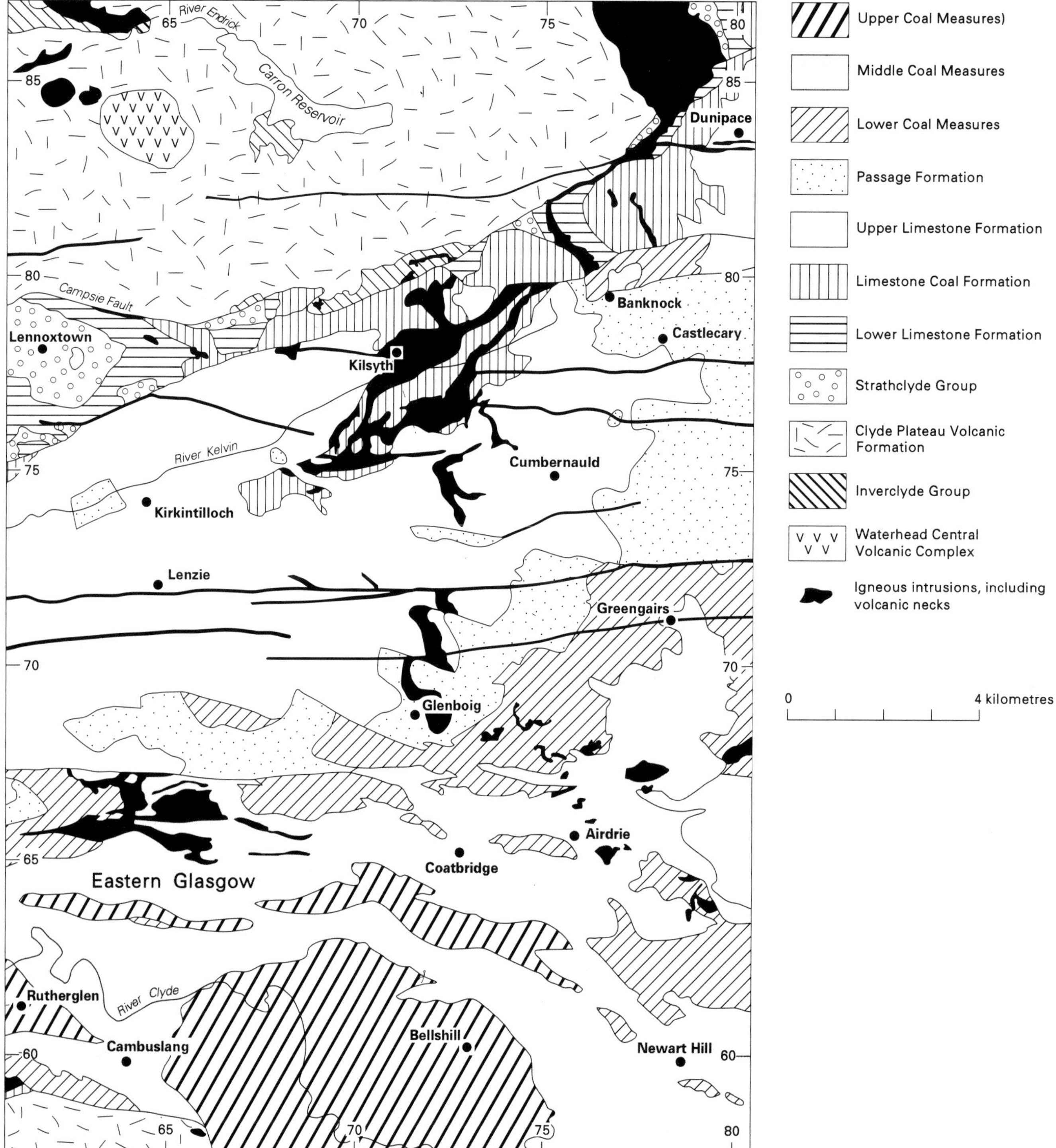

Figure 1 Outline geology of the Airdrie district.

ONE

Introduction

The Airdrie district, which is described in this memoir, comprises the area covered by Sheet 31W of the 1:50 000 geological map of Scotland. In the northern part the district encompasses the Kilsyth Hills, the eastern part of the Campsie Fells and the southern part of the Gargunnock Hills which together form a 6 km-wide block of high ground bounded along its southern margin by a bold scarp controlled by the Campsie Fault. To the south of these hills is lower undulating ground which extends as far as the Clyde valley and then rises again in the south-west to the Cathkin Braes. Differential resistance to erosion of the different rock types is clearly reflected by the nature of the topography. Almost all the features of prominent relief are due to the presence of extrusive or intrusive igneous rocks. The greater part of the high ground in the north, and the Cathkin Braes in the south, are formed by the resistant lavas and associated intrusions of the Lower Carboniferous Clyde Plateau Volcanic Formation (Figure 1). Older strata, also of Lower Carboniferous age, consisting of the fluvial sandstones and cornstones of the Kinnesswood Formation and the marginally marine mudstones with cementstones of the Ballagan Formation, are only seen in small areas north of the Campsie Fault where the scarp has been eroded back, in the lower ground of the Endrick valley and south of the Carron Valley Reservoir (Figure 1). South of the Campsie Fault the lower ground is occupied by a complete sequence of younger, less resistant cyclic sedimentary rocks of Lower and Upper Carboniferous age. During the late Carboniferous and Permian these rocks were intruded by sills and dykes of doleritic composition which now give rise to prominent low flat-topped hills with abrupt escarpments and long, wall-like features. The undulating nature of this area is also formed by numerous drumlins deposited by glaciers during the Quaternary and by two broad valleys, the Kelvin–Bonny Valley and the Clyde Valley, which run across the district.

The Carboniferous strata consist of sandstones and mudstones with limestones, coals, ironstones and seatrocks, which were laid down in fluvial and fluviodeltaic environments that were established after the submergence of the volcanic rocks. The succession shows the effects of tectonic activity, being punctuated by unconformities and nonsequences (Figure 2). The most important of these occurred in mid-Dinantian times when erosion of strata preceded the outpouring of the subaerial lavas of the Clyde Plateau Volcanic Formation, but the presence of sandstones with erosive bases, notably near the top of the Limestone Coal Formation, and throughout the Upper Limestone and Passage formations, indicates intermittent tectonism throughout most of the Carboniferous. Subsequently, suites of quartz-dolerite and alkali-dolerite rocks were intruded into the sedimentary sequence during the late Carboniferous and Permian respectively.

During the Quaternary, the district was covered on several occasions by ice sheets which moulded the topography and laid down extensive deposits of till, partly in the form of drumlins, and fluvioglacial sand and gravel.

The coal seams, ironstone bands and the seatrocks, which were sources of fireclay, became the raw materials for the heavy industry which flourished in this area. Several large conurbations grew up round the centres of industry and include the eastern part of Glasgow, Airdrie, Coatbridge, Cumbernauld, Kilsyth, Kirkintilloch and the northen part of Motherwell, making this one of the most densely populated areas in Scotland.

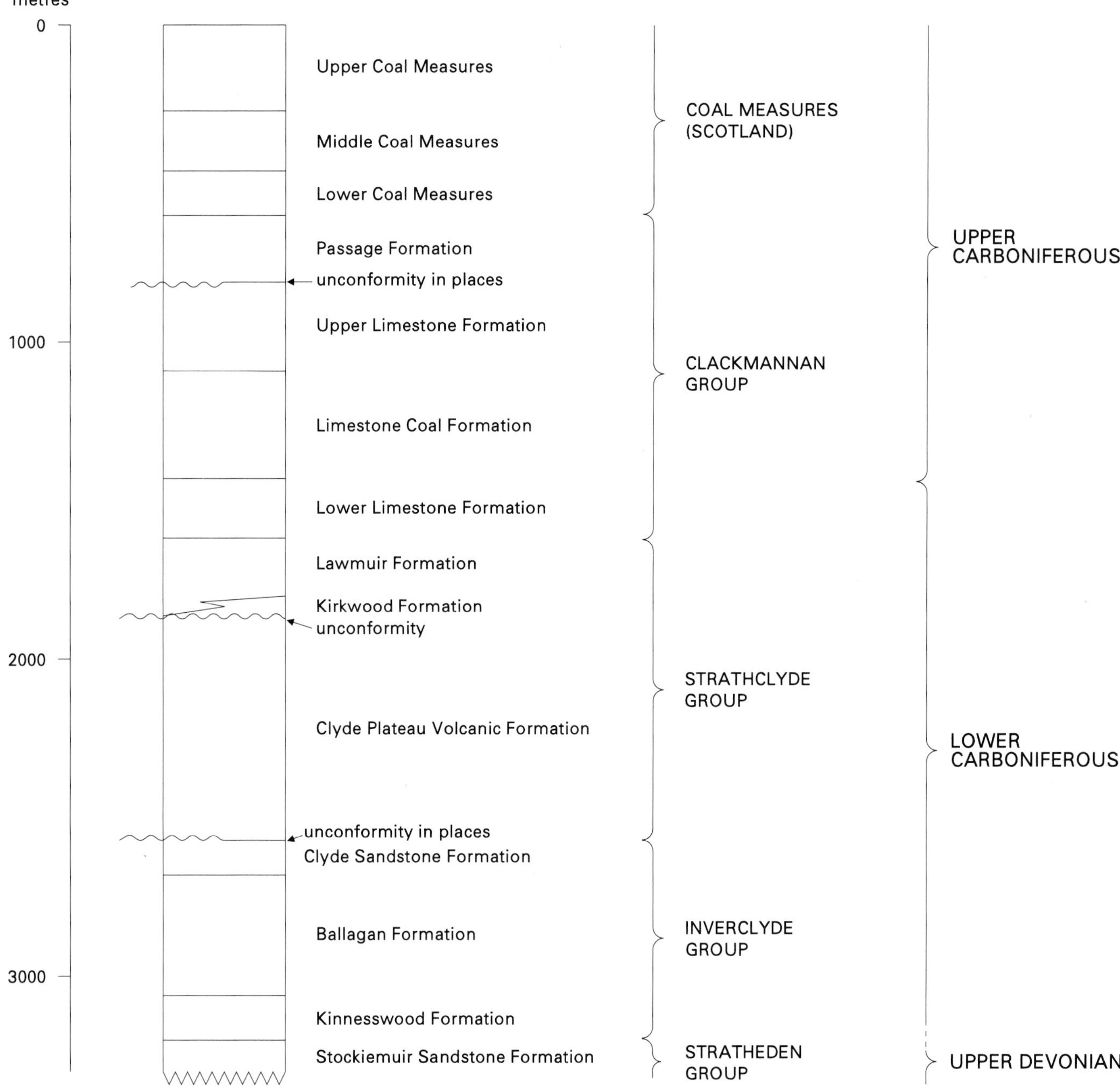

Figure 2 Generalised sequence of Devonian and Carboniferous rocks in the Airdrie district.

TWO
Devonian

Strata of Devonian age do not crop out within the Airdrie district. However xenoliths, thought to be of Lower Devonian strata, occur in intrusions north-west of Lennoxtown and the upper part of the Upper Devonian was intersected in a borehole drilled north of Kilsyth.

LOWER DEVONIAN

Xenoliths of probable Lower Devonian material occur in two narrow NW-trending dykes which lie about 1.5 km to the north-west of Lennoxtown [624 796]. The more northerly dyke has an extraordinary concentration of cobble-like quartzose and granitic rocks in a teschenitic matrix. The cobbles are very similar to those found in Lower Devonian conglomerates which occur along the Highland Boundary Fault zone at Balmaha on the east side of Loch Lomond. Thin-section examination shows the quartzose rocks to have suffered severe thermal and possibly metasomatic effects with the production of glass, now devitrified, and tridymite, now inverted (written communication, A Herriot, May 1991). The southerly dyke encloses a large subrounded block of baked sandstone.

UPPER DEVONIAN

The 36 m of strata drilled below the base of the Kinnesswood Formation in the BGS Tak-ma-doon Borehole [7291 8053] (Figure 3), are thought to be of Upper Devonian age and have been assigned to the Stratheden Group (Paterson and Hall, 1986). They consist of red, and grey-purple, medium- and coarse-grained sandstones with scattered mudstone clasts and quartz pebbles overlain with a sharp contact by fine- and medium-grained whitish, pale green or pink sandstones without clasts or pebbles of the Kinnesswood Formation. Cross-lamination in the Upper Devonian sandstones is common, cementation is poor in places and locally calcareous; small rather diffuse concretions occur patchily throughout.

The sandstones are very similar in lithology to those assigned to the Upper Old Red Sandstone (Gargunnock Sandstones of Read, in Francis et al., 1970) which occurs at the same stratigraphical horizon along the northern side of the Gargunnock Hills, some 6 km to the north of the district. The Gargunnock Sandstones are normally brick-red in colour, but locally are bleached to a whitish or pale greenish colour by the thermal affects of dykes and by leaching below a local unconformity. Both mechanisms may have been operative to cause the bleaching of the sedimentary rocks from the Tak-ma-doon Borehole.

THREE

Carboniferous — general

The entire area of the Airdrie district is underlain by strata of Carboniferous age. The oldest are unfossiliferous sedimentary rocks of the Kinnesswood Formation, the lowest unit of the Inverclyde Group, and are probably mostly of early Carboniferous age. These strata, which are mainly red and white sandstones with thin beds of concretionary limestone, were deposited in an environment transitional between the arid or semiarid conditions in which the red fluvial and aeolian sandstones of the Upper Devonian were laid down and the humid environment in which the mainly grey fluviodeltaic and marine Carboniferous rocks were deposited. A return to semiarid conditions occurred in the late Carboniferous when the region was uplifted and the Upper Coal Measures were oxidised and reddened. These climatic changes were due to the position of the Midland Valley relative to the equator, drifting from some distance south of the equator in the late Devonian to low latitudes in the early Silesian and well north of the equator by the end of the Carboniferous.

During Lower Carboniferous times normal sedimentation was interrupted by a period of major subaerial volcanic activity during which over 400 m of alkali basalts were erupted. These volcanic rocks cover a surface area of more than 100 km^2 in the Airdrie district and are thought to occur at depth under a considerable area of the younger Carboniferous strata.

CLASSIFICATION

A formal lithostratigraphical nomenclature has recently been applied to the late Devonian and early Carboniferous of the central and western parts of the Midland Valley of Scotland (Paterson and Hall, 1986), whereby formation and group names have been erected and defined. Subsequently, the group names have been applied to and new formations proposed for the sequence in Fife (Browne, 1986). In the Lothians the group names were also found to be valid (Chisholm et al., 1989) and in that area further new formations were erected and defined.

The classification erected by Paterson and Hall included all the Lower Carboniferous up to the base of the Hurlet Limestone (Table 1). Above this unit the presence of widespread limestones, marine bands and coal horizons allows correlations to be made across the Midland Valley on a basis of marker-band stratigraphy. All the units mapped above the base of the Hurlet Limestone are defined by marine bands which are considered to be lithological markers defining lithostratigraphical units. In accordance with the protocol established by the North American Commission on Stratigraphic Nomenclature (1983), these lithostratigraphical units are considered to be formations and have been assigned to newly established groups (Table 1). Since the definitions of lower and upper boundaries have not been changed, previous descriptions are still valid and in view of the general familiarity with longstanding names, these have been modified as little as possible in the new classification. Thus, the name Lower Limestone Formation replaces the term Lower Limestone Group.

Lithostratigraphy of the Lower Carboniferous (Table 1)

Classification of all except the highest part of the Lower Carboniferous has been discussed, type sections erected and formal names defined by Paterson and Hall (1986) and Chisholm et al. (1989). The lithostratigraphy so defined includes all the strata up to base of the Hurlet Limestone, traditionally taken as the top of the Calciferous Sandstone Measures. These strata are overlain by a dominantly argillaceous cyclic sequence with sandstones, thin limestones and a few coals. This sequence, which occurs between the base of the Hurlet Limestone and the top of the Top Hosie Limestone, was long referred to as the Lower Limestone Group; it has now been renamed the Lower Limestone Formation and has been placed in the Clackmannan Group.

Lithostratigraphy of the Upper Carboniferous (Table 1)

The Upper Carboniferous starts with the Limestone Coal Formation (formerly the Limestone Coal Group). The formation comprises a sequence of dominantly arenaceous cyclothems with mudstones, seatrocks, coals and ironstones. Two marine bands and several *Lingula* bands are present but marine limestone occurs only very locally. Stratigraphically above is a succession of dominantly arenaceous cyclothems with mudstones, marine limestones and thin coals forming the Upper Limestone Formation (formerly the Upper Limestone Group). The succeeding strata, which are mainly sandstones with thin marine bands, comprise the Passage Formation (formerly the Passage Group). The overlying fluviodeltaic coal bearing sequence is divided into Lower, Middle and Upper Coal Measures at the Vanderbeckei (Queenslie) and Aegiranum (Skipsey's) marine bands respectively. The Lower Limestone Formation, the Limestone Coal Formation, the Upper Limestone Formation and the Passage Formation have been assigned to the newly erected Clackmannan Group. The Lower, Middle and Upper Coal Measures are considered to be informal units and are placed in the Coal Measures (Scotland).

Table 1 Classification of the Carboniferous.

Subsystem	Series		Stages	Miospore zones	Lithostratigraphical units	
Upper Carboniferous (Silesian)	Westphalian	C	Bolsovian	XI		Coal Measures (Scotland)
				X	Upper Coal Measures	
				IX	Aegiranum Marine Band	
		B	Duckmantian	VIII	Middle Coal Measures	
				VII	Vanderbeckei Marine Band	
		A	Langsettian	VI	Lower Coal Measures	
				SS	Lowstone Marine Band	
	Namurian		Chokerian–Yeadonian	FR	Passage Formation	Clackmannan Group
				KV		
				SO		
			Arnsbergian	TK	Castlecary Limestone Upper Limestone Orchard Limestone	
			Pendleian	> NC	Formation Index Limestone	
					Limestone Coal Formation	
Lower Carboniferous (Dinantian)	Viséan		Brigantian	> VF	Top Hosie Limestone Lower Limestone Formation Hurlet Limestone	
			Asbian >	> NM > TC	Lawmuir Formation / Kirkwood Formation	Strathclyde Group
			Holkerian Arundian		Clyde Plateau Volcanic Formation	
			Chadian >	> Pu	Clyde Sandstone Formation	Inverclyde Group
	Tournaisian		Ivorian and Hastarian >	> CM	Ballagan Formation	
					Kinnesswood Formation	

Chronostratigraphy and biostratigraphy

The base of the Carboniferous is internationally defined by the presence of certain marine fossils. These fossils have not been found in Scotland; consequently the base cannot be defined chronostratigraphically. Miospores are the only fossils of any biostratigraphical significance in the lowest Carboniferous strata in Scotland. The Ballagan Formation is placed in the CM Miospore Zone, the earliest zone which can be recognised in Scotland (Table 1). At least two lower Carboniferous miospore zones can be recognised elsewhere; in the Airdrie district these lower zones are thought to be represented by at least the top part of the unfossiliferous Kinnesswood Formation. Hence, at least part of the Kinnesswood Formation is considered to be of Lower Carboniferous age.

The top of the Dinantian is taken at the lowest recorded occurrence of the goniatite *Cravenoceras* about 1 m below the Top Hosie Limestone.

The overlying Silesian strata are divided into the Namurian and Westphalian series which in turn are subdivided into stages, although only some of the diagnostic goniatites are present. The base of the Westphalian is defined by the presence of *Gastrioceras subcrenatum*. This goniatite has not been found in Scotland and the base of the Lower Coal Measures has been taken at a suitable arbitrary position which, within the present district, is the Lowstone Marine Band (Table 1). Miospore evidence from boreholes in the Kincardine area suggests that one of the marine bands in the group collectively known as No. 6 Marine Band of the Passage Formation is the equivalent of the Subcrenatum Marine Band and consequently the base of the Westphalian may lie within the upper part of the Passage Formation. However, in the present district, No. 6 Marine Band group is represented by one *Lingula* band and that is only known in the Castlecary area.

FOUR

Lower Carboniferous (Dinantian)

The Lower Carboniferous strata are assigned to the Inverclyde Group, comprising the Kinnesswood Formation, the Ballagan Formation and the Clyde Sandstone Formation; to the Strathclyde Group, consisting of the Clyde Plateau Volcanic Formation, the Kirkwood Formation, and the Lawmuir Formation; and to the Lower Limestone Formation, the lowest unit of the Clackmannan Group (see Table 1).

INVERCLYDE GROUP

Rocks of this group are exposed in the Airdrie district only to the north of the Campsie Fault along the southern margin of the Kilsyth Hills, and in the Carron Valley.

Kinnesswood Formation

The rocks of the Kinnesswood Formation consist of red, yellow, grey-purple and white cross-bedded sandstones with nodules and thin beds of concretionary limestone (cornstone). Fossils have not been found in these strata, either in the Airdrie or adjacent districts, but general considerations suggest that they are probably mostly of early Carboniferous age (Paterson and Hall, 1986). The rocks, which only crop out in small faulted areas north and north-west of Kilsyth, were laid down on an alluvial plain which occupied a large part of the Scottish Midland Valley at this time. The cross-bedded sandstones were deposited in river channels and the cornstones formed in soil profiles that developed under the influence of a semiarid climate on the associated floodplains.

The only good exposures of Kinnesswood Formation strata within the Airdrie district occur about 2 km north of Kilsyth, where about 40 m of the lower part of the formation is seen in the Garrel Burn [713 795] in a faulted block and, upstream [712 797], the top 50 m of the succession are exposed. In the lower part of the sequence, fine-grained rather friable, tan-coloured sandstones are interbedded with coarser, paler sandstones with a siliceous cement in places. Small quartz pebbles are present in both facies but are much more common in the coarser sandstones. These sandstones formed from typical channel-fill sediments of a braided river system. Finer-grained sedimentary rocks with calcareous concretions which occur at the top of this section are thought to represent overbank deposits. The top 50 m of the Kinnesswood Formation, seen further upstream in the Garrel Burn, comprise medium-grained, red-yellow and grey-purple sandstones interbedded with dark red or purplish, fine-grained sandstones, siltstones and mudstones. The medium-grained sandstones contain scattered quartz pebbles and are commonly cross-laminated. They are interpreted as channel-fill deposits and the finer-grained rocks are thought to have formed as overbank deposits. Cornstones are usually found in the overbank sediments, but calcrete nodules and incipient concretions are found throughout the sequence. Silicification is not uncommon in the cornstones.

A complete sequence of the Kinnesswood Formation, comprised largely of sandstone, was drilled nearby in the BGS Tak-ma-doon Borehole [7291 8053] where the thickness was found to be 146 m (Figure 3). Here, cornstones are not developed in the basal 40 m, though some small carbonate concretions are present throughout the whole succession. Mudstone and carbonate clasts and small quartz pebbles are also present throughout, usually being more abundant at or near the base of sandstone units. Many of the medium- and coarse-grained sandstones are cross-laminated, fine upwards, and have erosive bases, typical of channel-fill deposits.

Rocks of the Kinnesswood Formation were also proved at depth in the BGS Clachie Bridge Borehole [6447 8368] which drilled 20 m of brecciated cornstone-bearing sandstone at the bottom of the borehole (Figure 3 and Craig, 1980).

To the north of the Airdrie district, Read (in Francis et al., 1970), recorded 400 m of Kinnesswood Formation strata at the western end of the Gargunnock Hills [620 915], the succession thinning eastwards to just over 100 m in the Gargunnock Burn [708 934], some 10 km to the east.

Ballagan Formation

The succeeding Ballagan Formation, consisting of grey mudstones with thin nodular beds of dolomitic limestone (cementstone), was deposited in a coastal-plain environment subject to fluctuating salinity and periodic dessication. There are no good natural sections of Ballagan Formation strata in the Airdrie district. Outcrops are restricted to small isolated areas along the southern flanks of the Kilsyth Hills and a small area in the Endrick valley [625 865] where the formation has been mapped on the basis of the presence of small, usually degraded, exposures of grey mudstone with thin nodular limestone beds. The lithologies are typical of those of the Ballagan Formation seen in adjacent areas, for example the Stirling district (Read in Francis et al., 1970) where the formation has a thickness of about 300 m and thins eastward.

The BGS Clachie Bridge Borehole [6447 8368] drilled 166 m of vent breccia composed dominantly of Ballagan Formation lithologies (Figure 3). This gives an approximate thickness for the sequence in this area. The BGS

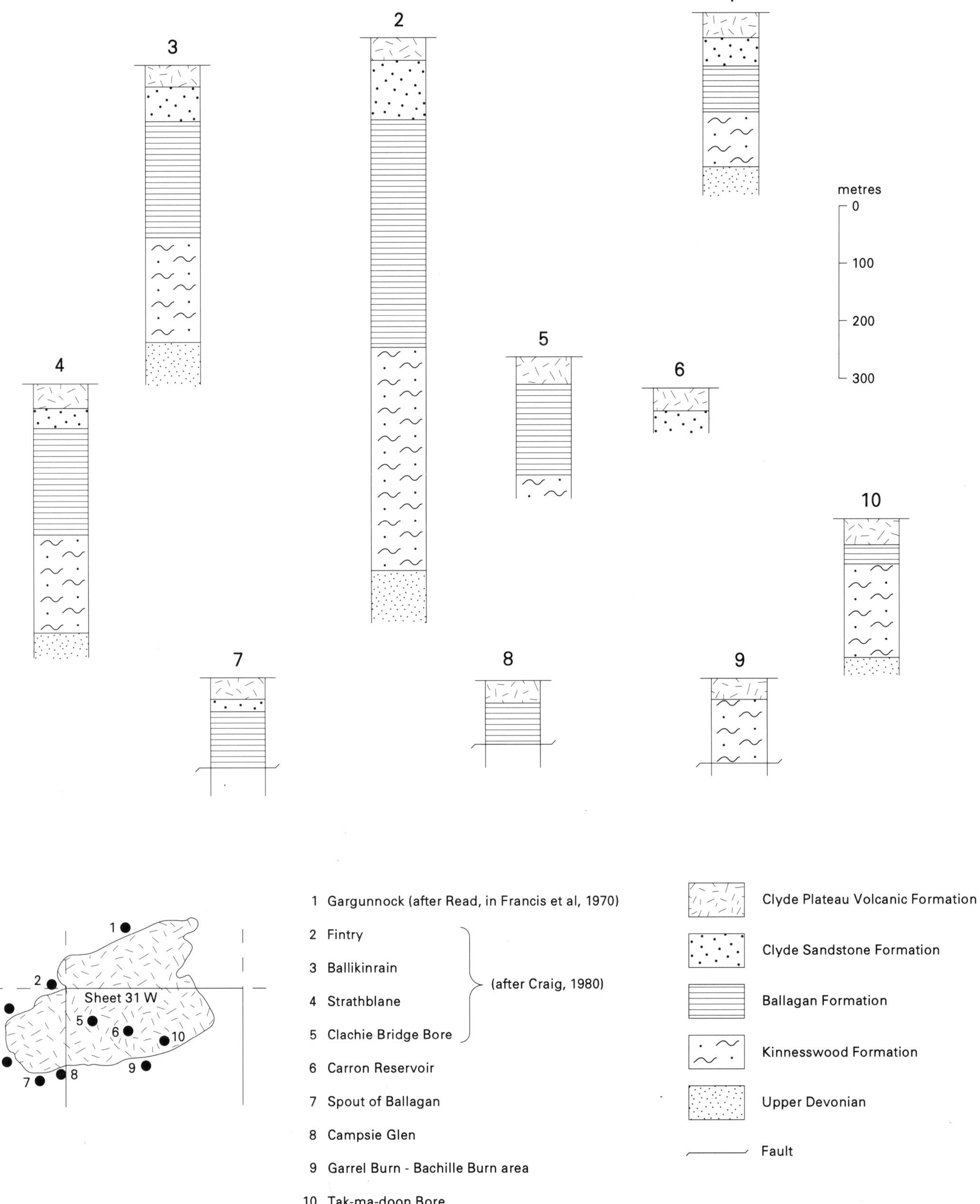

Figure 3 Correlation of the Inverclyde Group in and around the Campsie–Kilsyth Hills.

Tak-ma-doon Borehole [7291 8053] proved the Ballagan Formation to be only 20 m thick in that area and 2 km to the west, in the Bachille Burn [707 793], the lowest flow of the Clyde Plateau Volcanic Formation appears to lie directly on strata of the Kinnesswood Formation (Figure 3). The 20 m sequence drilled in the Tak-ma-doon Borehole was dominantly grey mudstone and siltstone interbedded with many dolomitic cementstones, which are predominantly 10–15 cm thick but range up to 0.5 m. Similar lithologies also occur in sporadic outcrops in the Drumnessie Burn [731 803].

The few fossils which have been found in Ballagan Formation strata in the Airdrie district are ostracods, an isolated fish scale in the Tak-ma-doon Borehole and one occurrence of an algal limestone with ?*Spirorbis* in the Corrie Burn [6771 7896]. In adjacent areas, the principal evidence for a marine influence on sedimentation is the presence of gypsum and salt pseudomorphs. Only gypsum has been recorded in the district, seen in small quantities in the Tak-ma-doon Borehole.

Clyde Sandstone Formation

A return to a fluviatile depositional environment is seen in the overlying Clyde Sandstone Formation, the youngest division of the Inverclyde Group. The sandstones of the formation are coarser than those of the Kinnesswood Formation and, though commonly calcareous and concretionary, do not develop true cornstones.

The Clyde Sandstone Formation is present only in small areas near Fintry and south of the Carron Valley Reservoir. At Fintry [620 859] its presence is largely inferred by extrapolation from known occurrences to the north where the sequence is 100 m thick. South of the Carron Valley Reservoir [685 832] poor exposures of sandstones with a concretionary limestone have been assigned to the Clyde Sandstone Formation but 4 km to the west they appear to be absent in the Clachie Bridge Borehole. They are absent along the southern margin of the Kilsyth Hills in the district.

STRATHCLYDE GROUP

A period of localised uplift and erosion at the beginning of Strathclyde Group times, thought to be due to magmatic updoming, was followed by a major volcanic episode which produced the Clyde Plateau Volcanic Formation of the Kilsyth and Cathkin hills. Uplift was greatest along the southern flanks of the Kilsyth Hills and may be related to the development of a linear vent system which was active in this area at the start of volcanicity. The lavas comprising the Clyde Plateau Volcanic Formation are predominantly olivine-basalt of Markle and Jedburgh types, with subordinate trachybasalt and mugearite, and were erupted from different centres at different times. Early lavas, mostly Jedburgh type or trachybasalt, were erupted from linear vent systems situated along the present northern and southern margins of the lava block. Most of the later lavas were of Markle type with subordinate mugearites and were derived from a major central volcano which developed in the Waterhead area. Evidence for contemporary subsidence and submergence below lake or sea water is seen in the eastern part of the lava pile where two pillow lava horizons occur high in the sequence.

Subsequent uplift and erosion produced volcanic detritus of the Kirkwood Formation which was deposited locally along the margin of the lava block. Elsewhere, at this time, the largely fluvial sandstones, siltstones and mudstones of the Lawmuir Formation were being deposited.

Clyde Plateau Volcanic Formation

The Clyde Plateau Volcanic Formation marks the most extensive of a series of volcanic episodes which took place during the Lower Carboniferous in the Midland Valley of Scotland. Within the Airdrie district volcanic rocks cover an area of more than 100 km^2, forming the high ground of the Kilsyth Hills, which is the south-eastern part of the more extensive Campsie Block (Campsie Fells, Kilsyth Hills, Denny Muir). The formation also occurs in a small area in the south-west where it occupies the high ground of the Cathkin Braes. In the Kilsyth Hills volcanic rocks show a markedly unconformable relationship to the underlying sedimentary strata of the Inverclyde Group. In contrast, on the north scarp of the Touch–Gargunnock Hills some 5 km to the north in the Stirling district (Sheet 39W), the volcanic formation apparently overlies the Clyde Sandstone Formation without angular unconformity (Read in Francis et al., 1970). Near Fintry and on the south side of the Carron Valley Reservoir the volcanic rocks rest on sandstones of the Clyde Sandstone Formation whereas on the southern flanks of the Kilsyth Hills they mostly lie on a thin sequence of Ballagan Formation rocks and, in one small area [707 793], they lie directly on the Kinnesswood Formation. The lavas also lie directly on Ballagan Formation strata in the Clachie Bridge Borehole [6447 8368]. In the Cathkin Braes, the relationship with the underlying rocks is unknown as the lavas occur in a fault-bounded block surrounded by younger strata.

In the Kilsyth Hills the volcanic pile is comprised of an accumulation of lavas with thick tephra deposits developed around vents, which were active in different localities at different stratigraphical levels. Many of these vents, which are interpreted as small- to medium-sized central volcanoes, are aligned in four ENE-trending linear vent systems (Figure 4). These systems were active during the first main phase of extrusion when a large volume of mainly microporphyritic lavas was produced. During this period there was a progressive migration of activity within the northern vent systems towards the south-east which finally became focused in a large central stratovolcano (Figure 4). The latter gave rise to a large number of more evolved felsic and distinctive macrofeldsparphyric flows. The total thickness of the volcanic pile is in excess of 400 m (Craig, 1980). Vulcanicity appears to have been largely subaerial, though at least one lava at the eastern margin of the Kilsyth Hills at the top of the sequence [779 828] has well-developed pillow structures indicative of subaqueous deposition. The bulk of the volcanic pile is comprised of lava flows which in general are characterised by their lateral persistence, particularly in the Kilsyth Hills. Interflow volcaniclastic material forms a very small proportion of the lava pile in distal facies sequences but the proportion increases rapidly around active vents where tephra cones comprising tuffs, agglomerates and breccias, with interbedded highly vesicular lava tongues, were developed. In distal facies sequences the lava sheets, which are mostly massive in character, are separated by weathered zones. Typically these weathered zones have a crudely stratified layer of scoriaceous volcanic debris overlain by fine red-brown, bole-like material. The bole-like material has ghost stratification and is thought to be tuff rather than weathered lava top. In proximal facies sequences, fragmental rocks with blocks, scoria bombs, spatter and stratified tuffaceous material form a high proportion of the sequence. The lava flows in this facies are highly vesicular and commonly compound, often comprising two or more flow units. The texture of the lavas is coarser than that found in distal facies lavas.

Classification

The classification which has been used in this account is essentially the one devised by MacGregor (1928). The more basic rocks mostly contain plagioclase, olivine and pyroxene phenocrysts in varying amounts and are allocated to six main types (Table 2). Dalmeny, Hillhouse and Dunsapie types are olivine-basalts and the more mafic Craiglockhart type is an ankaramite. Particularly in the Kilsyth Hills, the feldsparphyric Markle and Jedburgh types include Markle and Jedburgh types with little or no visible olivine. Analyses indicate that these rocks include basaltic hawaiites and hawaiites but these have not been distinguished on the Airdrie Sheet because they occur intimately associated with basalts. Following normal practice, pale grey or pinkish lavas with pronounced platy jointing, caused by flow-alignment of small feldspar crystals, have been classed as mugearites. Trachybasalts with alkali feldspar and plagioclase, and a few pink-weathering trachytes, also occur. A restricted rhyolite occurs in the Campsie Fells just to the west of the Airdrie district. Transitional varieties between the main types and variation within a single flow, particularly in abundance and size of phenocrysts, are common. Thus a Jedburgh lava may pass into a Markle type along its length by increase in the number of plagioclase macrophenocrysts. Composite flows, however, are rare in this district, only two having been positively identified. Both examples show markedly varying proportions of feldspar macrophenocrysts between the components. These composite flows suggest the mixing of magmas simultaneously derived from different zones within the subsurface reservoir.

The majority of lavas show varying degrees of alteration. The more basic flows are usually less altered, although olivine is almost always pseudomorphed by green or brown bowlingite. Albitisation, chloritisation,

Table 2 Nomenclature of basic igneous rocks of Carboniferous age.

Basalt types of MacGregor (1928)	Phenocrysts		Chemical classification, after Macdonald (1975)	Type locality
	abundant	sparse		
Macroporphyritic (phenocrysts > 2 mm)				
Markle	plag	ol, Fe-oxide	plag + ol + Fe-oxides-phyric basalts, basaltic hawaiites or hawaiites	Markle Quarry East Lothian (flow)
Dunsapie	plag+ ol + cpx	Fe-oxide	ol + cpx + plag + Fe-oxides-phyric basaltic hawaiites, or ol + cpx + plag-phyric basalts	Dunsapie Hill, Edinburgh (vent intrusion)
Craiglockhart	ol + cpx		ankaramite	Craiglockhart Hill, Edinburgh (flow)
Microporphyritic (phenocrysts < 2 mm)				
Jedburgh	plag	ol, Fe-oxide	plag + ol + Fe-oxides-phyric basalts, basaltic hawaiites or hawaiites	Little Caldon, Stirlingshire (plug)
Dalmeny	ol	cpx, plag	ol + cpx-phyric basalt	Dalmeny Church West Lothian (flow)
Hillhouse	ol + cpx		ol + cpx + phyric-basalt (rarely basanite)	Hillhouse Quarry West Lothian (sill)

plag = plagioclase
ol = olivine
cpx = clinopyroxene
Fe-oxide includes titanium.

carbonation, oxidation and occasionally zeolitisation all occur, leading to considerable difficulty in classifying the rocks either petrographically or petrochemically.

ERUPTIVE CENTRES

About a hundred centres where significant transfer of lava to the surface took place, have been identified in the Campsie Block (Craig, 1980) (Figure 4). Approximately one third occur within the Airdrie district but many of the volcanic centres outwith the district also supplied lava to the area of the Kilsyth Hills. Eruptive centres are most easily recognised where necks or vents have remnant tephra cones or where adjacent proximal facies lava sequences have been preserved.

No eruptive centres have been identified in the Cathkin Braes and the source of these lavas is unknown.

NORTH CAMPSIE LINEAR VENT SYSTEM

This system of vents is situated along the north-western margin of the Campsie Block and is the north-eastern part of the major volcano-tectonic lineament extending from Dumbarton to Fintry (Whyte and Macdonald, 1974). Although this system lies almost entirely outwith the Airdrie district, it has had a major influence on the development of the volcanic pile in the Kilsyth Hills and supplied a large volume of the early Jedburgh type and trachybasalt lavas.

SOUTH CAMPSIE LINEAR VENT SYSTEM

This system is aligned parallel with the Campsie Fault which forms the southern margin of the Kilsyth Hills. A large number of plugged conduits occurs between Craigdouffie [748 809] and Brown Hill [663 786] and are considered to constitute part of a volcano-tectonic lineament as important as the Dumbarton to Fintry vent system (Craig and Hall, 1975). It is thought that the west-south-west extension of this vent system is buried below younger sedimentary rocks beyond the Corrie area [693 792] where the Campsie Fault cuts across the main line of necks (Craig, 1980). The South Campsie Linear Vent System, which is about 15 km long and 2 km wide, has several necks with associated tephra cones occurring at low levels in the volcanic pile. These necks are thought to have been active at about the same time as those of the North Campsie Linear Vent System and also to be major sources of the early Jedburgh-type lavas. The remaining necks are mostly associated with activity later in the development of the volcanic pile.

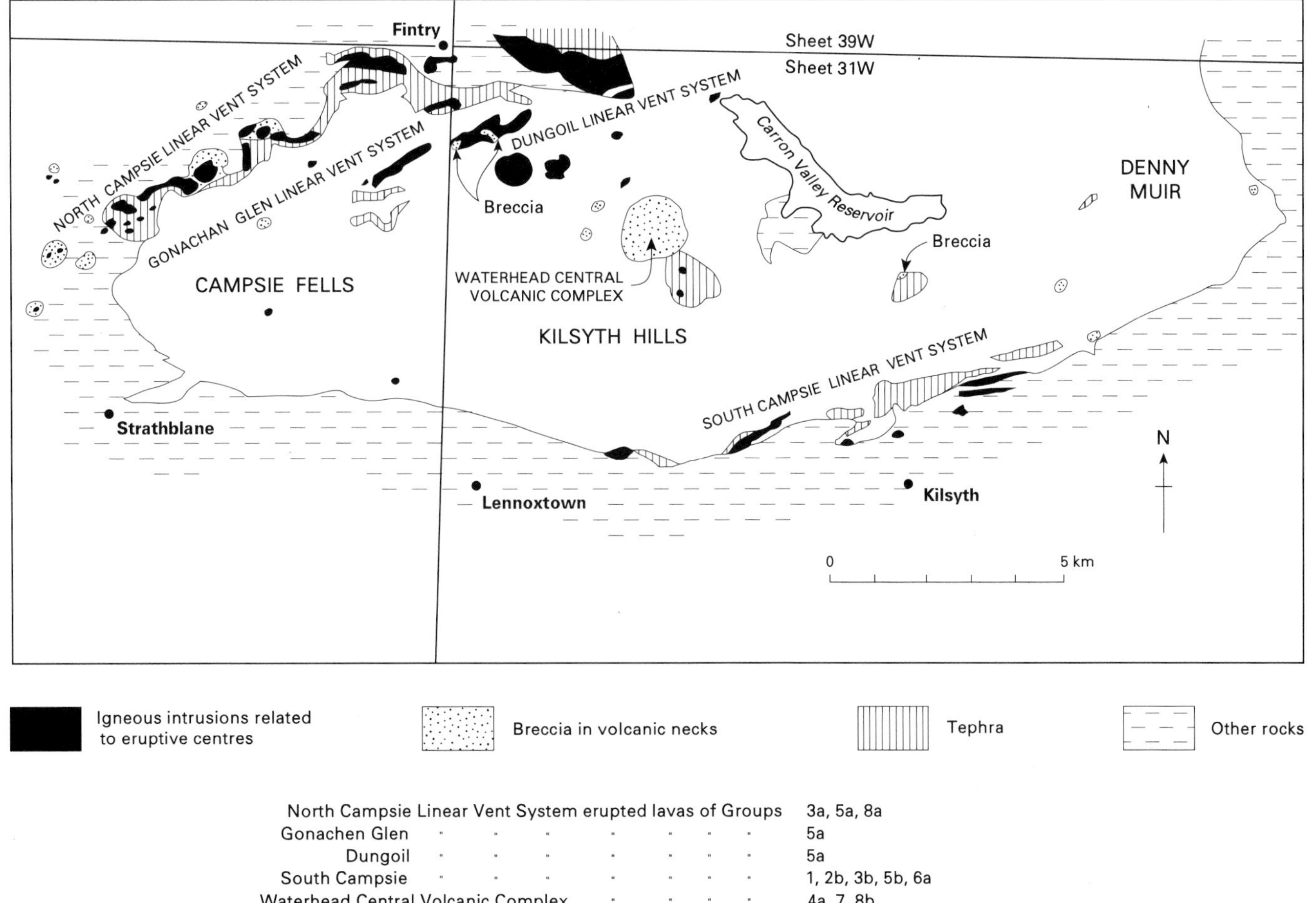

Figure 4 Major eruptive centres of the Campsie Block, see Table 3 for explanation of lava groups.

Gonachan Glen Linear Vent System

The earliest microporphyritic lavas derived from the North Campsie Linear Vent System are cut by vents aligned along Gonachan Glen [618 848–635 856]. This system has a similar trend to the other vent systems, is about 12 km long and extends beyond the Airdrie district both to the west-south-west and the east-north-east. Apart from the Cringate area [682 874] to the north-east of the Kilsyth Hills, no contemporary tephra deposits are exposed. In Gonachan Glen itself, there is a complex multiple intrusion cut by breccia-filled necks (Plate 1). These necks are thought to have produced trachybasalt and Jedburgh-type lavas contemporary with the second phase of effusion from the North Campsie Linear Vent System.

Dungoil Linear Vent System

This system lies parallel to and about 1 km to the south of the Gonachan Glen Linear Vent System. It is less extensive than the other vent systems, includes eight necks and is about 10 km long. Contemporary tephra deposits are preserved at each extremity of the vent system, the eastern deposits occur on Cairnoch Hill [701 863] and lie within the Airdrie district. The stratigraphical level of these tephra deposits indicates they formed during extrusive activity immediately prior to, or contemporaneous with, the earliest flows from the Waterhead Central Volcano (see below). A feature of interest in this vent system is a plugged neck at Dungoil [633 843] with maximum and minimum diameters of about 900 m and 650 m respectively. The plug is composed of Jedburgh type basalt which commonly shows columnar jointing. The attitude of the columns, field relations and its size suggest that the Dungoil neck represents the highest level of a flared, trumpet-shaped conduit. A second neck on the eastern slopes of Dungoil [640 842] is not part of the linear vent system but is thought to be related to the younger Waterhead Central Volcanic Complex (see below). Two small necks [642 850 and 639 849] to the north-east of Dungoil and included in the vent system are the earliest in which trachytic intrusions and fragments have been observed in the Kilsyth Hills.

Waterhead Central Volcanic Complex

All the vents considered so far have been aligned in ENE-trending linear systems of roughly contemporaneous extrusion. During later stages in the vulcanicity activity became focused in one central area, the Waterhead Central Volcanic Complex. The complex, which at the present level of erosion occupies 6 sq km, is aligned NW–SE (Figure 4). This phase of volcanic activity gave rise to distinctive Markle-type lavas, mugearites and trachybasalts.

The complex is dominated by a huge multiple neck [660 832] with a diameter of about 1500 m and comprising a wide variety of rock types ranging from basic to acid in composition and exhibiting textures from aphyric to feldsparphyric. The neck occupies the south-eastern half of a caldera which is an oval structure about 2.5 km by 2 km with its long axis running NW–SE and bounded by the Waterhead Ring Fault (Figure 5). Several other smaller necks occur both outside and inside the caldera. These show a linear trend running NW–SE and are also plugged by a wide variety of rock types. A regional gravity survey identified a major positive anomaly centred under Waterhead (Cotton, 1968). The anomaly was interpreted as indicating the presence of a large basic intrusion measuring about 8 km by 6 km running NE–SW and extending from 500 m below the surface to a depth of 6 km. Cotton (1968) suggested that this intrusion could represent a

Plate 1 Accessory agglomerate in or near conduit of a vent, Gonachan Glen near Fintry [6199 8482] (D 1867).

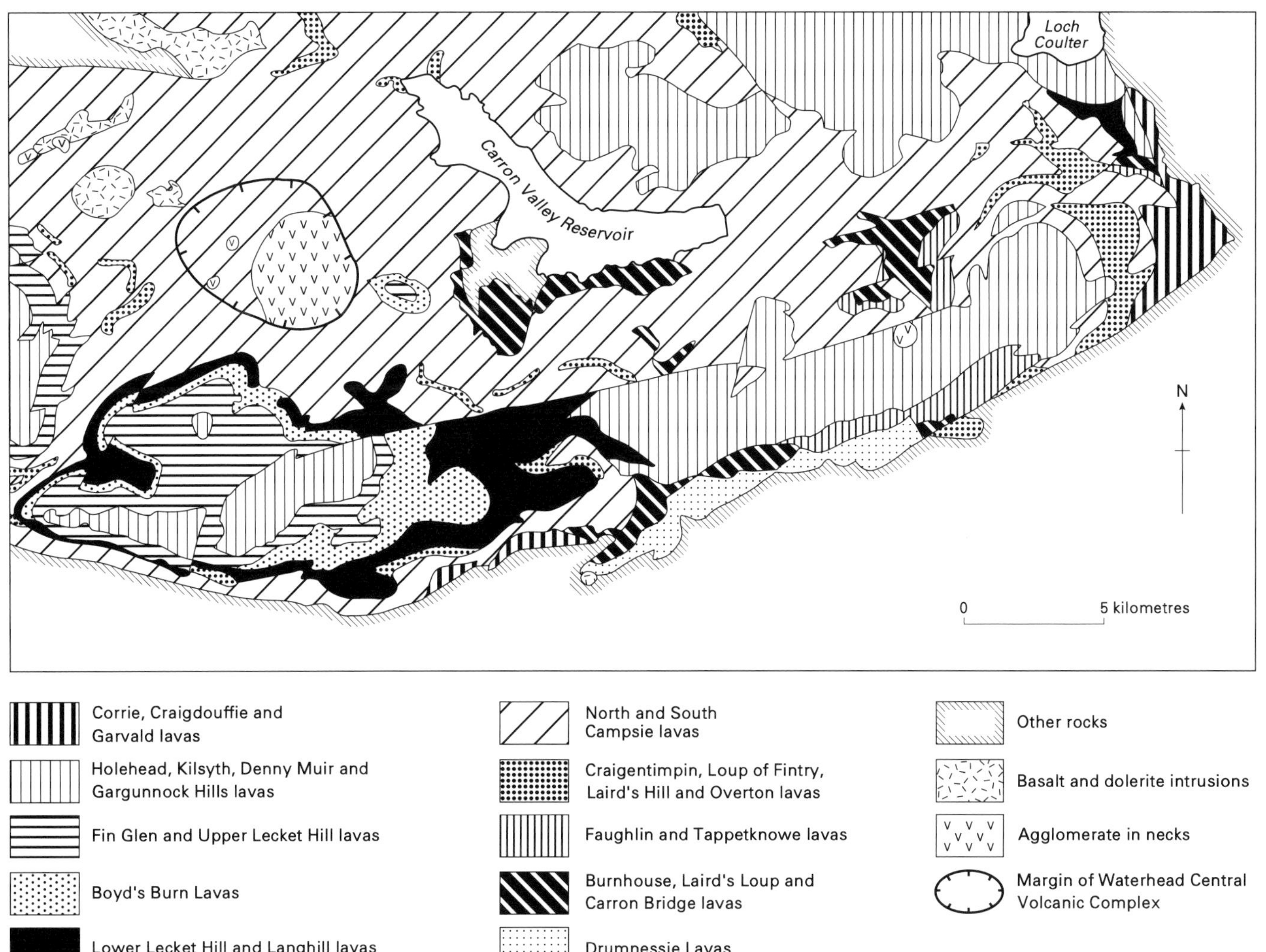

Figure 5 Stratigraphical divisions of the Clyde Plateau Volcanic Formation in the Campsie–Kilsyth Hills (see also Table 3).

high-level magma chamber from which many of the lava flows of the Campsie Block may have been erupted. Where early lavas overlie the site of this proposed magma chamber, they have been affected by considerable hydrothermal alteration and intruded by a large number and variety of dykes (Macdonald, 1973). This is consistent with the interpretation that they occur in the roof zone of a magma chamber. The rock occupying the neck on the east side of Dungoil [640 842] exhibits coarse doleritic and gabbroic textures. Such textures suggest that the present level of exposure of this neck is several hundred metres below the contemporary surface and indicate that it was emplaced at a late stage in the vulcanicity. The tephra deposits on Meikle Bin [667 822] are part of the Waterhead Complex. They occur at a high stratigraphical level showing that the central volcano was active after the linear vent systems to the north. However, the stratified tuffs within the caldera in Clachie Burn [643 837] indicate effusive activity at a much earlier period. It is thought that this area was the site of sporadic minor activity before the development of the major central volcanic complex which dominated the later phases of extrusion.

Other eruptive centre

A few other lava source areas occur away from the linear vent systems and central volcanic complex. Three of these areas, east of Carron Bridge [748 837], south of the Carron Valley Reservoir [710 820] and near Burnhouse [683 824], are identified by their coarse tephra and proximal facies Markle-type lavas. Although these occur at a low stratigraphical level, they are younger than the Markle lavas occurring at the base of the eastern half of the volcanic pile for which no source is known. A small neck on the north shore of the Carron Valley Reservoir [695 841]is associated with some of the later Markle lavas.

Dykes

A large number of dykes occur within or closely associated with the lava block. The great majority are 0.5–3.0 m wide and have little lateral extent. Most lie within the linear vent systems with which they share the same trend, or are related to the Waterhead Central Volcanic Complex where they lack any preferred orientation. The composition of the dykes ranges from acid to basic. In some of the multiple dykes different phases may have different compositions and textures. A few dykes, such as one exposed in Fin Glen in the Glasgow district (Sheet 30E) [599 800], show evidence of an early degassing phase causing metasomatic alteration of the adjacent lavas. Whyte and Macdonald (1974) suggested that much of the Markle basalt in the Campsie Block was erupted from fissures now represented by Markle dykes. Some lava may have been extruded through fissures now filled by dykes such as the one in Fin Glen, but the evidence suggests that most of the Markle-type lava was erupted from the Waterhead Central Volcanic Complex, with minor additions from small necks such as the one on the north shore of Carron Valley Reservoir.

Sequence in the Kilsyth Hills

A stratigraphical classification of the volcanic sequence in the Campsie Block was established by Craig (1980). The succession is divided informally into ten subdivisions most of which have several laterally equivalent groups of flows which could be considered to have member status. All ten subivisions are represented in the Kilsyth Hills (Table 3).

Drumnessie Lavas (1a)

This group of lavas occurs in much faulted outcrops at the base of the lava pile and can be traced for a distance of 5 km along the southern escarpment of the Kilsyth

Table 3 Lava succession in the Kilsyth Hills (modified after Craig, 1980).

Lava sub-division	Members	Eruptive sources	Petrographical types	Maximum thickness (m)
10	a Knowehead Lavas*	Local	B^M, B^{Du}, R	50 +
	b Corrie Lavas	Local	B^M, W	30 +
	c Craigdouffie Lavas	Local	B^M, W	15 +
	d Garvald Lavas	Local	B^M, W, B^{Du}, B^J	50 +
9	a Holehead Lavas	WCVC	B^M, W	100 +
	b Kilsyth Hills Lavas	WCVC	B^M, $B^{J/M}$, B^J, $B^{M/Du}$	200 +
	c Denny Muir Lavas	WCVC	B^M, W, W^M	85 +
8	a Fin Glen Lavas	Local & NCLVS	B^J, W, W^M, T	110 +
	b Upper Lecket Hill Lavas	WCVC	B^J, W, W^M, T	65
7	a Boyd's Burn Lavas	WCVC	B^M	50
6	a Lower Lecket Hill Lavas	SCLVS	B^J, W, W^M	50
	b Langhill Lavas	?	W	35
5	a Upper North Campsie Lavas**	NCLVS, GGLVS DLVS	B^J, W, W^M	215
	b Upper South Campsie Lavas**	SCLVS	W	60
4	a Craigentimpin Lavas	WCVC	B^M	30
	b Loup of Fintry Lavas	?	B^M	30
	c Laird's Hill Lavas	?	B^M	20
	d Overton Lavas	?	B^M	35
3	a Lower North Campsie Lavas**	NCLVS	B^J, W	70
	b Lower South Campsie Lavas**	SCLVS	B^J	135
	c Faughlin Lavas	?Local	W^M	35
	d Tappetknowe Lavas	?Local	W^M, W, B^M	40
2	a Burnhouse Lavas	Local	B^M, B^J	20
	b Laird's Loup Lavas	?SCLVS	B^M	65
	c Carron Bridge Lavas	?	B^M	50 +
1	a Drumnessie Lavas	SCLVS	$B^{J/D}$, B^{Ck}	60

Abbreviations: DLVS–Dungoil Linear Vent System, GGLVS–Gonachan Glen Linear Vent System, NCLVS–North Campsie Linear Vent System, SCLVS–South Campsie Linear Vent System, WCVC–Waterhead Central Volcanic Complex; B^J–Jedburgh, B^D–Dalmeny, B^M–Markle, B^{Du}–Dunsapie, B^{Ck}–Craiglockhart, W–Trachybasalt, W^M–Mugearite, T–Trachyte, R–Rhyolite.

* Part of the Kilpatrick Hills succession (Hall et al., in press)

** Not shown separately on Figure 5.

Hills, north of Kilsyth. It has a maximum thickness of about 60 m comprising several lava flows of typical proximal facies interbedded with thick tephra deposits. With one exception, all the flows are transitional between Jedburgh and Dalmeny basalts. The exception is a flow of Craiglockhart type, unique in the Kilsyth Hills. It is classed as an ankaramite, being rich in macrophenocrysts of augite and olivine but lacking in prominent plagioclase phenocrysts. The intercalated tephra deposits, which make up about half the total thickness, include essential agglomerate, stratified tuffs and lapilli tuffs composed of accidental and accessory material. The tephra and several of the flows are well exposed in the Garrel Burn area [701 805] where they exhibit many of the characteristics of a proximal-facies sequence. Several nearby necks belonging to the South Campsie Linear Vent System are plugged by basalt of similar type, for example near St Mirren's Well [721 795], and are probable sources of this group of lavas.

BURNHOUSE LAVAS (2a)

This group of lavas occurs at the base of the lava pile in the area south of the Carron Valley Reservoir and extends over a distance of about 3.5 km. The lavas are mainly Markle type with a few thin intercalated Jedburgh-type flows. The flows show typical proximal facies characteristics being only 2–3 m thick and having interbedded tephra deposits. Good exposures of the lavas and associated tephra are seen in the Burnhouse Burn [688 823] and March Burn [709 830] areas. The tephra deposits comprise a series of well-stratified, red-weathered tuffs with blocks and bombs, commonly up to 0.5 m in diameter, of various microporphyritic and macroporphyritic lava types. Blocks of cementstone and scoria are also incorporated. Near Burnhouse Burn, they are so coarsely agglomeratic in places that very close proximity to a source vent is indicated. In the March Burn area the character and extent of the tephra deposits also point to an obscured vent in the vicinity. To the north-east, along the southern shores of the Carron Valley Reservoir, the Markle-type lavas are more massive and the plagioclase phenocrysts are seen to be variable in size and distribution.

LAIRD'S LOUP LAVAS (2b)

These lavas overlie the Drumnessie Lavas along the southern escarpment of the Kilsyth Hills for about 3.5 km from the Takmadoon Road [730 805] to Corrie [692 797]. The lavas near Craigdouffie, some 3 km to the east, are also included in this group. The lavas, which are predominantly Markle type, are best seen in the Laird's Loup area of the Garrel Burn [703 804] where six flows form a 50 m outcrop. Individual flows range from 6 to 15 m, though some of the flows vary laterally in thickness. The vent at Craigdouffie [747 809] has been identified as a possible source of these lavas since the neck is filled with breccia of similar material and the lava outcrops near the vent show proximal facies characteristics.

CARRON BRIDGE LAVAS (2c)

Lavas of this group are well exposed in the River Carron above and below the bridge [741 835], in the Faughlin area to the south [735 827], and near Langhill [775 844]. All these flows are of prominently feldsparphyric Markle type but, unlike the lavas of the previously described groups, are massive and show typical distal facies characteristics. Nowhere is the base seen, but the group is over 50 m thick with some individual flows in excess of 15 m. The lavas are characterised by having particularly high concentrations of plagioclase phenocrysts which tend to be elongate, up to 6 mm in length, and flow aligned. There is no indication of source or direction of derivation of this group.

CAMPSIE LAVAS: LOWER (3a) AND UPPER (5a) NORTH CAMPSIE LAVAS; LOWER (3b) AND UPPER (5b) SOUTH CAMPSIE LAVAS

These groups of lavas are made up of Jedburgh-type flows ranging in composition from basalt to hawaiite. There is a considerable range of modal compositions, particularly with respect to the clinopyroxene content. Many of the flows derived from the south contain significantly more clinopyroxene than those derived from the north where it is distinctly lacking. Despite mineralogical differences, however, it is impracticable to distinguish North and South Campsie groups in the middle of the block, where interdigitation of lavas of both groups is believed to occur. Where no group 4 lavas are present, neither the North nor the South Campsie Lavas have been separated into Upper and Lower divisions. The Campsie Lavas as a whole have a maximum thickness of about 200 m in the north-west, reducing to less than 100 m in the south and east.

LOWER NORTH CAMPSIE LAVAS (3a)

Lavas which can be definitely assigned to this group occur in the north-western part of the district where they have been traced away from proximal facies flows associated with the North Campsie, Gonachan Glen and Dungoil linear vent systems. There are no good sections of these lavas within the Airdrie district but where sampled, they prove to be Jedburgh type or trachybasalt, generally with small amounts of augite, moderate amounts of microporphyritic olivine, and abundant microporphyritic plagioclase of a rather sodic andesine composition.

LOWER SOUTH CAMPSIE LAVAS (3b)

Lavas of this group occur along the southern escarpment and eastern part of the Kilsyth Hills. Good sections are exposed in streams between Forking Burn [653 790] and Burniebraes Burn [661 788]. In the Forking Burn section, the base of the group rests on a thin tephra bed which lies on sedimentary rocks of the Ballagan Formation. The top of the sequence is also exposed in this section where it is overlain by Craigentimpin Lavas (4a). The group includes about ten flows of Jedburgh basalt totalling 80 m in thickness and all showing proximal facies features. In other sections the Craigentimpin Lavas are absent and the Lower South Campsie Lavas pass directly up into the Upper South Campsie Lavas. These are identical in character and not readily separable. Individual flows are generally thin (3–8 m) and are separated by slaggy agglomerate which makes up about a quarter of the total thickness. They have features typical of pahoehoe flows. Most of the flows have been altered by carbonate replacement, particularly of olivine and augite and sometimes of plagioclase. In the Garrel Burn section, 4 km to the north-east, individual flows are thicker but the overall thickness of the unit is reduced to 50 m. Here the lavas show distal facies characteristics and are less altered.

Upper North Campsie Lavas (5a)

Though lavas of this group occur over a wide area in the northern part of the lava block, there are no good sections through the sequence. In the Muir Toll Burn area [628 828] the total thickness is about 40 m, comprising a series of Jedburgh-type flows. Further east, on Cairnoch Hill [690 852], Haugh Hill [682 842] and Little Bin [674 830] thick distal facies sequences are present, but poorly exposed. Most of the flows are Jedburgh type and trachybasalts, though mugearites also occur.

Upper South Campsie Lavas (5b)

This group is best exposed in the southern part of the Campsie Block to the west of the Airdrie district where it consists of four flows of trachybasalt, 40 m thick in total. Where the group occurs within the Airdrie district, as in the River Carron [768 847], interdigitation with flows derived from the north always occurs. Here also, the lavas are trachybasalts.

Faughlin Lavas (3c)

The Faughlin Lavas occur in a small area south and east of the Faughlin Reservoir [744 830] and in the River Carron [777 840]. These flows are predominantly mugearitic with a total thickness of 35 m. They are probably derived from a local source.

Tappetknowe Lavas (3d)

These lavas are confined to the eastern end of the south scarp of the Kilsyth Hills. They are poorly exposed, but near Tappetknowe [750 815] include mugearites, trachybasalts and rare Markle-type flows. They occupy the same stratigraphical position as the Lower South Campsie Lavas which appear to have been excluded from this area. The total thickness of the Tappetknowe Lavas is about 40 m and they were probably erupted from a nearby source.

Craigentimpin Lavas (4a), Loup of Fintry Lavas (4b), Laird's Hill Lavas (4c) and Overton Lavas (4d)

These are all thin groups of Markle-type lavas which occur in geographically separated areas between the Upper and Lower Campsie lavas. The Craigentimpin Lavas (4a) occur in the western part of the district and are well exposed in the Sloughmuclock area [627 795] where there are two flows with a maximum thickness of 30 m. The lavas are distinctive Markle type with very large, prominent, platy phenocrysts of calcic labradorite. Average phenocryst orientation is consistent with derivation from the Waterhead area (Whyte and MacDonald, 1974). The Loup of Fintry Lavas(4b) occur in the northern part of the district. Near the Loup of Fintry [662 862] there are two flows separated by a thin tephra bed with a combined thickness of 30 m. The lower lava is a prominently feldsparphyric Markle type and the upper a composite flow with intermingling of aphyric and feldsparphyric components. The Laird's Hill Lavas (4c) occur in the south and central parts of the district. The group comprises just one or two flows and has a maximum thickness of about 20 m. In the Garrel Burn [689 804] there are two flows, a mugearite overlain by one of Markle type. Where only one flow is present, it is the upper one. The Overton Lavas (4d) are about 35 m thick and occur in the eastern part of the district. Sections in the River Carron [764 843] and the Overton Burn [772 835] expose at least one Markle-type flow overlying one of mugearite.

Lower Lecket Hill Lavas (6a)

These lavas crop out extensively along the western half of the south scarp of the Kilsyth Hills, in the Lecket Hill [645 812] and Meikle Bin [667 822] areas. A maximum thickness of 50 m occurs in the Alnwick Burn [632 805] where seven flows ranging in composition from Jedburgh basalt to mugearite are exposed. On the south scarp, a thinner sequence is seen in the Goat Burn [637 793] comprising three flows with interbedded tephra deposits totalling 30 m in thickness. An analysis from the lowest flow in the Goat Burn has been described as compatible with a mugearite (Macgregor et al., 1925) but the chemical parameters are akin to those of benmoreite (Craig, 1980). The Lower Lecket Hill Lavas are thought to be derived, at least in part, from the South Campsie Linear Vent System.

Langhill Lavas (6b)

The Langhill Lavas are confined to a small area in the eastern part of the Kilsyth Hills where they are exposed in the River Carron [769 847]. The group consists of four flows of typically platy-jointed trachybasalt with a total thickness of 35 m.

Boyd's Burn Lavas (7a)

This group has a similar outcrop distribution to the Lower Lecket Hill Lavas which they overlie. Their maximum thickness of about 50 m is developed in the Boyd's Burn area [650 814], where at least four proximal facies flows occur, with well-developed interflow tephra deposits. These Markle-type flows have a hawaiite composition and show marked variation in the concentration and size of plagioclase phenocrysts, both between flows and within the same flow. The group is thought to be derived from the Waterhead Central Volcanic Complex.

Fin Glen Lavas (8a)

The Fin Glen Lavas only occur in the western part of the Airdrie district where they are 60 m thick. Further west in the Campsie Block, they are more widespread and attain a thickness of more than 100 m. The group is exposed in Clachie Burn [622 835] and on Campsie Muir [625 829] where the flows include Jedburgh basalt, trachybasalt and mugearite. The basal flow over part of this area is a distinctive trachyte. Another trachyte occurs higher in the sequence elsewhere in the area. The petrography of the basal trachyte is very similar to that of the plug of phonolitic trachyte near Fintry [614 863] which is part of the North Campsie Linear Vent System and which may be the source of the lava. The other lavas in this group show proximal facies characteristics and are thought to be of local derivation.

Upper Lecket Hill Lavas (8b)

This group of lavas only occurs in the south-west of the Kilsyth Hills around Lecket Hill [645 812] and the summit of Little Bin [673 829]. It consists of generally felsic flows including Jedburgh type, trachybasalt, mugearite, and trachyte, totalling 65 m in thickness. The proximal facies sequence exposed to the north-east of Lecket Hill [647 813] suggests derivation from the adjacent Waterhead Central Volcanic Complex.

Holehead Lavas (9a), Kilsyth Hills Lavas (9b) and Denny Muir Lavas (9c)

These groups include the structurally highest flows of the Campsie lava pile. They occur in geographically isolated areas but are all considered to represent parts of the large central volcano which developed around the Waterhead Central Volcanic Complex. Within the Airdrie district, the Holehead Lavas are confined to the eastern margin of Outer Black Hill [620 820]. A good section of these lavas is exposed just to the west of the district, in the Aldessan Burn [606 812]. The sequence comprises Markle basalt and Markle-type flows of more hawaiitic composition, with one intercalated flow transitional between trachybasalt and mugearite. The highest group of lavas in the south of the area is referred to as the Kilsyth Hills Lavas. They occur on Tomtain Hill [721 814], where they are 160 m thick, the high ground east of Crighton's Cairn [625 799], and around Lecket Hill [645 812]. They are also predominantly Markle basalts, the lower flows being transitional with Jedburgh basalt and the higher having affinities with Dunsapie basalt. There is a local intercalation of microporphyritic basalt, transitional between Jedburgh and Dalmeny types, on Hunt Hill [715 813]. In the eastern part of the lava block, on Denny Muir [750 820] and north to Tarduff Hill [756 837], the highest group is referred to as the Denny Muir Lavas. They are petrographically similar to groups 9a and 9b but include rare flows of mugearite and trachybasalt. The basal flow east of Darroch Hill [754 827] is composite with intermingled components of Markle and Jedburgh basalt.

Knowehead Lavas (10a), Corrie Lavas (10b), Craigdouffie Lavas (10c) and Garvald Lavas (10d)

These groups of lavas are all preserved in isolated down-faulted blocks and are thought to be the stratigraphically highest flows in the Campsie Block. The Knowehead Lavas occur south of the Campsie Fault north-west of Lennoxtown [618 794] but are best exposed in Fin Glen [604 794], just to the west of the Airdrie district. They range from Dunsapie basalt to rhyolite and have numerous intercalations of coarse tephra, indicating that their source is nearby. This group is included in the Kilpatrick Hills succession (Hall et al., in press). The Corrie Lavas are restricted to a small area south of the Campsie Fault and north of Corrie [692 795]. The sequence comprises Markle-type lavas, trachybasalts and coarse tephra beds, totalling over 30 m in thickness and thought to be of local origin. The Craigdouffie Lavas are only seen in a very small area west of Craigdouffie [750 807]. This group consists of alternating Markle-type lavas and trachybasalts, all showing proximal facies characteristics, and is thus of local derivation. The Garvald Lavas occur in the eastern part of the lava pile at the top of the succession but are in faulted contact with underlying members. The angular unconformity at the top of the lavas is seen in the Garvald Burn section [781 838] where beds of volcanic detritus and sandstone rest on progressively older flows towards the south. Other sections are exposed in the River Carron [781 829] and Overton Burn [779 837] where varied assemblages are seen. The lowest flow seen is a Jedburgh-type lava showing pillow structures. This is the only evidence of subaqueous eruption within the Campsie Block. The overlying sequence includes a Dunsapie basalt, Markle-type flows, trachybasalts and Jedburgh type lavas. These flows are thought to be of local derivation.

Correlation with adjacent areas

A stratigraphy for the lava successions which occur in the Fintry, Gargunnock and Touch hills was erected by Read (in Francis et al., 1970). The Fintry–Touch Lava Block, which lies mostly to the north of the Airdrie district, is separated from the Campsie Block by the Carron Valley Reservoir and the Endrick Valley. To the west, the sequence established in the Kilsyth Hills can be followed throughout the Campsie Block. The correlation from the western end of the Campsie Block to the Touch Hills is shown in Figure 6. The Upper and Lower North and South Campsie lavas (3a, 5a, 3b, 5b) can be traced from the Campsie Fells in the west, where they are more than 200 m thick, to the Touch Hills in the north-east where they are represented by about 30 m of the Spout of Ballochleam Group lavas. Underlying these are various thin groups which do not extend for any great distance. The other group of lavas which extends from the Campsie Fells to the Touch Hills comprises the Markle-type flows erupted when the Waterhead Central Volcano became fully established. They are represented by the Holehead (9a), Kilsyth Hills (9b) and Denny Muir (9c) lavas in the Campsie Block and the Fintry Hills and Gargunnock Hills groups in the Fintry–Touch Block. Over most of the area the tops of these groups are defined by the present-day erosion surface. Their true thickness is unknown, but they show residual thicknesses of 50 m to more than 100 m.

The BGS Rashiehill Borehole [8386 7301], put down about 2 km to the east of the Airdrie district, encountered 380 m of lavas below about 800 m of Carboniferous strata. The lavas comprise an upper group, mainly basic olivine-rich basalts of Dalmeny and Hillhouse types 315 m thick, and a lower group of feldspathic olivine-basalts of Jedburgh and Markle types accompanied by

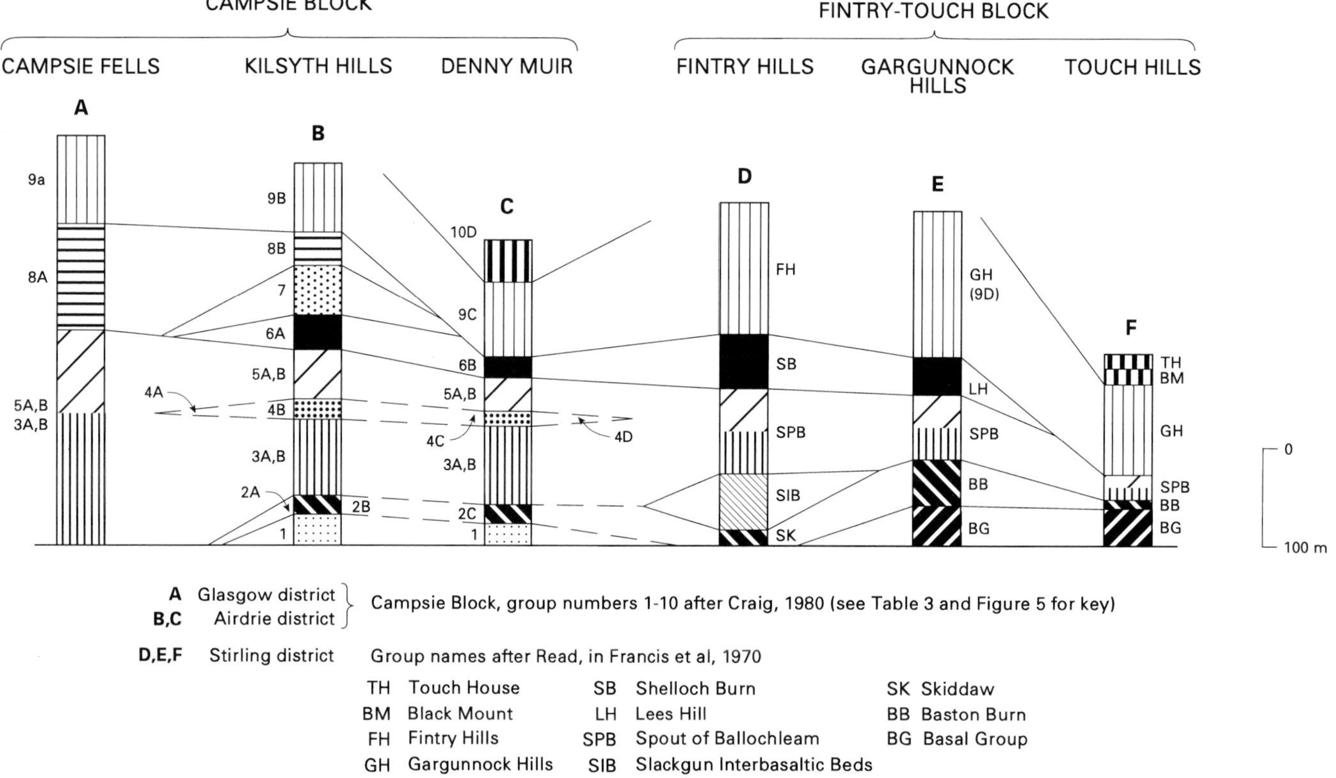

Figure 6 Composite sections showing correlation of Clyde Plateau Volcanic Formation within the Campsie Block and with adjacent areas (for key see Table 3).

some less basic flows more than 65 m thick. The upper and lower groups were correlated with the lavas of the Bathgate Hills and the Clyde Plateau Volcanic Formation respectively (Anderson, 1963). The correlation with the Clyde Plateau Volcanic Formation suggests that the lavas of the Kilsyth Hills extend, at depth, south of the Campsie Fault for a considerable distance.

Sequence in the Cathkin Braes

The eastern part of a faulted outlier of Clyde Plataeu Volcanic Formation occupies about 10 km^2 in the extreme south-west of the Airdrie district. The sequence in this area comprises two groups of alkali olivine-basalt lavas with interbedded pyroclastic deposits. Individual flows vary from a few metres to over 20 m in thickness and, in general, dip to the south. The lowest part of the lower group is not well exposed in the district but appears to comprise a series of Dalmeny and Jedburgh flows with an intercalation of Markle type near Fernhill School [622 592] and a further intercalation, at a higher level, of Dunsapie type near Cathkin [629 586]. Above this, the remainder of the lower group of the Dalmeny–Jedburgh basalt sequence is well exposed on the north scarp of the Cathkin Braes in the Glasgow district [605 587] as a series of well-defined trap features. The exposed thickness of the lower group in this area is about 80 m. The base of the upper group forms a distinct feature along the escarpment and was formerly exposed in Cathkin Quarry [622 582] where a macroporphyritic Markle–Dunsapie flow was seen to overlie the highest Dalmeny flow of the lower group and a metre or so of tuff. The succeeding flow in the upper group, which overlies a variable thickness of bedded tuff, is of Dalmeny–Dunsapie type and is more than 20 m thick. At Cathkin Quarry, these lower two lavas are overlain by two thin Dunsapie flows which thicken away from the quarry in all directions. These two thin flows, and all succeeding flows, have a general dip to the south-east. An intercalation of Hillhouse and Dalmeny basalts occurs above the two Dunsapie flows and is overlain by further Dunsapie flows. The upper group has a maximum thickness of about 50 m. Neither the source of the Cathkin Braes lavas nor their relationship with other lava blocks is known.

Petrology

The lavas are all members of a mildly alkaline, alkali-basalt series intermediate between the sodic alkali-basalt series of the British Tertiary Province and the potassic alkali-basalt series described from Tristan da Cunha. They belong to the series ankaramite-basalt-hawaiite-mugearite-benmoreite-trachyte-rhyolite with the end-members being less common and benmoreite possibly absent (Figure 7). The available analyses show that although a few of the more basic rocks are nepheline-normative, most are hypersthene-normative and most of

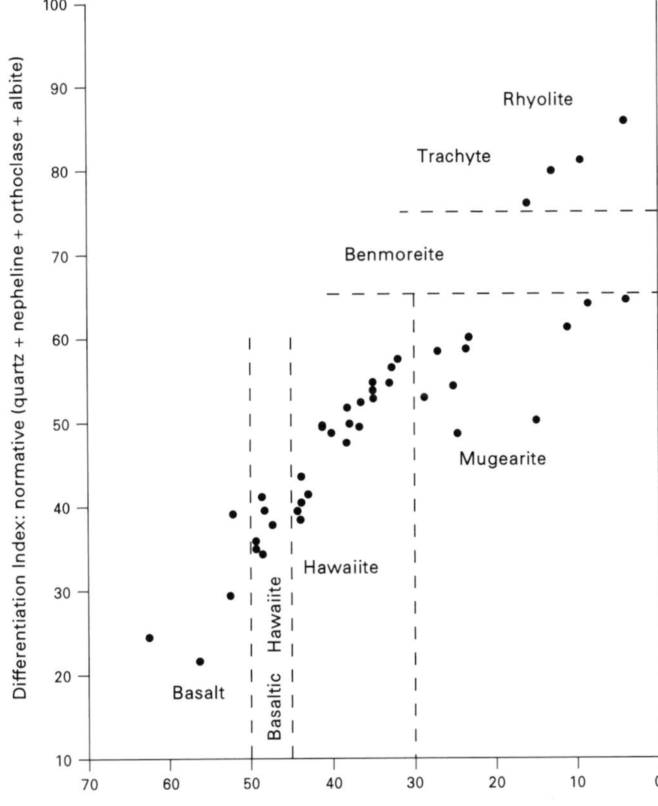

Figure 7 Compositional range of lavas within the Kilsyth Hills, after Craig, 1980. The classification is based on CIPW norm calculations, after Coombs and Wilkinson (1969) and Macdonald (1975).

the less basic, more fractionated rocks are hypersthene-quartz-normative.

Studies by Macdonald (1975), Macdonald et al. (1977), Craig (1980), MacDonald and Whyte (1981) and Smedley (1986, 1988) suggest that the lava series in the Campsie Block is derived by fusion of sublithospheric upper mantle material. Such magmatism is typical of that which occurs in continental rift environments throughout the world. The evolved condition of the lava flows indicates high-pressure fractionation of clinopyroxene at pressures in excess of 10 kb. This would effect the transition from basalt to basaltic hawaiite. Subsequent lower-pressure fractionation at higher levels, dominated by crystallisation of olivine, plagioclase and oxide assemblages, would give rise to the other members of the series. Extraction of substantial amounts of clinopyroxene from parental magma is supported by the relative paucity of clinopyroxene in many of the lavas (Craig, 1980). The variation seen in the lava types erupted from the Waterhead Central Volcano may have been due to low-pressure fractionation in a long-lasting magma reservoir situated beneath it. The volcanicity took place in a regional tensional stress regime. This regime caused normal faulting which gave rise to differential subsidence of fault-bounded blocks, such as the Campsie Block, within the Midland Valley graben.

Kirkwood Formation

After volcanism ceased there was a period of uplift and erosion, and volcanic detritus comprising the Kirkwood Formation (Paterson and Hall, 1986) was deposited locally along the margin of the lava block. Elsewhere the largely fluvial sandstones, siltstones and mudstones of the Lawmuir Formation were being deposited at the same time. The Kirkwood Formation only occurs in isolated outcrops along the margins of the Kilsyth Hills.

Along the eastern margin of the Kilsyth Hills, north of the Campsie Fault, the Kirkwood Formation varies from being absent to a maximum of about 15 m in thickness. Around Loch Coulter Reservoir, in the north [769 860], the Kirkwood Formation is absent and the Lawmuir Formation lies directly on the Clyde Plateau Volcanic Formation. South of the reservoir, at localities [773 853–784 838] a quartz-dolerite sill is in contact with the lavas. Further south, the Kirkwood Formation thickens from 1 m at [784 836] to about 15 m near the Campsie Fault. The basal part of the Kirkwood Formation is usually conglomeratic near the fault, and includes rounded pebbles of volcanic material and, locally, boulders up to 30 cm in diameter. The conglomerate is dark purple or red and has a variable amount of sandy matrix. At higher levels it contains intercalations of grey, nonvolcanic sandstone.

South of the Campsie Fault the Kirkwood Formation occurs in two small areas. One area is 1 km north of High Banton [750 808] where about 15 m of poorly exposed volcanic detritus is overlain by grey sandstones of the Lawmuir Formation. The other area is at Corrieburn [675 787], where deposition of volcanic detritus continued much longer than in adjacent areas such that the volcanic deposits are interbedded with normal fluvial sediments and a marine horizon which is thought to be equivalent to the Hollybush Limestone of the Glasgow district. At Corrieburn the Kirkwood Formation is overlain by marine mudstones and limestone correlated with the Blackbyre Limestone of the Glasgow district. The highly diachronous and localised nature of the Kirkwood Formation is shown by the fact that the Blackbyre Limestone occurs over 100 m above the base of the Lawmuir Formation west of Glasgow indicating that here, the Kirkwood Formation is laterally equivalent to a large part of the Lawmuir Formation further west.

Lawmuir Formation

The Lawmuir Formation includes all the strata between the Kirkwood Formation and the Lower Limestone Formation, the base of which is now drawn at the base of the Hurlet Limestone, not the Hurlet Coal. The Lawmuir Formation was previously known as the Upper Sedimentary Group of the Calciferous Sandstone Series, or Measures. The type section is the Lawmuir Borehole in the Glasgow district (Hall et al., in press). The main outcrops are around Lennoxtown, with smaller occurrences to the east. Elsewhere little is known about the Lawmuir Formation, except for the topmost beds which were intersected by the Dumbreck No. 1 [7040 7850], Cardowan No. 13 [6706 6876] and Wester Gartshore [6823 7239] boreholes. The thickness of the formation is not known but in the Lennoxtown area it is thought to be at least 185 m and may reach 200 m. East of Lennoxtown it thins markedly to 10–12 m at Corrieburn where it is partly replaced by the Kirkwood Formation but may reach 60 m north-west of Banknock. The formation is therefore subject to such marked lateral variation that each area is best described separately. The marine faunas have been described by Wilson (1989).

The Lawmuir Formation was laid down on an irregular and variably subsiding land surface of basalt lavas, the hollows in which had been partly filled by the volcaniclastic sediments of the Kirkwood Formation. Most of the strata in the Lennoxtown area consist of fluvial sandstones derived largely from nonvolcanic sources outwith the area, and some overbank mudstones. It is uncertain if the marine incursion represented farther west by the Dykebar and Balmore marine bands reached Lennoxtown, but the next two incursions did, introducing rich faunas including corals. The second incursion was followed by a period of nonmarine inundation with conditions favouring ostracods and producing a limestone which may, in part, be a chemical precipitate. This limestone subsequently became part of the seatearth during the prolonged episode of plant colonisation now marked by the Hurlet Coal. This episode was ended by the final marine incursion which produced the pyrite- and alum-rich Alum Shale (and later the Hurlet Limestone). Subsidence in the Lennoxtown area was considerable and more-or-less continuous during this period. However, only a few kilometres to the east, at Corrieburn, subsidence began later and was relatively slow, fluvial sand being largely excluded from this area. The last two marine incursions marked periods when sedimentation just kept pace with subsidence.

Lennoxtown

The Lawmuir Formation around Lennoxtown consists mainly of sandstones, with poorly bedded mudstones (sometimes called fireclays or marls). The formation also comprises several coal seams, all less than 0.4 m thick except the Hurlet Coal. At least two major marine bands occur in bedded mudstones with limestone bands. The nonmarine Baldernock Limestone and, at the very top, the Alum Shale also occur.

The sandstones are mostly cross-bedded, fine- to medium-grained and off-white to pale grey in colour. Scattered exposures occur in several stream sections. The lowest marine incursion in this area is represented by the Craigenglen Beds, whose type locality is in Glenwhapple [6216 7571–6221 7563]. Here, there are at least 5 m of very shelly calcareous mudstones, containing in particular *Latiproductus* cf. *latissimus* together with *Siphonodendron* and other corals, whose presence indicates a correlation (Figure 8) with the Hollybush Limestone of Paisley and Limestone G of the Bannock Burn section in the Stirling district (Francis et al., 1970, pp.170, 181). The second major marine incursion formed the Balgrochan Beds (type locality at [6276 7874]), which lie about 30 m above the Craigenglen Beds and consist of several metres of very fossiliferous mudstones with limestone bands. The Balgrochan Beds are exposed in two streamlets [6387 7840] and [6390 7828]. The correlation with the Blackbyre Limestone of Paisley and Limestone F of the Bannock Burn section is supported by the rich brachiopod fauna. In addition it is now suggested that Limestone E, which is partly leached by roots, is equivalent to the upper part of the Balgrochan Beds since it is now considered both Limestones E and F belong to the same marine episode and are differentiated largely by the leaching that has affected Limestone E (Figure 8).

The Baldernock Limestone lies immediately above the Balgrochan Beds and is 0.6–3.0 m thick. It was also known as the Entomostracan Limestone (on account of its fauna of nonmarine ostracods such as *Carbonita*) or the White Limestone, from its pale-cream or fawn colour, ascribed to leaching by roots. This limestone generally forms part of the seatbed of the Hurlet Coal. Exposures occur in Muirhead Glen [6238 7688], in Burnel Rannie [6278 7877] and at Bencloich Mill Dam [6390 7840]. The Baldernock Limestone is reported to have been worked on the slopes north of Glorat House [6415 7780]; an analysed sample from here contained 83.20% $CaCO_3$, 2.17% $FeCO_3$, 2.63% $MgCO_3$ 'and moisture', 0.13% iron pyrite and 11.87% 'insoluble matter', although locally the rock is dolomitic (MacGregor et al., 1925). To the south, the limestone persists at least as far as Cardowan No. 13 Borehole [6706 6876] and the Wester Gartshore Borehole [6823 7239], where it is 1.37 m thick (Forsyth and Wilson, 1965).

The Hurlet Coal is about 1.0 m thick and was extensively mined. It is dirty and pyritous but has good coking properties. South-east of Lennoxtown it splits into several leaves, the top one passing locally into blackband ironstone. The highest marine band is contained in the Alum Shale, which is generally 1–2 m thick, and lies between the Hurlet Coal and the Hurlet Limestone. The shale was formerly extracted with the coal and limestone to manufacture alum at Lennoxtown. The marine shells are generally pseudomorphed in pyrite: they are mostly molluscs such as *Actinopteria persulcata* and *Sanguinolites abdenensis*. To the south of Lennoxtown, the marine mudstones between the coal and the limestone thicken to 3–4 m.

Corrieburn

The best section of the Lawmuir Formation in the Corrieburn area [68 78] is the following one [6833 7881]:

	Thickness m
Base of Hurlet Limestone	
Shale with marine shells including *Actinopteria persulcata* and *Sanguinolites abdenensis*; thin ironstone near base	5.0
Hurlet Coal (said to have been mined — ?thicker in workings)	0.15
Seatclay	0.3

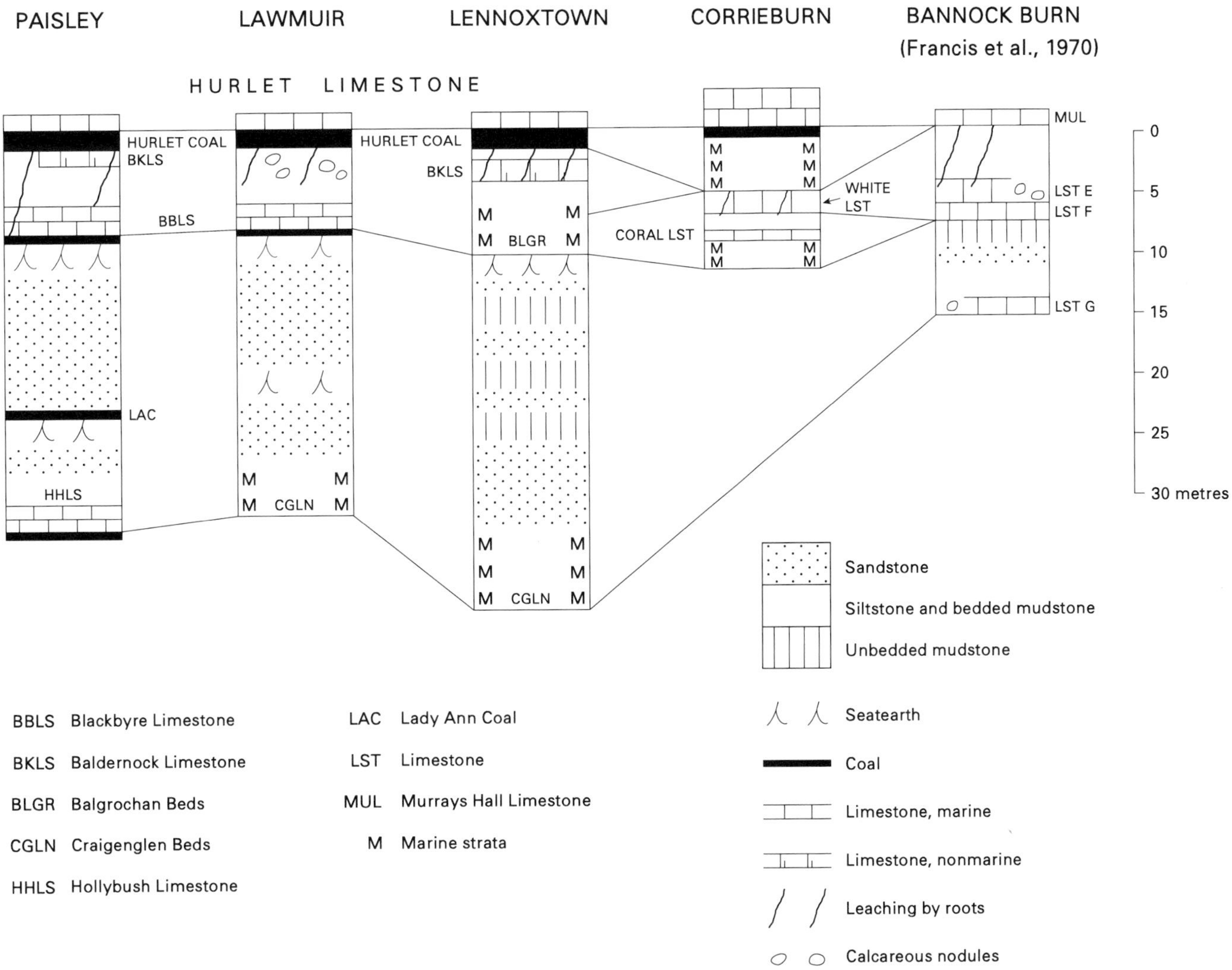

Figure 8 Comparative vertical sections of the upper part of the Lawmuir Formation.

	Thickness m
White Limestone, full of rootlets at top; brachiopod and crinoid debris	1.1
Mudstone, off-white	0.3
Coral Limestone with *Diphyphyllum, Siphonodendron* and many brachiopods	0.75
Mudstone with rich marine fauna	2.75
Ironstone, silty	0.3
Shale with ironstone bands and nodules; *Lingula* sp. and *Naiadites crassus*	0.75
	11.4

Sandstone is absent and only one thin coal is present. This area is one of minimal subsidence and, in consequence, the sequence is largely marine or quasimarine, richly fossiliferous and highly calcareous. The absence of *Latiproductus* cf. *latissimus*, however, argues against any correlative with the Hollybush Limestone, which may be represented by a mudstone with productoid fragments lying below a mudstone with *Curvirimula* and *Euestheria*; the two mudstones occur as intercalations within the underlying Kirkwood Formation.

The top part of the section is similar to that seen in the Dumbreck No. 1 Borehole, 2 km to the east-south-east except for the absence of the Baldernock Limestone. The correlation of the White and Coral limestones with Limestone E of the Bannock Burn section (Francis et al., 1970, pp.170–171) is here modified to include Limestone F (Figure 8).

High Banton

The small outcrop north of High Banton [750 801] is marked by scattered exposures of sandstone, siltstone and shale; a thin coal with a marine mudstone above it was formerly exposed. The Hurlet Coal is known from boreholes to be 0.2–0.3 m thick in this area. The mudstones at the top of the sequence are 4–5 m thick with several ironstone bands near their base. One of the ironstones was mined from a shaft 22 m deep [7591 8031].

Northfield

Little is known about the Lawmuir Formation around Northfield [802 856] but a few old boreholes and scattered surface exposures indicate that 25–30 m of sandstones, siltstones and mudstones occur above a quartz-dolerite sill. Similar strata occur within the sill between Hallquarter [783 860] and Boards [791 858], and below the sill on the east side of Loch Coulter [769 860].

CLACKMANNAN GROUP (Dinantian part)

Cyclic sequences became the established pattern of sedimentation after the deposition of the Hurlet Coal and, in general, the strata are more widespread and allow correlation over much of the Midland Valley. This type of sedimentation, which characterises the Clackmannan Group, persisted until the establishment of coal measure-type cyclic deposition in the Lower Coal Measures at the start of the Westphalian. The Group consists of four formations, the Lower Limestone Formation of Dinantian age, and the Limestone Coal Formation, Upper Limestone Formation and Passage Formation of Silesian age (described in Chapter Five). Detailed descriptions are given in Forsyth, 1993.

Lower Limestone Formation

The Lower Limestone Formation is present at outcrop intermittently in a WSW–ENE belt across the northern part of the Airdrie district, from Lennoxtown to the north-east corner. Exposures are quite numerous, mainly in stream sections. To the south, the formation occurs at depth and has been reached by several boreholes (Figure 9), three of which (Dumbreck No. 1, Cardowan No. 13 and Wester Gartshore) proved the whole sequence (Forsyth and Wilson, 1965). The maximum thickness of 210 m was attained at Wester Gartshore, north of which the formation thins to about 100 m at Corrieburn. It probably also thins farther south but this has not been proved within the district.

The Lower Limestone Formation is much more uniform than the underlying Lawmuir Formation. It consists of up to seven cycles of sedimentation, each starting with a thin marine limestone, followed by a dark grey bedded mudstone, the lower part of which usually has a marine fauna. The mudstone passes gradually up through siltstone to a sandstone that is generally fine grained. A thin seatearth and a thin coal may be present in the upper part. Clayband ironstones are common in some of the mudstones. Nonmarine limestones with ostracods occur below the Blackhall Limestone and were formerly regarded as part of it, but the name is now restricted to the marine limestone only. Faunal lists for the strata within this formation are given in Wilson (1989).

Marine influences were stronger during the deposition of the Lower Limestone Formation than at any other time in the Carboniferous. Several times shallow seas covered most if not all of the Airdrie district for prolonged periods. The clear shallow waters were rich in a variety of brachiopods, gastropods, bivalves, and at times some polyzoa, a few corals and goniatites. Subsidence was greatest in the central part of the sheet. Northward thinning of units plus changes in facies, for instance of the Hurlet Limestone, suggest that the northern part of the district may have escaped some of the marine invasions. Channel sandstones of fluvial origin are rare, most of the silt and sand laid down during Lower Limestone Formation times being deposited in the central part of the district. These sediments, which occur in upward-coarsening cycles, were probably part of a large delta which occupied much of the central part of the Midland Valley at this time. The top of the delta rarely and usually only locally emerged sufficiently to allow vegetation to cover it. A mudstone and siltstone dominated sequence in the Lennoxtown area suggests that it may have been situated in an interdistributary bay during this period.

Hurlet Limestone cycle

The lowest cycle occupies the interval between the base of the Hurlet Limestone and the base of the Shields Bed. The Hurlet Limestone, a crinoidal bioclastic bed, is visible at Finniescroft [6232 7685] and is usually 0.75–1.5 m thick, but is up to 3.7 m thick at Sculliongour [63 79] and up to 6.5 m at Corrieburn [684 799]. The limestone is normally crinoidal except where it is unusually thick, as in this area, where it is shelly (mostly brachiopods) and flaggy with argillaceous partings. It was quarried and mined, together with the underlying Alum Shale and Hurlet Coal, at Sculliongour and more extensively north of Milton of Campsie and south of Lennoxtown on the South Brae of Campsie. As the Murrayshall Limestone it was also quarried in the north-east corner of the district. The mudstones above the Hurlet Limestone are not generally very fossiliferous, but locally a few marine shells, including goniatites, occur near the base and *Lingula*, *Curvirimula*, *'Euestheria'* and fish debris have been recorded at higher levels. In the Wester Gartshore and Cardowan No. 13 boreholes the cycle is about 50 m thick with mudstone passing very gradually up into fine-grained sandstone, which gives way to siltstone and mudstone just below the top of the cycle. In Dumbreck No. 1 Borehole a medium-grained sandstone, 9 m thick, sits on the mudstone and is overlain by a coal 0.15 m thick in a cycle only 27 m thick. In the Lennoxtown area 10 m of mudstones occupy the whole of the interval between the Hurlet Limestone and the Shields Bed. Indeed, in this area the Shields Bed and some clayband ironstones are the only other beds to occur in 40 m of mudstones between the Hurlet and Blackhall limestones. These mudstones are well exposed in Glenwhapple [6154 7647–6193 7620] and in the Spoutbrae and Burniebrae burns near Shields Cottage [658 776]. In the Corrieburn area this cycle is thin (11–12 m including the enlarged limestone) but includes two sandstones. The upper one is a shelly bed 1.1 m thick that weathers to rottenstone [6855 7924] and lies immediately below the Shields Bed. In the north-east corner of the district this cycle is 20 m

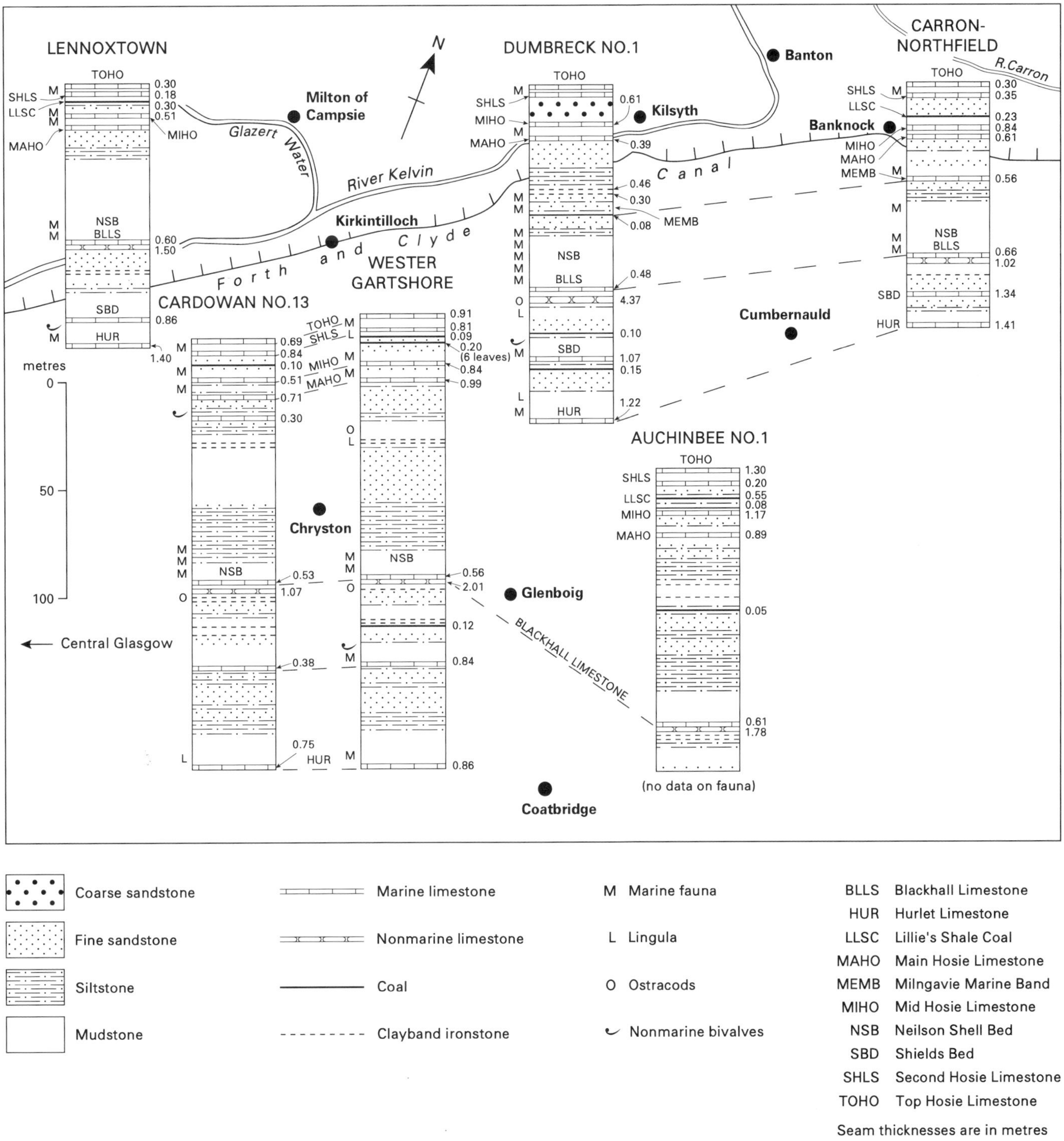

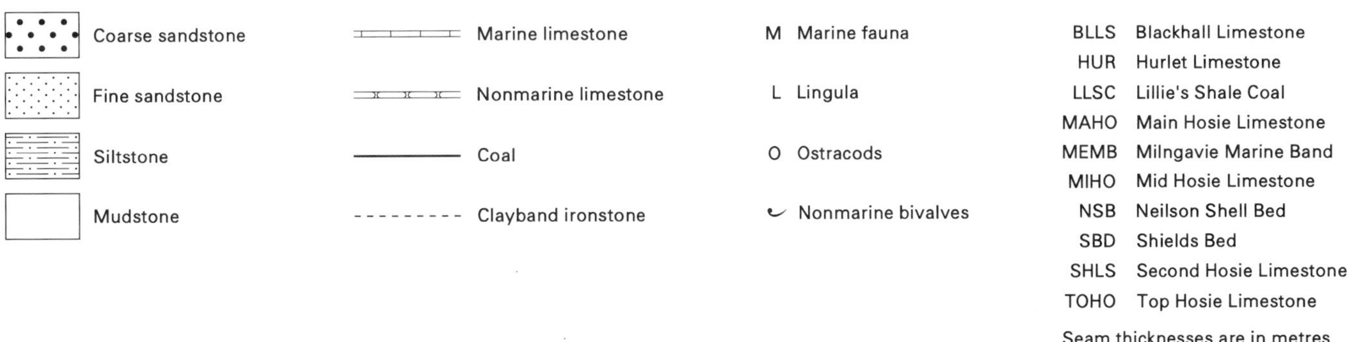

Figure 9 Comparative vertical sections of the Lower Limestone Formation, superimposed on a sketch-map to show approximate sites.

thick and consists mainly of mudstones, passing up into sandstone with a coal 0.1–0.2 m thick at the top.

Shields Bed cycle

This cycle comprises the strata between the base of the Shields Bed and the base of the Blackhall Limestone. The Shields Bed is a sandy crinoidal limestone up to 1.34 m thick which thins westwards and dies out near the western margin of the Airdrie district. The type locality [6579 7751] is in the Burniebrae (or Shields) Burn near Shields Cottage, where the bed is 0.75 m thick. It is also exposed at several places nearby in Spouthead Burn, in an unnamed streamlet [6423 7835] and in a tributary [6850 7916] of the so-called Middle Burn in the Corrieburn area. At Dunipace the bed has been known by its Stirling name of Limestone C. In parts of the Lennoxtown area mudstones, 30 m thick, occupy the whole cycle but elsewhere thin siltstones and sandstones also occur. This interval also contains the Campsie Clayband Ironstones and, locally, at the top several beds of nonmarine limestone with abundant ostracods. The sandstones thicken eastwards and are prominently exposed in the Middle Burn at Corrieburn. In Dumbreck No. 1 Borehole a coal 0.1 m thick lies between 8 m of mudstone, in which *Curvirimula* succeeds a marine fauna, and 7 m of sandstone that is overlain by 4 m of mudstone with *Lingula*. The nonmarine limestones below the Blackhall Limestone are unusually thick (4.37 m in 5 beds). The cycle thickens markedly south of the outcrop to about 40 m, with siltstones and sandstones well represented, and the coal reappears at Wester Gartshore.

Blackhall Limestone cycle

This cycle occupies the interval from the base of the Blackhall Limestone to the Milngavie Marine Band. The Blackhall Limestone is a persistent, bioclastic, crinoidal limestone, generally 0.45–0.65 m thick. It is the equivalent of the upper, marine part of the Fankerton Limestone of the River Carron [7902 8325], where it is almost the lowest bed seen above the quartz-dolerite sill. The limestone is also exposed at Maiden Castle [6433 7844], in the Burniebrae Burn [6600 7766] and in the Middle Burn at Corrieburn [6854 7870–6856 7908]. The mudstone above the limestone contains the Neilson Shell Bed (Wilson, 1966), with its exceptionally rich and diverse fauna of brachiopods, molluscs (including goniatites) and a few solitary corals. The fauna includes in particular *Crurithyris urii*, *Tornquistia youngi*, *Glabrocingulum atomarium*, *Straparollus carbonarius*, *Euchondria neilsoni*, *Pernopecten fragilis* and *Posidonia corrugata gigantea*. In Dumbreck No. 1 Borehole marine fossils persist for almost 40 m above the limestone (the fauna in the upper half being somewhat different from the lower assemblage) in a gradually upwards coarsening sequence from mudstone to siltstone. A few marine fossils were also found 24 m above the limestone in Cardowan No. 13 Borehole, but they are usually abundant only in the basal few metres, for instance at Wester Gartshore. Two other deep boreholes, Bedlay No. 2 [7139 7065] and Auchinbee No. 1 [7323 7566], also reached the Blackhall Limestone. The thickness of mudstone and siltstone combined reaches a maximum of 58 m in Bedlay No. 2. The best exposure of the mudstones is in the east bank of the Middle Burn at Corrieburn [6856 7864–6857 7908], where they are at least 18 m thick and contain abundant ironstone nodules. Other exposures of the mudstones occur in several streams flowing south off the Campsie Fells and in Muirhead Glen [6120 7679–6180 7677]. The overlying fine- to medium-grained sandstone varies in thickness from 3 m in Dumbreck No. 1 Borehole to 24 m in the Wester Gartshore Borehole. The sandstone is exposed above the mudstones at Corrieburn and in streams and hillside exposures (including old quarries) along the North Brae of Campsie from Burniebrae Burn westwards to Meikle Reive Fort [639 789]. In this last area the sandstone may be continuous with the Hosie Sandstone in the absence of the Milngavie Marine Band. In Dumbreck No. 1 and Auchinbee No. 1 boreholes a thin coal occurs near the top of the cycle.

Milngavie Marine Band cycle

This cycle is represented by the strata between the Milngavie Marine Band and the base of the Main Hosie Limestone. The Milngavie Marine Band shows a very varied development. It was first noted in this district in the River Carron section (Dinham and Haldane, 1932, p.30) occurring in 0.9 m of 'micaceous strata' which contained crinoid columnals 'and traces of other definitely marine fossils'. The correlation suggested therein with the Mill Hill Marine Band of west Fife is now regarded as correct. Forsyth and Wilson (1965, p.71) named the marine band on the basis of its development in the Glasgow district in Milngavie Nos. 5 and 6 boreholes (and also in Balmore No. 2 Borehole). Surface exposures of the band in the district occur in two of the head streams of the Banton Burn, east of Drumnessie [736 804]. Here the band is represented by shelly calcareous sandstone, locally decalcified to rottenstone. The band has not been found in the Lennoxtown area. A crinoidal limestone 0.3 m thick in Cardowan No. 13 Borehole may be the Milngavie Marine Band, but it appears to be rather high in the succession. In Dumbreck No. 1 Borehole the band is in two leaves of siltstone separated by 2.5 m of sandstone. The fauna is a restricted one of brachiopods and molluscs. The overlying mudstone, 5–10 m thick, contains several clayband ironstones and a fauna of *Curvirimula*, ostracods and fish debris. It passes up through siltstone and silty sandstone into the Hosie Sandstone, a mainly medium-grained bed up to 13 m thick. Unusually for a Scottish Carboniferous sandstone, the top contains crinoid and shell debris. The sandstone is split in the Burnlip Borehole [7339 6786] by an 18 cm coal overlain by mudstone with *Lingula*, and in Auchinbee No. 1 Borehole, by siltstone and coaly mudstone on seatearth. The latter also has a coal 2.5 cm thick just below the Main Hosie Limestone. Otherwise coal is absent from this cycle.

Hosie Limestone cycles

The top three cycles in the Lower Limestone Formation are much thinner than the preceding four. Each starts with one of the Hosie Limestones and the Top Hosie Limestone completes the formation. The total thickness of the three cycles ranges from 22 to 34 m, with the Main Hosie cycle 6.7 to 10.6 m thick, the Mid Hosie cycle 12 to 15 m thick and the Second Hosie cycle 2.4 to 7 m thick. These cycles are incomplete, being mainly composed of mudstones which along with the limestones are the only lithologies that are everywhere present. Sandstone does not occur in the sheet area between the Second and Top Hosie limestones. Dumbreck No. 1 Borehole is unique in having at least 12 m of mainly coarse-grained sandstone in the Mid Hosie cycle. Coal is present only in the Mid Hosie cycle, where the highly variable Lillie's Shale Coal is up to 0.55 m thick and locally is split into leaves. The Main, Mid and Second Hosie limestones are all bioclastic and crinoidal. They are 0.6–1.0 m, 0.35–1.15 m and 0.38–0.83 m thick respectively. The Top Hosie Limestone is of the cementstone type, that is, highly argillaceous, fine grained and less conspicuously fossiliferous than the other limestones. The occurrence of outlines of *Euphemites urii* on weathered surfaces led to its old name of Bellerophon Limestone. The mudstones all have rich faunas of brachiopods and molluscs, including (usually indeterminate) goniatites and orthocones. The Main Hosie cycle has the richest fauna and is the only one to include corals and bryozoa.

The Main Hosie Limestone is exposed in the headwaters of both the Spouthead Burn [6549 7844] and the Banton Burn [7399 8026], and in a decalcified state in the River Carron [7918 8328]. The Second Hosie Limestone is visible in the Burniebrae Burn [6605 7816], the Banton Burn [7403 8021] and the River Carron [7922 8325]. The Top Hosie Limestone is the best displayed in Burniebrae Burn [6605 7818], two unnamed streamlets [6750 7778, 6821 7808], the eastern burn at Corrieburn [6870 7874], Banton Burn [7403 8017] and the River Carron [7925 8324].

Typical Hosie cycles were found in several deep boreholes including Burnlip [7339 6786], Nethercroy No. 2 [7297 7690], Dalshannon [7289 7288], Cardyke No. 3 [6515 7025], Langdale No. 3 [6992 7037] and Thankerton Farm [7671 6134]. The last named is of particular interest because it is the only section in the southern part of the district.

The section from Thankerton Farm is as follows:

	Thickness m
Top Hosie Limestone, with brachiopods and gastropods	0.30
Calcareous mudstone with productoids	0.81
Dark mudstone with *Posidonia corrugata*	2.19
Second Hosie Limestone, crinoidal	0.51
Mudstone, shelly and crinoidal at top; rest carbonaceous, rooty in places	1.19
Mudstone, shelly, with *Lingula*, productoids and bivalves (Mid Hosie horizon)	0.23
Sandstone, hard, grey, rooty, with shell fragments at top	1.07
Sandstone and siltstone, interbanded	2.13
Mudstone, shelly, with abundant *Spirifer*	1.07
Main Hosie Limestone, crinoidal	0.69

The Hosie cycles in the borehole at Thankerton Farm are barely 12 m in total thickness (the least amount known in the district) but the coal and three of the limestones are present, with the fourth limestone represented by a marine band. The borehole continued through 12.67 m of sandstone and siltstone and ended in 2.03 m of mudstone.

FIVE

Upper Carboniferous (Silesian)

The Upper Carboniferous strata are assigned to the upper part of the Clackmannan Group, comprising the Limestone Coal Formation, the Upper Limestone Formation and the Passage Formation, and to the overlying informal group, the Coal Measures (Scotland) which is made up of the Lower, Middle and Upper Coal Measures. The boundary between the two lithostratigraphical groups almost coincides with the Namurian and Westphalian boundary. Detailed descriptions are given in Forsyth, 1993.

CLACKMANNAN GROUP (Silesian part)

The part of the Clackmannan Group of Silesian age, consists of the Limestone Coal Formation, the Upper Limestone Formation, and the Passage Formation, and is characterised by the continuation of the cyclic sedimentation which started in the upper Dinantian. All three formations consist of arenite-dominated sedimentation cycles with mudstones, limestones and coals occurring in different proportions in the different formations.

The top of the Limestone Coal Formation is taken at the base of the Index Limestone, the top of the Upper Limestone Formation at the top of the Castlecary Limestone, and the top of the Passage Formation at the Lowstone Marine Band.

Limestone Coal Formation

The Limestone Coal Formation is the lowest part of the Namurian sequence and belongs entirely to the Pendleian (E_1) Stage (Table 1). It occurs, either at surface or at depth, throughout most of the Airdrie district, only being absent in the northern part and the south-west corner. Outcrops occur mainly around Kilsyth and Dunipace. Exposures are largely confined to stream sections on the Kilsyth Hills, such as Queenzie Burn, where the Black Metals, dark grey mudstones, 20–30 m thick, with several clayband ironstones, are visible at [694 786], the Garrel Burn, the Banton Burn, where much of the lower part of the formation can be seen above Banton [750 792], and locally along the Castlerankine Burn and the River Carron, both of which traverse the whole of the formation. The Black Metals are also visible [712 762–712 764] on the south side of the Forth and Clyde Canal and in a quarry [752 801–752 804] east of Banton. The stratigraphy of the formation, however, is based largely on the numerous boreholes proving the sequence. The Limestone Coal Formation is thinnest (177 m) in the Thankerton Farm Borehole [7671 6134]; in the north-east, at Dunipace, it is 260 m thick. Elsewhere the formation is over 300 m thick, reaching 360 m in north-east Glasgow and substantially above 330 m at Kilsyth.

The distinction between the mainly argillaceous lower part and the coal-cyclic upper part of the Limestone Coal Formation, which is very marked to the west of the district, becomes progressively less marked eastwards.

The lower part (Figure 10) of the formation, up to the top of the Black Metals, is largely composed of mudstone in the west but siltstone and sandstone become more abundant eastwards (Forsyth, 1978c). Coals are largely, but not entirely, confined to that part of the sequence between the Johnstone Shell Bed and the Black Metals. They are generally thicker in the north-east than in the west. The Kilsyth Coking Coal in particular thickens markedly to 1.5 m around Kilsyth (where it was mined very extensively), a thickness only exceeded by the Bannockburn Main Coal around Dunipace in the upper part of the formation. The number of thin coals within and below the Johnstone Shell Bed increases eastwards. Clayband ironstones are less abundant than they are to the west of the district except in the Black Metals in the Banton area where nine occur, three of which were formerly worked. The Garibaldi Clayband Ironstone was mined at Banton as the Finestone, but the Johnstone Clayband Ironstone is thin or absent. The only widespread blackband ironstone is the Banton seam, which was quite extensively mined around Kilsyth and Banton, but elsewhere usually passes into coal. It is the equivalent of the Lower Garscadden Ironstone of the Glasgow district (Sheet 30E); there is no equivalent of the Upper Garscadden Ironstone in the Airdrie district.

The upper part of the Limestone Coal Formation (Figure 11) is a coal-cyclic sequence very similar to that found in the Glasgow district, with up to 25 cycles which have been traced from Glasgow to Stirling (Forsyth and Read, 1962). The cycles usually consist, in upward sequence, of coal, mudstone, siltstone, sandstone (generally the thickest item), siltstone and seatearth (usually thin and commonly sandy). The cycle that starts with the Kilsyth Cloven Coal is usually the thickest (8–15 m). The most extensively mined of the coals is the Meiklehill Main, which is rivalled in thickness only by the Bannockburn Main Coal of Dunipace and the Kilsyth Coking Coal in the lower part of the formation. Other extensively mined seams include the Kilsyth Cloven, Dumbreck Cloven and Meiklehill Wee coals. Seven other coals (Figure 11) are known to have been exploited to a lesser extent. Nine of the coals pass laterally into blackband ironstones, six of which were mined, the Kilsyth No. 3 seam quite extensively. These ironstones tend to be restricted to certain areas, for example, they occur in northern Glasgow, Kilsyth–Banton and Dunipace but are absent in the eastern Glasgow, Kirkintilloch–Lenzie,

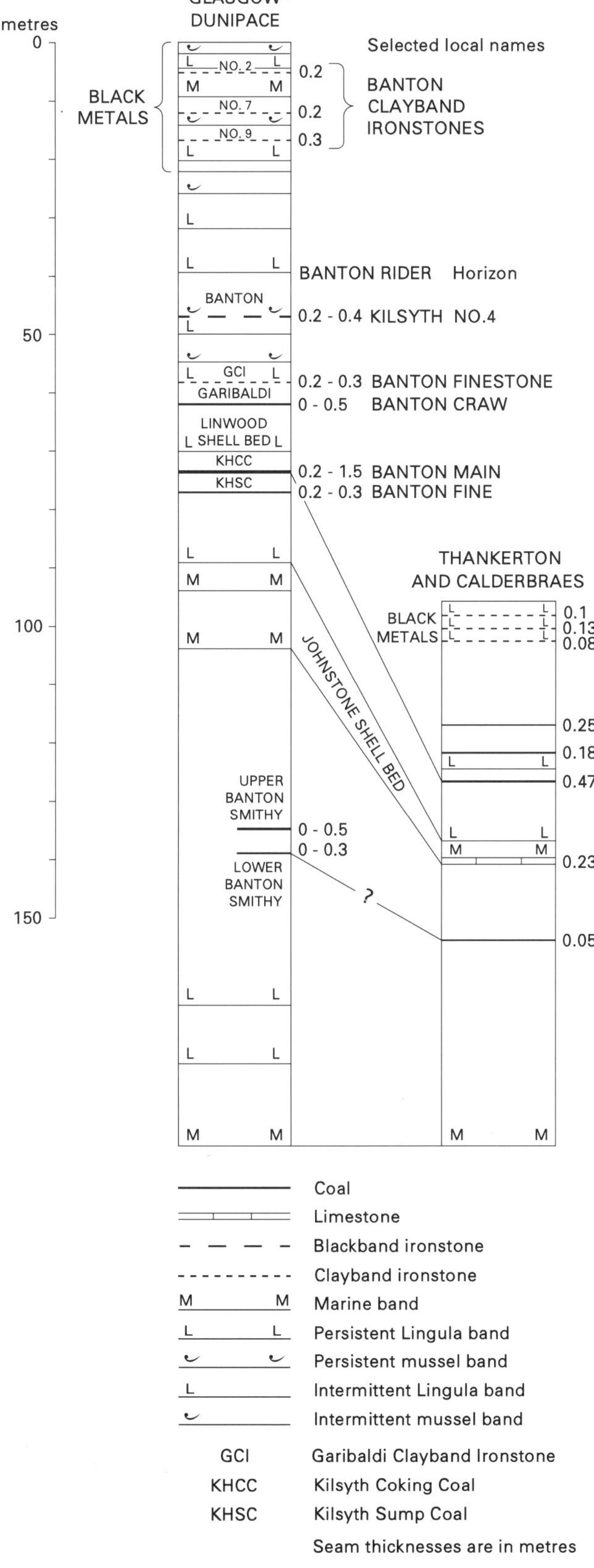

Figure 10 Vertical sections to show south-eastward thinning of the lower part of the Limestone Coal Formation.

Glenboig, Dullatur and Cumbernauld areas. The Banton Blackband Ironstone in the lower part of the formation is also of local occurrence.

Sandstones

Most of the sandstones are hard, fine grained, up to 6 m thick and contain sideritic micaceous ripple laminae. Several coarser and thicker channel sandstones, some with notably erosive bases, occur mainly in the upper part of the formation. In the lower part of the succession the only notable sandstone occurs between the Linwood Shell Bed and the horizon of the Garibaldi Coal. It is 15–22 m thick and causes little basal erosion. Above the sandstone the Garibaldi Coal is absent, probably because reduced subsidence over the sandstone prevented its formation.

The Cowlairs Sandstone at the top of the formation is generally absent along the northern margin of the outcrop and is best developed at its type locality in northern Glasgow. It occurs, mainly at depth, in a sinuous belt that extends east-south-east from Cowlairs almost to Coatbridge, then swings north-east through Cumbernauld, where it reaches 22 m in thickness, and on to Banknock. A subsidiary development, in which the sandstone is up to 17 m thick, extends east-south-east from Torrance through Kirkintilloch. In both belts there is erosion at the base of the sandstone, which appears to lie in channels coming from a large area of thick sand accumulation north and north-west of Glasgow.

The most persistent sandstone in the upper part of the formation is the Nitshill Sandstone which reaches 20 m in thickness. It occurs in a sinuous belt 1.5–2 km wide extending from west of the present area through eastern Glasgow to Dunipace (where it is exposed in the Castlerankine Burn). It cuts out the underlying Ashfield Rider Coal and where it is thickest, its incompactibility prevented the development of the Fourteen-Inch Under Coal, together with its seatearth and overlying mudstone. Other thicker and coarser sandstones locally cut out the Possil Wee and Possil Rider coals and the Berryhills Limestone, mainly along the northern margin of the outcrop from Torrance [620 742] to Dunipace [803 833].

Faunal bands

The lower part of the Limestone Coal Formation in the Airdrie district contains a number of faunal bands. The thick mudstone above the Top Hosie Limestone has a marine fauna at the base, dominated by *Posidonia corrugata*, and up to four *Lingula* bands higher up. *Naiadites* occurs sparsely between and above these bands. The Johnstone Shell Bed is usually in two or three leaves, separated by sandstone and siltstone. The lowest leaf generally has the richest fauna, the highest contains *Lingula* above marine fossils and the middle leaf, if present, may have *Lingula* or other marine shells as well. Exceptionally, in a cross-cut mine in Gartshore No. 11 Pit [7034 7389] two marine bands and three *Lingula* bands were reported (Robertson and Haldane, 1937, p.54).

The Linwood Shell Bed (Forsyth, 1978c, p.8) is fully developed in the western part of the district. Towards the east *Paracarbonicola* disappears, *Naiadites* becomes scarce

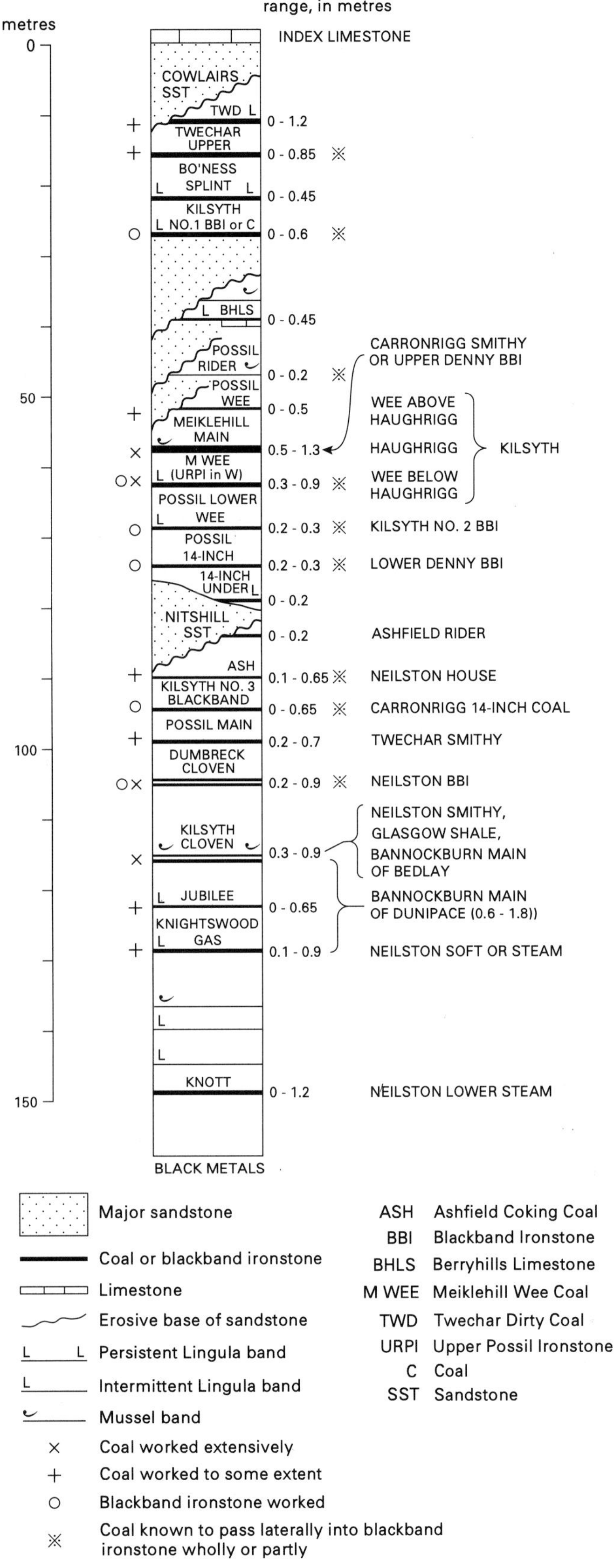

Figure 11 Vertical section of the upper part of the Limestone Coal Formation.

and tends to occur above the persistent *Lingula* band that identifies this horizon, even in the thin sequence seen in the Thankerton Farm and Calderbraes boreholes (Figure 10). *Naiadites* (above) and *Lingula* (below) both occur locally above the Garibaldi Coal. The *Lingula* band below the Banton Blackband Ironstone and *Naiadites* above the seam both occur persistently from eastern Glasgow to Glenboig, but the former is absent and the latter rare in the Kilsyth area. The *Lingula* band above the horizon of the rarely developed Banton Rider Coal has a similar range. Well-preserved *Naiadites* occur just below the Black Metals in eastern Glasgow. The Black Metals Marine Band has a less-rich fauna than the Johnstone Shell Bed. The Black Metals contain up to four *Lingula* bands, some lying above and others below the marine band; *Naiadites* is also locally present.

The upper part of the Limestone Coal Formation in the district contains 11 *Lingula* bands, only one less than the number found in the Glasgow district, but more than anywhere else in the Midland Valley (Forsyth, 1979). Of the eleven *Lingula* bands only that band above the Bo'ness Splint Coal, which has locally yielded *Orbiculoidea* and a few marine bivalves, can be described as persistent. The lowest three marine bands (Figure 11) occur only in the western part of the district. The band above the Jubilee Coal, however, persists eastwards, almost to Coatbridge, although in the north it has not been found east of Kirkintilloch. The band above the Fourteen-Inch Under Coal has only been recorded at five localities, four from between Glasgow and Coatbridge, and one at Dullatur [748 771]. The next band is known as the Sub-Hartley *Lingula* Band (Francis et al., 1970) which occurs persistently below the Hartley Coal in the Stirling and Clackmannan Coalfield. In the Airdrie district it has been found intermittently in the Dullatur, Kilsyth and Kirkintilloch areas and reaches eastern Glasgow, which appears to be its western limit. It is exceptional among Limestone Coal Formation *Lingula* bands in that it dies out gradually south-westwards from the Kincardine Basin. The band above the Meiklehill Wee Coal has been confirmed only in Torrance No. 3 Borehole [6354 7296], but has also been reported to occur in north-east Glasgow in the equivalent seam, the Upper Possil Ironstone. The *Lingula* bands above the Berryhills Limestone and Kilsyth No. 1 Blackband Coal are both of localised occurrence, most records coming from eastern Glasgow. The band above the Twechar Dirty Coal is rare and occurs only in the Kilsyth and Dullatur areas.

Nonmarine bivalves, mostly *Naiadites*, have been found at several horizons but occur commonly only above the Kilsyth Cloven Coal. Whether or not they also occur in the blackband ironstones is not known.

The thinness of the Limestone Coal Formation in the Thankerton Farm and Calderbraes boreholes has already been indicated. The former borehole proved the whole formation to be 177 m thick, with the upper part 81 m thick and the lower part 96 m thick. In the Calderbraes borehole the upper part of the formation is 89 m thick. The Johnstone Shell Bed contained a crinoidal limestone, 0.23–0.25 m thick, in both boreholes. This limestone has not been identified in the remainder of the

Airdrie district. The three coals found in the boreholes between the Johnstone Shell Bed and the Black Metals are probably the Kilsyth Coking, Garibaldi and Banton coals respectively with a *Lingula* band representing the Linwood Shell Bed. The Black Metals are thin and contain three *Lingula* bands. Therefore, all the main horizons in the lower part of the succession can be recognised in the borehole sections despite the reduction in thickness of the formation by about one-third. The thickness reduction in the upper part is greater and affects the stratigraphy so much that no marker horizon can be identified. The sequence consists of irregular alternations of sandstones, siltstones, mudstones and unusually thick seatearths with a few coals up to 0.38 m thick but faunal bands are absent. The successions from the two boreholes are quite different in detail, but both are generally similar to the Hamilton Bridge Borehole [7380 5621] in the Hamilton district (Sheet 23W), (Macgregor, 1937) the Rashiehill Borehole [8386 7301] (Anderson, 1963, pp.50–51) and the Forrestfield Borehole [8604 6707], both in the Falkirk district (Sheet 31E). All these boreholes are in the central zone of the Central Coalfield syncline and proved the formation to be 150 to 200 m thick, a good deal less than the thickness found on either flank. The structural syncline is therefore superimposed on an area of reduced subsidence that persisted throughout most of the Namurian but had little effect on Westphalian strata.

Palaeogeography

The depositional basin continued to subside during the deposition of the Limestone Coal Formation but marine influences were much weaker than in the underlying Lower Limestone Formation. Quiet backwater conditions prevailed, at first, to the west of the district, but farther east deltaic conditions quickly became dominant and vegetation occasionally colonised the delta top. Increased subsidence brought about the major marine incursion represented by the Johnstone Shell Bed but only in the south-east corner of the district was the sea clear enough to permit even impure limestone to form. Deltaic clastic deposits alternated with quasimarine muds towards the end of the marine episode.

The marine incursion was followed by the onset of a paralic environment in which several periods of coal formation alternated with the entry of quasimarine or nonmarine waters accompanied by *Lingula* or *Naiadites*, or, for one period, by both plus *Paracarbonicola*. Locally, accumulations of decaying vegetation were accompanied by iron precipitation to form blackband ironstone. Fluvial channels were uncommon during this episode. Subsequently, as the main part of the delta retreated, probably to the north-east, marine and quasimarine muds covered the whole district for a prolonged period. This was followed by a return to paralic conditions with many episodes, some of them prolonged, of colonisation of the delta top by plants. Decaying vegetation accumulated, with periodic iron precipitation, over considerable periods of time. Fluvial channels remained uncommon but one has been identified and traced across the entire district from west-south-west to east-north-east. The presence of other channels to the north-west may indicate an origin in that direction. Frequently the delta top was sufficiently submerged for *Lingula* to become established locally.

Upper Limestone Formation

The Upper Limestone Formation occurs in most of the central and southern parts of the Airdrie district. It is largely outcropping in the central parts, and buried below Coal Measures in the southern part. The lower part of the formation belongs to the Pendleian (E_1) stage of the Namurian and the upper part, above the Orchard Limestone, has been assigned to the Arnsbergian (E_2) stage (Ramsbottom, 1978). This chronostratigraphical division is mirrored by lithological changes (see below). Surface exposures were formerly quite abundant in stream sections and quarries but have now deteriorated in both number and quality. The Index Limestone is rather poorly exposed in the Castlerankine Burn [7952 8228] and is seen to be baked hard by an underlying sill at Craigroot Quarry [691 776] and beside the adjacent Queenzie Burn. Near the Queenzie Burn, the overlying mudstones are 6 to 8 m thick and the Bishopbriggs Sandstone has conspicuous laminated burrows. Strata between the Index and Lyoncross limestones, including the Huntershill Cement Limestone, are exposed in the headstreams of the Wood Burn [6743 7756–6790 7712; 6818 7779–6804 7729]. The mudstones above the Orchard Limestone and the Glenboig Marine Band are exposed in a railway cutting [619 707]. The Calmy Limestone was formerly visible in several quarries in north-east Glasgow and around Cumbernauld. Now it can only be seen in a waterfall [7847 7728] at Cumbernauld, in part in a streamlet [7637 7770] at Hirst and in Cowie's Glen [6603 7705] where the *Edmondia punctatella* band is visible. In the Luggie Water, on either side of Luggiebank, [763 728] strata above (Plate 2) and below the limestone are exposed. The overlying mudstones are visible in quarries beside the stream and at Balloch [737 746]. The sandstone below Plean No. 1 Limestone and the limestone itself are displayed in Drumcavel Quarry [705 694]. The Red Glen at Cumbernauld provides several exposures of the strata associated with the Plean Limestones, including one of Plean No. 2 Limestone [7753 7520], which can also be seen in a quarry [7625 7415] in Glencryan Wood. The Castlecary Limestone is no longer visible around Castlecary or Cumbernauld.

The Upper Limestone Formation in most of the Airdrie district (Forsyth, 1982, fig. 5, p.16) is between 225 and 300 m thick, except in two areas.

The first area is in the south-east, where the Thankerton Farm and Calderbraes boreholes show thicknesses of 119 m and 136 m respectively. These boreholes were drilled into a NNE-trending positive area marked by reduced sedimentation in Namurian times. This feature now lies below the axial region of the Central Coalfield Syncline. The sequences in the two boreholes are similar to those in the Hamilton Bridge and Rashiehill boreholes (Macgregor, 1937; Anderson, 1963).

The second area is in a WSW–ENE belt extending from Torrance to Banknock. In this area, even allowing

Plate 2 Mudstone sequence with thin ironstone bands occurring above the Calmy Limestone (Upper Limestone Formation), Luggiebank Quarry, near Cumbernauld [765 725] (D 4869).

for the high dips encountered in Wester Shirva No. 1 Borehole [6865 7517], it appears that the formation locally exceeds 400 m in thickness and is more than 300 m thick throughout this area.

The overlying Passage Formation rests on various strata ranging from the Castlecary Limestone in the north to just above Plean No. 1 Limestone in the south-east. Although this has affected comparisons of total thickness from the south-west to the north-east, a real thickening of the succession is shown by comparison of various intervals. For example, the Index–Calmy interval shows a clearly defined thickness of 200–260 m in the north but to the south, it shows an easterly decrease from 180–213 m in eastern Glasgow to 156–182 m around Glenboig and 91 m at Thankerton Farm.

LITHOSTRATIGRAPHY

The Upper Limestone Formation can be divided into two parts reflecting both lithology and chronostratigraphy.

The lower part, up to the Orchard Limestone, consists mainly of coal-cyclic sequences similar to those in the upper part of the Limestone Coal Formation except that they are extensively replaced by erosive sandstones (Figure 12). The sequences are also interrupted by two major marine incursions. Evidence for the first begins at the Index Limestone, a typical Upper Limestone Formation bioclastic crinoidal limestone, characteristically containing algal bodies. This is overlain by several metres of mudstone that grade upwards through siltstone to the generally fine-grained Bishopbriggs Sandstone. The end of this marine phase is marked by the Huntershill Cement Limestone. The Bishopbriggs Sandstone locally contains abundant trace fossils and may be part of the marine episode. The second major marine incursion resulted in the formation of the Lyoncross Limestone and a few metres of mudstone. Several other minor marine episodes produced bands with *Lingula* and locally *Orbiculoidea* or a few marine bivalves. Nonmarine bivalves are rare, but *Naiadites* has been found. The thickest coal is the Chapelgreen Coal which was worked to a small extent [6972 7750] near Kilsyth and possibly also, as Gardner's Coal, at Meiklehill [6676 7401]. The Garnkirk Gas Coal of Cadder No. 16 Pit [6405 7007] (later named Wester Auchengeich) is a local development, probably about 10 m lower in the sequence. The Lyoncross Coal is not known to have been mined in the district.

The Bishopbriggs Sandstone is very variable in thickness and thins markedly eastwards from over 30 m at its type locality (just to the west in the Glasgow district) to less than 2 m over a distance of less than 5 km. By contrast the sandstones which lie between the Huntershill Cement Limestone and the Lyoncross Coal are generally much coarser and have erosive bases. The lowest of these sandstones is the Upper Dumbreck Sandstone which reaches almost 40 m in thickness and locally cuts out the Huntershill Cement Limestone. The next notable sandstone is the Cadgers Loan Sandstone, which is a very persistent bed up to 26 m thick that locally replaces one or more of the coals lying both above or below it. These two sandstones coalesce in places to form the Barrhead Grit. This facies occurs between eastern Glasgow and Glenboig reaching 50 m in thickness and locally containing quartz pebbles up to 2.5 cm in diameter. Above the Lyoncross Limestone the most notable of the coarser, erosive sandstones is the Giffnock Sandstone, which is best developed in the present sheet along the northern part of the outcrop, for example in Torrance No. 1 Borehole [6419 7359] where it is 22 m thick.

The upper part of the Upper Limestone Formation starts with two major Yoredale-type cycles. The lower cycle is 43–75 m thick and the upper one 36–55 m. Both cycles have basal limestone overlain by a thick mudstone (up to about 25 m thick) which usually passes gradation-

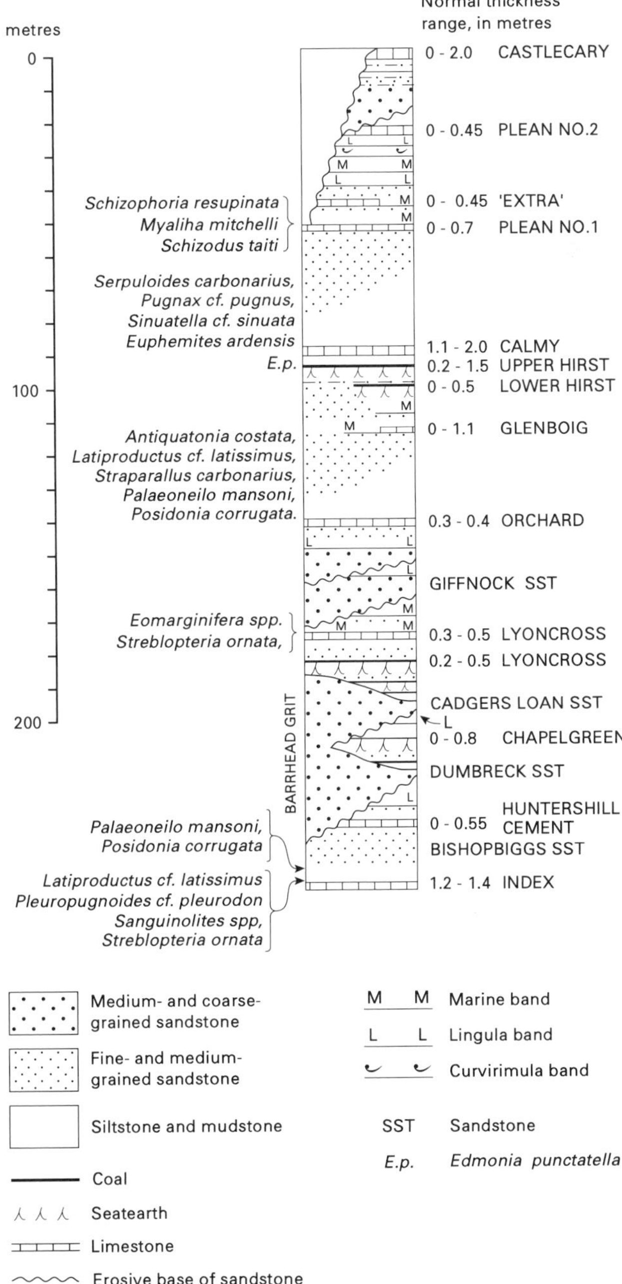

Figure 12 Vertical section of the Upper Limestone Formation.

ally through siltstone to fine- or medium-grained sandstone. The proportions of mudstone, siltstone and sandstone vary a great deal. The base of the lower cycle is marked by the Orchard Limestone. Locally, the sandstone overlying the Orchard Limestone, which reaches 37 m in thickness in Torrance No. 1 Borehole, is divided by the Glenboig Marine Band (Forsyth, 1978b), consisting of up to four beds of mudstone, and the Glenboig Limestone. The Lower and Upper Hirst coals at the top of the lower cycle are both very variable in thickness. The upper seam is up to 1.5 m thick and has been mined to a small extent. Immediately below the upper boundary of the cycle, defined by the Calmy Limestone, is the widely developed *Edmondia punctatella* band (Wilson, 1958), a thin band of carbonaceous shale in which *E. punctatella* occurs abundantly, with a few other marine shells.

The Calmy Limestone marking the base of the second cycle, is typically in two leaves, the upper of which is of 'calmy' type — hard, fine-grained, compact, pale grey, fawn or almost white in colour, conchoidal in fracture and not conspicuously fossiliferous but sufficiently so to establish its fully marine character. It is usually 1.3–2 m thick, but reaches 3 m, the maximum for an Upper Limestone Formation limestone in the district. The Calmy Limestone was formerly quarried at several widely scattered localities and is known to have been mined around Muirhead [693 695] and Cumbernauld. The mudstone above the Calmy Limestone is thick and grades up through siltstone into sandstone; the proportions of the three lithologies vary a great deal. Marine shells occur at intervals up to 25 m above the limestone. In this cycle coarser sandstones are known only from the Alexandra Parade Borehole [6177 6566], in which they occur in two beds, 7.5 and 8 m thick respectively. The beds are separated by 8 m of finer sandstones, seatearths and siltstones, with two thin coals and two thin mudstones with *Lingula* and *Curvirimula.*

The next part of the formation, known as the strata associated with the Plean Limestones, is 25–40 m thick and consists of up to six cycles, three of which include a thin coal locally.

At the base, Plean No.1 Limestone is shelly and crinoidal over much of the Airdrie district but locally develops a coralline phase. It is absent in the north-east where it may be represented by mudstone or, as in the Abronhill Borehole [7881 7564], by shelly calcareous sandstone. It usually has little or no coal below it, except in the north-east, where a seam which was mined to a small extent as the Navigation Coal, may lie at this horizon. There are two other limestones in this sequence, the lower of which is only locally developed and has the name 'Plean Extra'. Near the top of the sequence is Plean No. 2 Limestone which, although generally persistent, is locally cut out. Plean No. 3 Limestone is not known in the district. The mudstones contain several bands with *Lingula*, *Orbiculoidea* and a few marine bivalves. Two of the higher bands have *Curvirimula.*

The highest part of the Upper Limestone Formation is known only in the north where it reaches 35 m in thickness. It consists mainly of a coarse-grained sandstone up to 18 m thick with an erosive base. This major sandstone is overlain by sequences of sandstones and siltstones with one or two thin coals (Figure 12). The Castlecary Limestone at the top of the formation is also known only in the north, where it is 1.5–2.0 m thick, dolomitic and locally affected by contemporaneous leaching that reduced it to nodules in a clay matrix as seen in the Coneypark Borehole [7754 7888].

Condensed sequences of the Upper Limestone Formation were encountered in the Thankerton Farm and Calderbraes boreholes. These sequences comprise four cycles of limestone, mudstone and sandstone, plus

Plean No. 1 Limestone at the top. The Orchard Limestone has a thickness within its normal range; the Calmy Limestone (1.1–1.2 m) is slightly thinner; the Lyoncross and Index limestones (0.45–0.55 m and 1.8 m respectively) are actually thicker.

Palaeogeography

The Upper Limestone Formation shows marked contrasts in palaegeography. The whole of the Airdrie district (and much of the Midland Valley of Scotland) was inundated by a shallow sea on at least four occasions. The richest faunas known in western Europe (Wilson, 1967, p.466) thrived in these seas except that goniatites and corals were rare. These marine incursions were thought by Wilson (1967) to have come from the east, several were lengthy and included periods of sufficiently clear-water conditions to permit limestone formation. Their duration is uncertain because the absence of marine fossils in silty or sandy sediments does not preclude marine conditions; for example, in the interval between the formation of the Index and Huntershill Cement limestones. Several other shorter and possibly less-complete cycles of marine deposition took place with the final incursion marking the end of the formation. The Castlecary Limestone, produced in this event, was probably formed all over the district but was speedily removed from much of it by penecontemporaneous erosion. During the marine episodes the margins of the depositional basin probably receded well away from the Airdrie district. Between the marine incursions, paralic conditions prevailed as the long-established delta in the central part of the Midland Valley emerged and was periodically colonised by vegetation, though usually only briefly. The delta top was also crossed by major distributaries, particularly during deposition of the first part of the formation. These distributaries cut deep and wide channels which are now sand filled. Towards the end of Upper Limestone Formation times more widespread erosion resumed in the southern part of the district heralding the more powerful downcutting processes in Passage Formation times which removed variable amounts of the highest Upper Limestone Formation strata.

Passage Formation

The term 'Passage Group' was introduced by MacGregor (1960) to replace the previous name (Scottish) Millstone Grit, because the strata concerned are equivalent to only the top part of the English Millstone Grit, plus some of the English Lower Coal Measures. In the Central Coalfield the Passage Group originally included the strata between the Castlecary Limestone and the Crofthead Slatyband Ironstone but Francis et al. (1970, p.203) extended the group in the adjacent Stirling and Clackmannan Coalfield upwards to the base of the more persistent Lowstone Marine Band. This practice has been adopted in the Central Coalfield. The Passage Group has now been reclassified as the Passage Formation.

The Passage Formation is known (Neves et al., 1965) to include strata belonging to the Arnsbergian (E_2) Stage and either the Subdenian (H) Stage or the Kinderscoutian (R_2) Stage. The presence of both Marsdenian (R_1) and Westphalian A strata is indicated with some certainty by miospore evidence. It has not, however, proved possible to identify the *Gastrioceras subcrenatum* marine band at the Namurian–Westphalian boundary, although it is thought to be one of the bands in the No. 6 Marine Band group of the Passage Formation (Figure 13). In the Airdrie district No. 6 Marine Band group is represented by one *Lingula* band, known only from the Castlecary area. It follows that the Lowstone Marine Band together with the topmost beds of the Passage Formation are regarded as lying within Westphalian A.

The Passage Formation in the Airdrie district contains up to 12 marine or *Lingula* bands, identified by numbers (Figure 13). Numbers 0, 1 and 2 occur as single bands, usually with limestones. No. 0 is local, the other two are widespread except in the south-east part of the district. No. 3 Marine Band group is represented by a single band from Castlecary to Glenboig and is absent in eastern Glasgow. In the Alexandra Parade Borehole three bands occur close together and contain a fauna that suggests identification as No. 3 Marine Band group although the borehole is more than 25 km south-west of the nearest known occurrences. The nearby Beattie's Bakery Borehole [6186 6513] has a similar grouping of two marine bands, also in a section with no other Passage Formation marine or *Lingula* band. A single marine band occurs in the Castlecary–Bonnybridge area, between No. 3 Marine Band and No. 5 Marine Band group. It is suggested that the term No. 4 Marine Band be applied to this band, which is represented at Castlecary by a *Lingula* band but is not known elsewhere in the district. No. 5 Marine Band group includes four marine or *Lingula* bands at Castlecary, one more than Francis et al. (1970, p.210) could confirm in the Kincardine Basin. Elsewhere in the district, however, only one band (possibly two at Chapelhall) has been found, usually with *Lingula* alone. No. 6 Marine Band group is represented in the district by a single *Lingula* band, known only at Castlecary. Penecontemporaneous erosion certainly has played a part in the disappearance of these bands towards the south-west, but it is also likely that some of them died out in that direction.

The Passage Formation crops out in an irregular NE-trending belt across the middle of the Airdrie district extending below Coal Measures to the south. It also occurs in two small unexposed basins west and north-east of Kirkintilloch. In the eastern part of the main outcrop exposures, mostly in the lower part of the formation, are quite numerous in several stream sections, such as the Walton Burn, Luggie Water and Shank Burn. Previously, quarries also provided good sections but they are now all abandoned and some have been filled in. Greenfoot Quarry [734 700] still provides a section of the lower part of the formation.

The Passage Formation thins markedly westwards and southwards (Figure 13) from an estimated maximum of almost 200 m at Castlecary to 83 m in the Alexandra Parade Borehole [6177 6566] and 75 m in the Calderbraes Borehole [768 627].

The south and westward reduction in thickness particularly affects the upper part of the formation, in which

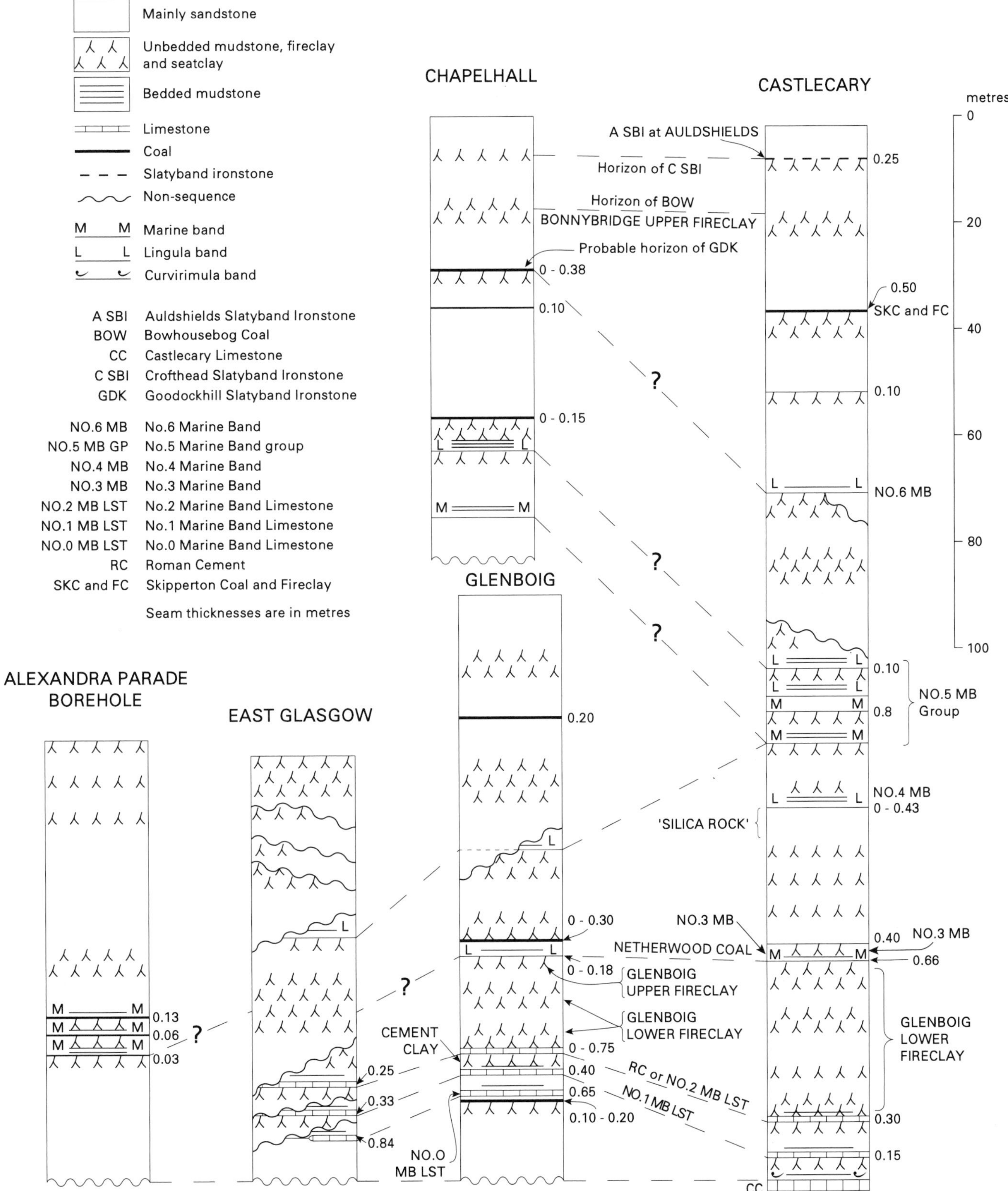

Figure 13 Comparative vertical sections of the Passage Formation.

the coals and marine bands recognised at Castlecary are cut out progressively, from the top down. Their removal is not the result of a single major non-sequence but rather the cumulative effect of erosion at the bases of the many sandstones. This erosive process was most notable in the upper part of the formation, although a widespread break prior to the deposition of No. 0 Marine Band occurs over most of the Airdrie district. This erosive event removed the Castlecary Limestone over the central and southern parts of the sheet area and locally cut down as far as Plean No. 2 Limestone.

The westward attenuation in the southern part of the district takes a different course. In the Chapelhall area (Figure 13) several boreholes show that the upper part of the formation is essentially intact, though reduced in thickness. The Bowhousebog Coal is absent but the Bonnybridge Upper Fireclay can be recognised. The Goodockhill Slatyband Ironstone is represented by a coal but the No. 6 Marine Band group is absent. An assemblage of mudstones, fireclays and a thin coal includes a *Lingula* band as a representative of No. 5 Marine Band group, to which a marine band 9 m below it may also belong. Below a coarse, pebbly sandstone, with a clearly erosive base, there is a thin crinoidal limestone that is tentatively identified as Plean No. 1 Limestone of the Upper Limestone Formation. If this correlation is correct, the Passage Formation is 80 m thick with the lower part entirely missing. In the Calderbraes Borehole, 2 km to the west, the formation is of similar thickness to the succession in the Chapelhall area but no faunal bands were detected.

Lithology

The Passage Formation consists mainly of sandstones with subordinate poorly bedded mudstones that are commonly termed fireclays regardless of their refractory properties. Bedded mudstones, siltstones, coals and limestones all occur but are very thin except from the base to the top of No. 2 Marine Band and within Nos. 3 and 5 Marine Band groups where the succession is clearly coal-cyclic with significant development of all the lithologies.

The sandstones are up to 24 m thick and range in grain size from fine to very coarse. Locally they contain pebbles, generally of quartz, up to 2.5 cm in size. The sandstones are mostly white in colour with a high silica content, for example the Silica Rock (Figure 13) which was formerly mined as refractory material at Castlecary and other beds which were worked at Heathfield [684 684] and Gartcosh [693 679]. None has been exploited for glass sand in the district. The sandstones are usually rather soft, and have been quarried for moulding sand at Gartverrie [733 688]. The proportion of sandstone in the succession tends to increase as the thickness decreases.

The unbedded mudstones include several seams that have been worked as fireclays. Indeed the Scottish firebrick industry began over 100 years ago in the area from Cardowan [668 686] through Garnkirk and Heathfield to Glenboig and Gartverrie. Later it spread north-eastwards to Cumbernauld and Castlecary. Sadly no extraction of fireclay is now taking place in the district. Most of the seams lie in the Passage Formation, including the one which was most extensively exploited, now named the Glenboig Lower Fireclay but widely known as the Lower Fireclay(s). It lies between the Roman Cement and the Netherwood Coal. At Castlecary it is divided into four leaves, all of them mined, the second lowest most extensively. The Glenboig Lower Fireclay yields material with over 40 per cent alumina and was quarried or mined almost throughout its outcrop from Heathfield to Castlecary. It is usually mottled in fawn, yellow, green, grey, red or purple and rarely shows much evidence of roots. Its provence may, therefore, be largely the product of intense bauxitic weathering of basaltic lavas, possibly exhumed parts of the Clyde Plateau Volcanic Formation (cf. Read, 1969).

At Glenboig at least two other fireclays (Figure 13) were mined, namely the Cement Clay and the (Glenboig) Upper Fireclay. The latter must not be confused with the much higher Bonnybridge Upper Fireclay to the east. Fireclays at or about these horizons were also mined at Castlecary, Gain [736 702] and Gartcosh. Other fireclays, mostly in the upper part of the Passage Formation, have been mined at Blochairn [617 662], Cardowan, Garnkirk, Gartverrie and Glentore [793 724], mostly under local names or numbers. The sequence is too condensed and lacking in marker bands to permit these local seams to be correlated. Some, such as the Captain's Fireclay at Glenboig, are probably in the Lower Coal Measures.

Most of these unbedded mudstones contain roots and are therefore seatclays, but in many cases decarbonisation makes the roots very difficult to detect. Some of the mudstones are conspicuously mottled in red, purple, yellow or green on a fawn or grey background. Clay ironstone nodules or clusters of sphaerosiderite granules are common with the latter, in particular, difficult to remove and therefore detrimental to their quality as fireclays. Clay ironstones also occur in the bedded mudstones but none are known to have been worked in this district.

The bedded mudstones are usually very thin (up to 1 m), dark grey to black and carbonaceous. Many contain roots which may largely obliterate the bedding. They are thickest and most abundant in the lower half of the formation. The very shaly or canneloid mudstone immediately above the Castlecary Limestone at Castlecary and Cumbernauld contains *Curvirimula*, fish debris and ostracods. The other mudstones are either barren or, more usually, yield *Lingula* or a sparse marine fauna.

There are up to three thin impersistent limestones near the base of the Passage Formation. The lowest is No. 0 Marine Band Limestone. It is the least persistent and can only be proved to occur by the presence of both the other two, as at Greenfoot Quarry and the nearby Haggmuir Borehole [7406 6877]. It may also be present in Queenslie No. 6 Borehole (Forsyth, 1961). The horizon is locally occupied by a marine or *Lingula* band. The absence of the band may, in general, be the result of non-deposition rather than penecontemporaneous erosion. No. 1 Marine Band Limestone is the thinnest (up to 0.45 m thick) of the three. It is almost as persistent as the Roman Cement or No. 2 Marine Band Limestone but is locally cut out, especially in the west, by an erosive sandstone. Nos. 0 and 1 Marine Band limestones are both argillaceous, bioclastic and crinoidal, in contrast to the No. 2 Marine Band Limestone, which consists largely of a 'lumachelle' of crushed orthotetoid and *Schizophoria* valves. This limestone is the most persistent but is locally cut out, and is the only one to occur in the outlier of Passage Formation west of Kirkintilloch, but it also is locally cut out. None of the limestones occurs in the south-east part of the district.

The coals are mostly very thin and impersistent. Most are thickest in the north-east at Castlecary. The Netherwood Coal takes its name from Netherwood Farm [775 784] and is not known to have been mined although it reaches 0.66 m at Castlecary. It persists as far south as Glenboig and may reappear in the Alexandra Parade Borehole. The Skipperton Coal is 0.5 m thick at Castlecary but elsewhere is not identifiable. The Bowhousebog Coal is known at Bonnybridge, just east of the sheet margin, but its presence has not been established within the sheet, even in the Banknock–Castlecary area.

The upper part of the Passage Formation was formerly notable for the occurrence of slatyband ironstones (defined as fissile ironstones composed of alternating clayband and blackband laminae), which were eagerly sought after in the 19th century. Although most of these impersistent but locally very rich ironstones occur to the east a few are located in the Airdrie district. The Auldshields Slatyband (or Lower Blackband) Ironstone is up to 0.25 m thick and is exposed in Auldshields Glen, south of Auldshields Bridge [770 715] where it was worked locally. It is probably a correlative of the better known Crofthead Slatyband Ironstone of the Falkirk district, as is the Earlshill Upper Slatyband Ironstone, whose workings, at depths of over 150 m, extend westwards into the Airdrie district at Stepends [804 671] and Easter Moffat [802 663]. This seam was exceedingly variable (from 0.05 m to 0.9 m) in thickness but very rich: a sample yielded 42 per cent of metallic iron, hence it was economically viable to mine at considerable depths. The Goodockhill Slatyband Ironstone of the Falkirk district is represented by a coal in the Chapelhall area; it is not recognised elsewhere in the district.

Palaeogeography

Read (1969, p.344) indicated that with the onset of the Passage Formation the paralic, probably mainly deltaic conditions that had prevailed in the Central Coalfield tended to retreat before a great influx of coarse-grained clastic sediments. He ascribed this regression to tectonic instability. The depositional basin probably contracted, some of the Dinantian lavas to the north and west may have been exhumed and fluviatile conditions prevailed. Sand filled the channels and mud formed overbank deposits. Mottling of the rocks, the presence of siderite concretions and desiccation cracks all attest to periods of lower water table; thus, although vegetation frequently colonised the depositional area, little coal-forming material was preserved. Marine incursions were frequent, but were mostly of too short a time scale to allow rich faunas to develop. The marine strata mostly die out to the west and south, the directions in which the Passage Formation thins markedly. This thinning reflects reduced subsidence, which would both inhibit penetration by the sea and favour penecontemporaneous erosion. Many small non-sequences and one larger one occur in the south-east. Here, the lower part of the formation, plus the top of the Upper Limestone Formation, appears to be missing.

COAL MEASURES (SCOTLAND)

The coal-bearing, cyclic, fluviodeltaic sediments which overlie the Passage Formation have long been known as 'coal measures'. In Scotland they were formerly divided into the Barren Red Measures overlying the Productive Coal Measures, the latter being split into Upper and Lower parts. MacGregor (1960) renamed the units as the Upper (Barren) Coal Measures and the Productive Coal Measures. He divided the latter into the Middle Coal Measures and the Lower Coal Measures. The top of the Middle Coal Measures was defined by Skipsey's (Aegiranum) Marine Band and the base by the Queenslie (Vanderbeckei) Marine Band. The base of the Lower Coal Measures was drawn at an arbitrary level, taken to be the Lowstone Marine Band (Francis et al., 1970). The base of the Lower Coal Measures as currently in use in Scotland is at a somewhat higher chrono-stratigraphical level than defined elsewhere. The term Coal Measures (Scotland) reflects the different usage in Scotland and because the top and bottom are not formally defined it is considered to be an informal unit of group status.

Lower Coal Measures

The Lower Coal Measures fall entirely within Westphalian A, both ending at the base of the Vanderbeckei Marine Band (Table 1). The base is now drawn at the Lowstone Marine Band which lies about 70 m above the base of Westphalian A at Castlecary and less than that elsewhere in the district. The Lower Coal Measures occur, either at surface or at depth, over most of the southern half of the Airdrie district and also in the Banknock Coalfield. Exposures are few. The basal beds are exposed in Auldshields Glen [77 71–77 72]. Some of the lower part of the succession is visible in the Shotts Burn, east of Chapelhall, and some of the upper part in the North Calder Water at Petersburn [78 64] and Calderbank [77 62]. The stratigraphy is therefore largely obtained from the numerous boreholes. The Lower Coal Measures are thickest (160 m) in the Banknock Coalfield, decreasing south-westwards to 96 m in central Glasgow (Forsyth, 1980), the thinning being most marked in the lower part of the sequence.

The Lower Coal Measures (Figure 14) are composed entirely of coal-bearing cyclic sedimentary rocks, the typical cycle consisting of coal, mudstone, siltstone, sandstone, siltstone and seatearth. In the lowest part of the succession, however, the sandstones and seatearths

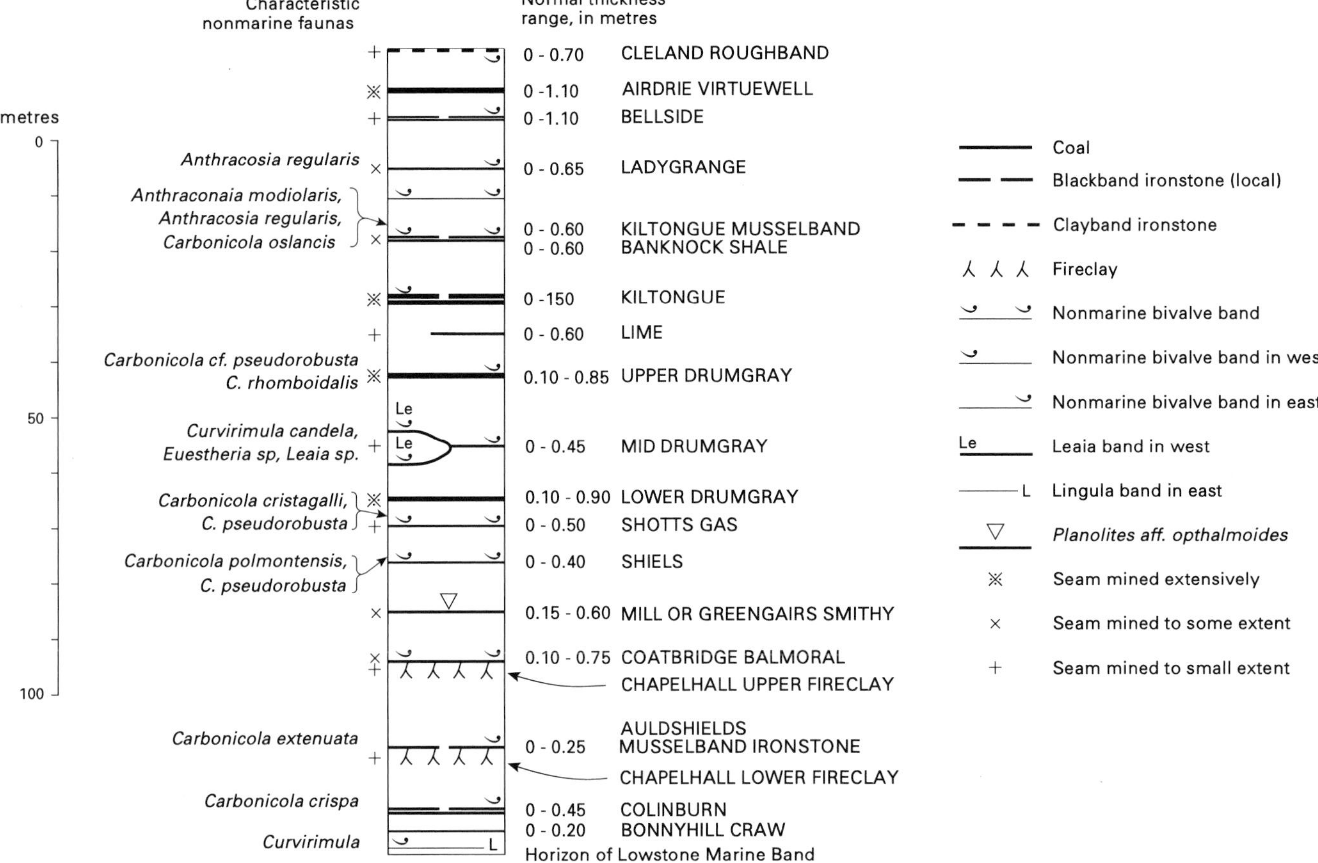

Figure 14 Vertical section of the Lower Coal Measures.

dominate. The number of cycles varies from 15 to 20 and decreases slightly towards the south-west, but the reduction of the total thickness from 160 to 96 m is largely due to the thinning of individual cycles. The sandstones are mostly fine or medium grained. In many, sideritic micaceous laminae show conspicuous ripple-lamination. Silty or carbonaceous laminae are also common. The few sandstones that show evidence of markedly erosive bases are mostly in the lowest part of the sequence or are located in the west. The mudstones commonly include bands or nodules of clay ironstone. Most contain faunas of nonmarine bivalves. The mudstones and siltstones between the Ladygrange and Airdrie Virtuewell coals are commonly pale grey in colour, in places with a greenish tinge. The only carbonate rock calcareous enough to be locally called limestone is at the top of the sequence and is more usually known as the Roughband Ironstone. This ironstone consists of nodules, which locally coalesce into a band, of unusually pale grey or fawn clay ironstone, with a speckled appearance. It occurs in the seatclay below the Vanderbeckei Marine Band and is best developed in the south-east part of the district, where it was mined. Seatearths are generally well developed and mostly argillaceous, especially in the lowest cycles. Two were mined as the Chapelhall Lower and Upper fireclays (Figure 14). The former may be the same as the Captain's Fireclay of Garnkirk. Other locally exploited fireclays of uncertain correlation may also lie in the Lower Coal Measures.

Coals

The coals (Figure 14) in the Lower Coal Measures are usually less than 1 m thick. The thickest developments are mostly in the Banknock Coalfield, where the whole succession resembles that found at Falkirk (Sheet 31E) and where a plethora of local names was used. Most of the coals persist over all or most of the sheet area and their horizons can usually be identified even where no actual coal is present. However, the Lime Coal of Greengairs dies out completely north of Airdrie; the two leaves of the Mid Drumgray Coal coalesce in the east and south-east and the Bonnyhill Craw Coal is absent over wide areas. Two persistent horizons, well defined by bedded mudstone on seatearth, rarely have any coal at all. One is named after the Auldshields Musselband, which is only found around the type locality [770 715]. The other lies between the Kiltongue Musselband and the Ladygrange Coal. At least fourteen coals have been mined (Figure 14). The four most extensively mined were: 1) the Lower Drumgray (mainly in the south-east, extending to the southern fringes of Airdrie and Coatbridge and the south-east fringe of Glasgow); 2) the Upper Drumgray (mainly in the east from Holytown to Greengairs, in eastern Glasgow and at Banknock); 3) the Kiltongue (mainly in a broad belt from Glasgow to Greengairs); and 4) the Airdrie Virtuewell (widespread but intermittent workings). Near the surface the seams were mined for many years. Working at depth occurred mainly in the 20th century and, at best, met with moderate success as the seams are generally thinner than those in the overlying Middle Coal Measures and dewatering of the mines was a considerable problem.

IRONSTONES

Blackband ironstones are rare in the Lower Coal Measures of the district. The Duntilland Parrot around Chapelhall includes blackband ironstone. The Auldshields Musselband Ironstone is sufficiently carbonaceous at Auldshields [770 715] to be included but the only seam known to have been mined for blackband ironstone alone is the Bellside Ironstone, a local development, up to 0.2 m thick, of the Bellside Coal in the Newarthill–Cleland area. Two other seams include ironstone. The upper part of the Kiltongue Coal passes locally into cannel, oil shale and ironstone in the Chapelhall area and was worked as the Calderbraes or Kennelburn Ironstone. The blackband ironstone is up to 0.38 m thick, the cannel up to 0.15 m thick and the oil shale up to 0.4 m thick. Nodular bands of clay ironstone up to 0.15 m thick also occur. The Kiltongue Musselband Ironstone is part of a complex seam which locally includes a coal up to 0.6 m thick, that was mined at Banknock as the Shale Coal. There are one or more ironstone bands with abundant bivalves, interleaved with oil shale, up to a total thickness of 0.6 m. This seam was mined around Greengairs and in northern Airdrie. Oil shale up to 0.35 m thick also occurs in places above the Airdrie Virtuewell Coal and was formerly exploited in northern Airdrie.

PALAEOGEOGRAPHY

The dominantly fluviatile conditions of the Passage Formation gradually gave way to a broad flat deltaic plain. The sea was almost completely excluded and quasi-marine conditions occurred only twice and probably only locally towards the east, indicating that the delta front was situated at a considerable distance from the area during this period. The delta continued to subside and receive large amounts of mud, silt and fine sand. The distributaries that brought this material initially eroded channels across the delta top; the channels were subsequently filled with coarser material. Colonisation by vegetation was frequent and sometimes prolonged. Subsequent to each episode of colonisation, the water level rose, usually preserving the vegetable matter to form coal and enabling nonmarine faunas, mainly *Anthracosia* and *Carbonicola*, to spread over most of the district. On some occasions these nonmarine faunas were unable to thrive and, particularly in the west, other genera such as *Curvirimula*, *Leaia* and *Euestheria* were common, being more suited to the local conditions.

Middle Coal Measures

The Middle Coal Measures (Forsyth and Brand, 1986) coincide exactly with the Westphalian B stage. Except for two small basins within the Banknock Coalfield, the rocks of the Middle Coal Measures are confined to the southern part of the Airdrie district, where there are extensive outcrops. They are covered by the Upper Coal Measures in the Lanarkshire Basin, at Rutherglen, in a west–east belt from Glasgow almost to Holytown, and in a small area in Coatbridge. The Middle Coal Measures are almost 200 m thick in the east, decreasing westwards to 160 m. There are few good exposures, and some of these, such as the opencast sites around Darngavil [785 690], have deteriorated in recent years. Stream sections, showing mostly sandstones, include the South Calder Water, beside which sandstone forms Ravens Craig [7835 5760], the north bank tributary that flows between Newarthill and Cleland, the North Calder Water at intervals from Monkland House [775 637] to its confluence with the River Clyde, and the River Clyde east of Glasgow, where sandstones near the top of the sequence are visible. The elucidation of the stratigraphy, however, has depended almost entirely on abundant borehole sections.

The Middle Coal Measures (Figure 15) consist throughout of a coal-cyclic sequence with the typical cycle consisting of coal, mudstone, siltstone, sandstone, siltstone and seatearth. The cycles are 20–25 in number and mostly between 5 and 10 m thick. Limestones are absent, but many of the mudstones, siltstones and seatearths contain bands or nodules of clay ironstone. Some of these bands are sufficiently rich in bivalves to be termed musselbands. One was worked for ornamental stone under the name Cambuslang Marble. The mudstones between the Glasgow Ell and Glasgow Upper coals are notably lacking in fissility and are greenish grey in colour. Most of the seatearths are mainly clay grade. The sandstones are mostly fine or medium grained (Plate 3) and many are rendered conspicuously ripple-laminated by sideritic, micaceous, or locally silty carbonacous laminae. Coarser and usually thicker sandstones, such as the Shettleston Sandstone, are largely confined to the strata above the Glasgow Upper Coal, where they locally cut out parts of the cyclic sequence. The Shettleston Sandstone is the approximate equivalent of the Devon Red Sandstone of the Clackmannan Coalfield. The few thicker sandstones in the rest of the sequence vary in their effects on the strata below and above them. Basal erosion is usually minimal and rarely reaches the underlying coal, but in some localities the overlying coal is abnormally thin or absent, even though the bedded mudstone above and the seatearth below are present. This is attributed to the thick body of incompactible sand preventing the coal-forming vegetation escaping oxidation below the water table. Examples include the effect of the Auchinlea Sandstone on the Airdrie Blackband Coal south-east of Newarthill and the thinness of the Humph Coal in eastern Glasgow. The very variable sandstone between the Glasgow Main and Pyotshaw coals has little effect on either seam.

COALS

The Middle Coal Measures (Figure 15) include a number of coals that were extensively mined in the past and are

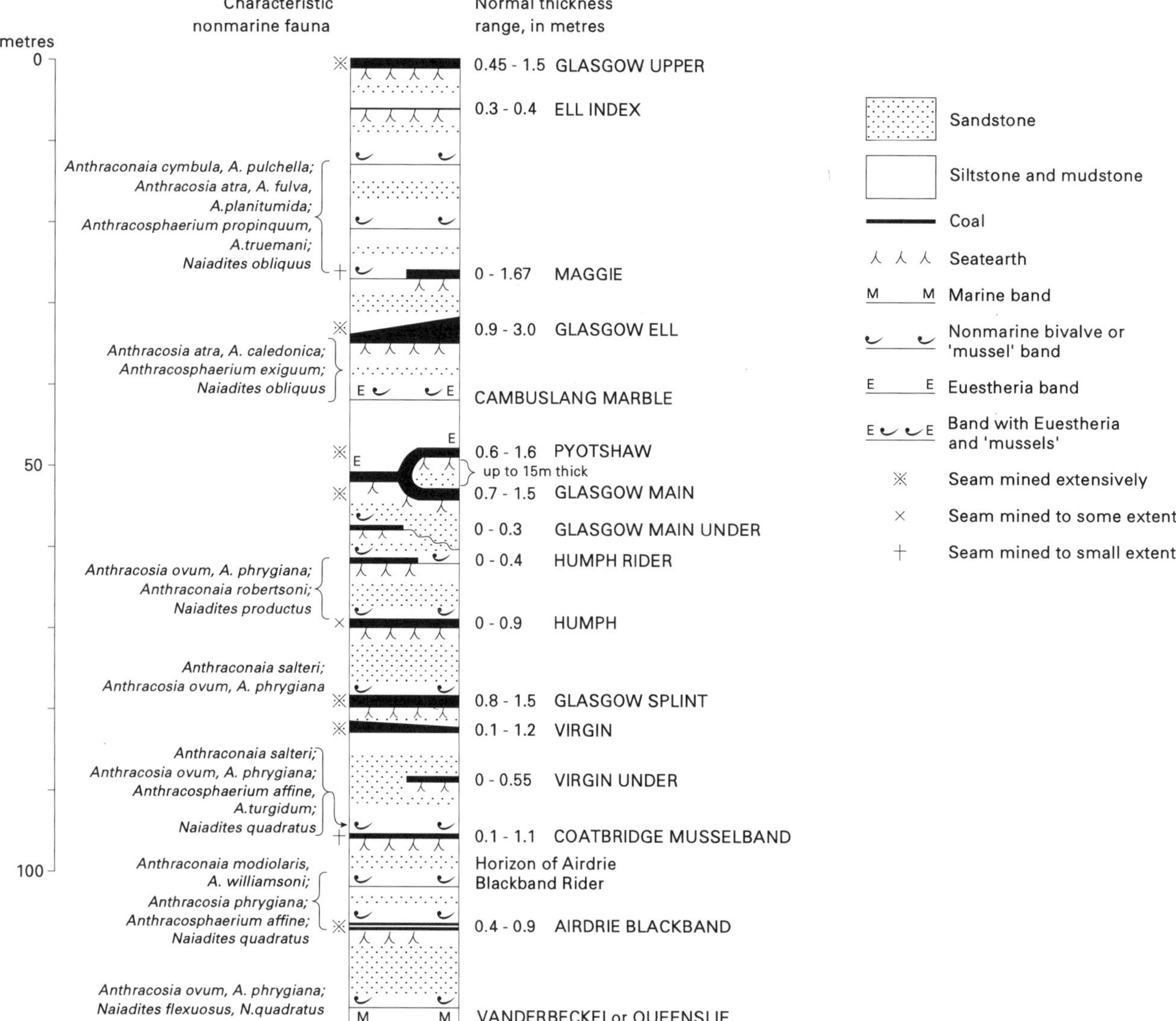

Figure 15 Vertical section of the Middle Coal Measures up to the Glasgow Upper Coal.

now virtually worked out. Mining of both coal and ironstone no longer takes place, although attempts have been made locally to remove 'stoops' (pillars of coal left behind in stoop-and-room or pillar-and-stall workings).

The Airdrie Blackband Coal was mined extensively except in Glasgow, where it is thin, and in Coatbridge and Airdrie, where the lower leaf is thin or absent and the upper leaf passes laterally into the Airdrie Blackband Ironstone (up to 0.45 m thick). This latter ironstone was almost completely extracted in the mid 19th century. The Coatbridge Musselband Coal was mined to a small extent in the Airdrie area, where it reaches its maximum thickness. The Virgin Coal is one of the most variable seams in the Middle Coal Measures, thinning eastwards and more markedly southwards. It was therefore most extensively mined in Glasgow, Coatbridge and Airdrie. The Glasgow Splint Coal was very much in demand, especially for use in furnaces, because of the hard splinty character of bands in the seam. Locally, in south-east Glasgow, the coal was 'burnt', that is, oxidised by fluids percolating down from thick, locally red-stained sandstones. The Humph Coal is also variable in thickness, being thin or absent in eastern Glasgow and generally in two leaves in the Coatbridge–Airdrie area, where mining was largely confined to the southern part of the district. The seam was extensively mined from south-east Glasgow to Bothwell, but only locally elsewhere. The Humph Rider and Glasgow Main Under seams both pass locally into blackband ironstone in Glasgow.

The Glasgow Main Coal is one of the thickest and best quality seams in the Middle Coal Measures and in consequence has been almost completely worked out. With the Pyotshaw Coal it forms a single seam up to 3 m thick in Glasgow and locally elsewhere, for example around Newarthill. The Pyotshaw Coal was also extensively mined where it occurs as a separate seam. The Glasgow Ell Coal is thickest in the south, where it locally exceeds 3 m and was much sought after. Northwards it thins and

Plate 3 Sandstones of the Middle Coal Measures showing large-scale cross-bedding, Cambuslang [645 595] (D 4870).

splits and workings become less extensive. To the north-west it thins but remains a single seam, which has been widely extracted. The Maggie Coal is a local development in the Holytown–Newarthill area. The Glasgow Upper Coal, which has been mined between Glasgow and Bothwell, is the highest of the important seams. Like the Virgin Coal it is thickest in the west, where it locally exceeds 2 m, but thins markedly south-eastwards and less so eastwards.

The coals in the upper part of the sequence, above the Glasgow Upper Coal, are thinner and more variable than those in the lower part of the succession. One or two of the seams have been mined to a small extent but their identity is uncertain. The variable Palacecraig Coal is up to 0.9 m thick and passes into the 0.3 m-thick Palacecraig Blackband Ironstone south of Airdrie. The ironstone was worked to some extent in the mid-19th century.

Seams in the Middle Coal Measures in the Banknock Coalfield have been mined using Central Coalfield names such as Virgin, Splint, Humph, Main and Pyotshaw. These usages may be correct but the stratigraphy in the Banknock Coalfield has not been established.

Palaeogeography

Sedimentation on the delta plain which prevailed during most of Westphalian A was interrupted by the major marine incursion that formed the Vanderbeckei Marine Band, but thereafter became reestablished during Westphalian B. The delta continued to subside steadily, repeatedly providing conditions in which first coal-forming vegetation and then nonmarine bivalves flourished.

For much of the time marine conditions were excluded, the type of conditions suitable for *Euestheria* to survive was very rare and distributary channels were also largely absent. Subsequently, conditions that suited both *Euestheria* and nonmarine bivalves began to occur and later, marine conditions made a limited and brief appearance. After this, the delta plain was subjected to more regular although brief and restricted marine incursions. These incursions allowed marine or quasimarine rather than nonmarine faunas to become established at regular intervals towards the end of Westphalian B. Coal-swamp conditions occurred frequently but briefly, and at times sandstones in distributaries caused penecontemporaneous erosion.

Upper Coal Measures

The Upper Coal Measures consist of the youngest Carboniferous strata preserved in the Airdrie district and belong mainly to the Westphalian C stage but may include some units of the overlying Westphalian D stage. The Aegiranum Marine Band which defines the base of the Upper Coal Measures is known in Scotland as Skipsey's Marine Band, although it is now believed (Forsyth and Brand, 1986) that the band originally discovered by Skipsey (1865) is the Drumpark Marine Band (Middle Coal Measures). The Upper Coal Measures succession is up to 270 m thick and is confined to the southern part of the district where the main outcrop is in the middle of the Lanarkshire Basin. The Upper Coal Measures also occur in the west, at Rutherglen, at Coatbridge and in a narrow west–east belt extending from central Glasgow almost to Holytown. Exposures are largely confined to the River Clyde and its tributaries. In the former, sandstones are visible at intervals from Uddingston [68 60] to Bothwell and are well displayed around Bothwell Castle [688 593] (Plate 4). There are extensive exposures in the South and Rotten Calder waters. Skipsey's Marine Band is visible in the North Calder Water [7519 6324]. The Bothwell Bridge Marine Band is exposed in the Clyde at its type locality [7069 5773]. No coal in the Upper Coal Measures is known to have been mined but a terra-cotta clay 2.6 m thick which occurs almost 50 m above the base was mined from 1955 to 1965 at Blantyreferme Nos. 4 and 5 mines [682 610]. The Westmuir Sandstone near the base was quarried at Westmuir [632 641] and Eastfield [631 611]. A higher sandstone was quarried at Fallside [713 604] and a red fireclay, 1.8 m thick, was quarried and mined from the bottom of the Fallside Quarry.

The Upper Coal Measures were deposited as coal-cyclic sequences but subsequent oxidation has reddened all but the lowest strata and the coals have mostly been destroyed or replaced by limestone (Mykura, 1960). A few thin coals have survived in the grey strata of the lower part of the succession. The sandstones vary in grain size from fine to coarse and in colour from white through pink and purple to red (Plate 4). Individual beds are up to 20 m thick but most have erosive bases which locally bring two

Plate 4 Reddened, cross-bedded Upper Coal Measures sandstone, Bothwell [688 593] (D 4872).

or more sandstones together with a total thickness of up to 50 m. The bedded mudstones are mostly bright red whereas the unbedded mudstones (some of which are certainly seatclays with decarbonised roots clearly visible) are mottled red, purple, green and yellow. There is considerable lateral variation in stratigraphy, largely caused by the impersistent and erosive nature of the thicker sandstones. For example, the two best borehole sections, Hallside [6694 5975] and Blantyreferme No. 1 [6839 5994], are only 1.5 km apart but have quite different lithological sequences, especially in the positions of the thicker sandstones. A three-fold lithostratigraphy for the lower part of the succession introduced by Clough et al. (1920, p.100) for the Hamilton district (Sheet 23W) can be recognised at Hallside but not at Blantyreferme, which is actually nearer Hamilton. In general, however, the tripartite division breaks down in the Airdrie district so that the lower part of the succession becomes dominated by sandstones to the west, as shown for example, by the succession in the Shettleston Borehole [6307 6414].

Deposition of the Upper Coal Measures was initially controlled by a marine incursion which formed the Aegiranum Marine Band. The fauna in this marine band becomes poorer to the west where limestone is also lacking, suggesting that the marine incursion was from the east. Thereafter conditions returned to those characteristic of late Westphalian B times, with delta plain sedimentation locally interrupted by sand-filled distributary channels and brief marine incursions. Subsequently oxidation, due to uplift and continental conditions, reddened most of the strata, and calcareous fluids altered the coals to limestones.

SIX

Carboniferous biostratigraphy and palaeontology

General discussions of the nature and palaeoecological significance of the marine faunas of the Dinantian and Namurian have been published by Wilson (1967; 1989), and some details from these accounts have been included here. Selected Dinantian and Namurian fossils are illustrated in Plate 5.

TOURNAISIAN–VISÉAN

The strata below the Clyde Plateau Volcanic Formation (the Ballagan Formation and the Clyde Sandstone Formation), where present in the Airdrie district, are generally unfossiliferous. Ostracods and an isolated fish fragment were found in the Ballagan Formation in the Tak-ma-doon Borehole [7291 8053] which, together with an algal limestone with ?*Spirorbis* in Corrieburn, are the sole macrofossils so far found in the district. Work on the miospores from this part of the sequence shows that a basal TC Miospore Zone assemblage is present at a similar horizon to the macrofossils in the Tak-ma-doon Borehole (B Owens, unpublished BGS reports). This contrasts with a Pu Miospore Zone assemblage from above the lava pile at Douglas Muir on the adjacent sheet to the west, and with CM-TC Miospore Zone assemblages recorded within the lava pile in the Kilpatrick Hills by Scott et al. (1984). Thus the precise position of the lava pile in the miospore zonal scheme remains undecided.

VISÉAN

Lawmuir Formation

In the Airdrie district this formation includes strata which are mainly of Brigantian age. Characteristic fossils include *Diphyphyllum lateseptatum*, *Lonsdaleia* sp., *Siphonodendron junceum*, *Angiospirifer trigonalis*, *Pugilis pugilis* and *Actinopteria persulcata*. As already noted *Latiproductus* cf. *latissimus* is common at the horizon of the Hollybush Limestone in most of the district, but otherwise is rarely present. Few conodonts have been recorded from the more calcareous marine beds and these are, in general, long-ranging forms. Foraminifera are present also, but so far have not proved stratigraphically significant. Miospores from this formation in the Lawmuir Borehole, drilled in the adjacent Glasgow district (Sheet 30E) are characteristic of the VF Miospore Zone and may thus be regarded as of Brigantian age.

Lower Limestone Formation

The marine fauna from this formation is more varied than that from the Lawmuir Formation and the individual marine episodes also show greater differences between each other. In general the Hurlet Limestone is not very fossiliferous, although in the Corrieburn area the mud fraction is reduced, with the result that the fauna changes and a wider variety of corals and brachiopods, together with *Limipecten dissimilis*, are present. The Blackhall Limestone, with the Neilson Shell Bed in the mudstones above it, carries one of the most varied faunas in the Lower Limestone Formation. Of particular interest are the rare occurrences of species of *Sudeticeras* at Corrieburn, although the various species recorded by Currie (1954, pp.584–590) are not in themselves diagnostic of any particular horizon. According to Moore (*in* Currie, 1954, p.533), the forms listed are high P_2 forms. The genus is principally characteristic of the P_2 Zone, although it does range up into lower E_1 according to Bisat (1950, p.23). Wilson (1966; 1989) has discussed the palaeoecological implications of the fauna of the Neilson Shell Bed, concluding (1989, p.113) that much of the outcrop area in the Airdrie district lay to the east of the mouth of a river system which was the source of some of the clastics at that time.

In localities along the southern margin of the Campsie Fells the lower two of the Hosie limestones contain isolated specimens of *Caneyella membranacea*, a bivalve common in the higher beds of P_2 Zone in the Pennine region of England. Their presence in the Airdrie district is unusual and it has been suggested that the species was not able to establish itself in the conditions prevailing in the Airdrie district at this time. Wilson (1989) has drawn attention to the richness of the faunas in these limestones where they have been examined.

There are marked differences between the faunas which occur in the Lower Limestone Formation in the north of the Airdrie district and those from the adjacent Hamilton district (Sheet 23W) to the south. However, little is known of the faunas of the formation in the intervening area below the wide outcrop of Coal Measures strata.

Miospore evidence from various sources suggests that rocks of the Lower Limestone Formation contain assemblages typical of the VF Miospore Zone and that this zone is represented in the Hosie limestones. It is not clear where exactly the change over to the overlying NC Miospore Zone takes place within the Hosie limestones. Conodonts described by Clarke (1960) and revised by Higgins (1975) from just below the Top Hosie Limestone indicate the presence of the upper part of P_2 Zone, that is, a late Brigantian age. The discovery of *Cravenoceras scoticum* in shales below the Top Hosie Limestone at East Kilbride (Sheet 23W) led Currie (1954) to take the base of the Pendleian stage below the Top Hosie Limestone. Thus the Viséan–Namurian boundary has been taken for convenience at the base of the Top Hosie Limestone.

Plate 5 Selected Dinantian and Namurian fossils.

a. *Streblopteria ornata* juv. (GSE 12257) ×5. Namurian, Upper Limestone Formation, Lyoncross Limestone, Queenslie No. 6 Borehole at 412.32 m [6813 6523].

b. *Eumorphoceras* sp. (GSE 12703) ×2. Namurian, Upper Limestone Formation, Calmy Limestone, Bowhousebog No. 1 Borehole at 213.51 m [8513 5877].

c. *Limipecten dissimils* (GSE 7838) ×1. Dinantian, Lower Limestone Formation, Hurlet Limestone, Corrie Burn [6840 7877].

d. *Latiproductus* cf. *latissimus* (GSE 12258) ×1. Namurian, Upper Limestone Formation, Index Limestone, Dumbreck No. 2 Borehole at 87.48 m [7029 7792].

e. *Aviculopecten inaequalis* (GSE 11824) ×1. Namurian, Limestone Coal Formation, Johnstone Shell Bed, Gartshore No. 11 Colliery [704 736].

f. *Posidonia corrugata gigantea* (GSE 12145) ×1. Dinantian, Lower Limestone Formation, Neilson Shell Bed, Wester Gartshore underground borehole at 203.23 m [6823 7239].

g. *Echinoconchus elegans* (GSE 8489) ×2. Dinantian, Lower Limestone Formation, Neilson Shell Bed, Glenwhapple Burn a little south of Craigenglen [6221 7556].

h. *Tornquistia youngi* (GSE 12184) ×2. Dinantian, Lower Limestone Formation, Neilson Shell Bed, Dumbreck No. 1 Borehole at 212.55 m [7040 7850].

i. *Prothyris scotica* (GSE 6442) ×1.5. Namurian, Passage Formation, No. 2 Marine Band, Greenfoot Quarry, Glenboig [734 699].

NAMURIAN

Limestone Coal Formation

Apart from the mudstones forming the roof of the Top Hosie Limestone only two major marine episodes, the Johnstone Shell Bed and the Black Metals Marine Band, are present in the Airdrie district. The Bo'ness Splint *Lingula* Band contains *Orbiculoidea* sp. and bivalves at a few localities. The mudstones above the Top Hosie Limestone exhibit an oscillation between *Lingula*-bearing and *Naiadites*-bearing strata. Towards the base mudstones which contain the arthropod *Pseudotealliocaris* have been regarded as indicative of brackish-water conditions. The area in which the arthropods are known appears to be restricted to the north-western corner of the district. The association of *Paracarbonicola* with fragmentary *Lingula* at other locations, perhaps indicates a different, but still brackish-water environment. *Paracarbonicola* is also found in the upper part of the overlying Johnstone Shell Bed and in the Linwood Shell Bed at some localities in the western part of the district. The fauna of the Johnstone Shell Bed also includes *Serpuloides carbonarius*, *Composita ambigua*, *Pleuropugnoides* sp., *Productus* spp., *Euphemites urii*, *Retispira* spp., *Palaeoneilo luciniformis*, *P. mansoni* and *Streblopteria ornata*. In the Linwood Shell Bed rare individuals of *Aviculopecten inaequalis* have been recorded from localities at the western margin of the district. The Black Metals Marine Band, as already noted, contains a less varied assemblage of forms than the Johnstone Shell Bed including *Serpuloides carbonarius*, *Buxtonia* sp., *Pleuropugnoides* sp., and *Streblopteria ornata*. Only the Bo'ness Splint *Lingula* Band, amongst the remaining faunal horizons, near the top of the sequence contains forms other than *Lingula*, and such occurrences are restricted to the northern margins of the coalfield.

Upper Limestone Formation

The faunas of this formation were studied by Wilson (1967) who listed them and showed the ranges of many species. He discussed the palaeoecology and derivation of the faunas and concluded that, while migration of faunas from the west could not be precluded, the nearest analogues to the Scottish Pendleian and Arnsbergian faunas are to be found to the east. Much of the fauna is common to the majority of the marine horizons in the formation and may be described as 'background fauna' which in terms of faunal lists has little value. Nevertheless variations in relative abundance of various species aid the process of distinguishing particular horizons. Few zonally significant goniatites are known, although at certain horizons, for example the Orchard and Calmy limestones, goniatites such as *Anthracoceras* are of regular occurrence. Specimens of *Eumorphoceras pseudobilingue* from the Index Limestone in Cardowan No. 1 Borehole [6855 6813] indicate the presence of E_{1b} Zone whilst specimens of *Cravenoceras gairense* from Robroyston have been compared with forms found in the main *Eumorphoceras bisulcatum* band (E_{2a} of England) by Ramsbottom (1977, p.327). Thus the Pendleian–Arnsbergian stage boundary has been taken at the Orchard Limestone (Wilson in Ramsbottom et al., 1978, p.34).

Little work has been done on the miospore content of coal seams since the work of Smith and Butterworth (1967). These workers established a series of Miospore Zones in which the NC and TK zones span the interval from within the Brigantian stage of the Viséan to near the top of the Arnsbergian stage of the Namurian; the base of the TK Zone approximating to the Pendleian–Arnsbergian (E_1–E_2) boundary. Smith and Butterworth (1967) also showed that the Chapelgreen Coal contains an assemblage typical of the NC Zone whilst the Hirst Coal contains an assemblage typical of the TK Zone. Clarke (1960) was able to show that limestones in the Upper Limestone Formation are recognisable by their foraminiferal content. Hutton (1965) showed that there was a marked variation of microfauna both with facies changes in individual limestones and also in the same limestone across the Midland Valley of Scotland. He also showed that there was a marked change in fauna above the Calmy Limestone. Clarke (1960) was able to show that the conodonts from the Upper Limestone Formation included species not present in earlier rocks, but he had insufficient data to distinguish individual limestones, although a faunal change was detected between the Index and Calmy limestones. Higgins (1985, p.215) drew attention to the presence of apotognathids, similar to those from the later Pendleian (E_{1c}) of the Stainmore Trough, in limestones in the lower part of the Upper Limestone Formation. He also recorded *Gnathodus bilineatus* in the Castlecary Limestone. This species occurs in conodont faunas of the E_{2b} Zone elsewhere in Britain.

Passage Formation

In this area the faunas of the various marine bands are mostly sparse, usually consisting of *Lingula mytilloides* alone or with rare small high-spired gastropods. Only No. 2 Marine Band contains, in general, a rather richer fauna characterised by species of *Schellwienella* and *Schizophoria*. The bivalves *Promytilus* sp. and *Prothyris scotica* are also present in a number of collections. Goniatites are rare in the Passage Formation in Scotland and have yet to be recorded within this sheet area. No work has been carried out on the miospore content of the Passage Formation in this district. However, at Bonnyside [835 793] close to the eastern margin of the district, Neves et al. (1965) showed that coals around No. 2 Marine Band contain a microflora comparable to that of the Upper Namurian A coals of the Pennines while coals within No. 3 Marine Band group contain microfloras which may be assigned a Kinderscoutian (R_1) age. Coals around No. 5 Marine Band group contained microfloras suggestive of a Marsdenian (R_2) age whilst the microfloras from seams higher up the local sequence denoted an horizon close to the Namurian–Westphalian boundary. Microfloras from coals about the Bowhousebog Coal indicate a Lower Westphalian age. Thus the closest approximation to the base of the Westphalian (the *Gastrioceras subcrenatum* Marine Band) lies within No. 6 Marine Band group. In the Airdrie district only one marine band is recognised and its exact equivalent within No. 6 Marine Band group has not been determined.

WESTPHALIAN*

Lower Coal Measures

There have been no records of the goniatites which characterise the principal Lower Coal Measures marine bands in Lancashire and the base of the Westphalian is thought to occur within No. 6 Marine Band group, where miospores indicative of a basal Westphalian A age have been found in adjacent districts. Above this level only the Lowstone Marine Band is well represented in the Airdrie district and that only in the east. In the western part of the district the marine band itself is largely, if not completely, absent, and *Curvirimula* sp. occurs at or very near the horizon.

Nonmarine bivalves are scarce in the lower part of the sequence and, where present, are poorly preserved. The faunas in the Duntilland Parrot phase of the Colinburn Coal include *Carbonicola crispa*, and in the Auldshields Musselband *Carbonicola extenuata* is present, thus enabling the recognition of the Lenisulcata Biozone in the eastern part of the district. The nonmarine bivalves become more abundant above the Coatbridge Balmoral Coal (Forsyth, 1978a) and less so above the Kiltongue Musselband. The Communis Biozone faunas are best represented in the eastern part of the district, though even here the faunas are not as abundant as they are in the adjacent Falkirk district (Sheet 31E). Westwards the faunas deteriorate and even the normally persistent bands such as those above the Shiels, Shotts Gas and Upper Drumgray coals become, at best, intermittent in occurrence. In the Glasgow area *Curvirimula* is found in association with *Euestheria* and *Leaia* in strata between the Shotts Gas and Upper Drumgray coals. The association is unusual for this part of the sequence and is not repeated elsewhere in the Central Coalfield. Near the base of the zone, above the Mill Coal, the trace fossil *Planolites* aff. *ophthalmoides* seems to be confined to this level in the district. The form is much larger than the type species, and has been recognised near the base of the zone in several northern coalfields. The band itself may have value in local correlation. The Kiltongue Musselband contains *Anthraconaia modiolaris*, *Anthracosia regularis* and *Carbonicola oslancis* and has been taken to mark the base of the Modiolaris Biozone. The horizon is generally well developed, although it is locally absent in Glasgow.

Middle Coal Measures

The Middle Coal Measures may be divided into three sections on the basis of the contained faunas. The lower part, up to the Pyotshaw Coal at the top of the Modiolaris Biozone, is dominated by several rich nonmarine bivalve bands (Figure 15). The only marine band is the Vanderbeckei Marine Band, originally described as the Queenslie Marine Band (Manson, 1957; Brand, 1977). Brand (1977) described the faunal phases of the band, showing it to be at its most varied in a cephalopod–pectinid facies in the Coatbridge–Airdrie area. In the Glasgow area a *Myalina* facies is present and the marine horizons may be interbedded with horizons containing stunted *Anthracosia* sp. and *Geisina arcuata*. *Euestheria* occurs in abundance at the base of the band at Airdrie but is otherwise very rare.

Nonmarine faunas deteriorate southwards and, at the horizon of the Coatbridge Musselband, they also deteriorate westwards. At the latter horizon rare examples of *Anthraconaia irvinensis* (Brand, 1991) occur in a restricted area between Glasgow and Coatbridge, supporting Macgregor's (1930) correlation of the Virgin and Splint coals of Glasgow with the Wee, Turf and Parrot coals of the Irvine area.

The middle part of the sequence extends to just above the Palacecraig Coal and is entirely within the Lower Similis–Pulchra Biozone. A prominent faunal horizon near the base, the Cambuslang Marble, contains *Euestheria* sp. as well as a varied fauna of species of *Anthraconaia*, *Anthracosia* and *Anthracosphaerium*. This may be the correlative of the "*Anthraconaia pulchella*" fauna of Ayrshire described by Calver (in Mykura, 1967, p.64) and thus another example of the widespread "*Estheria*" band of the English coalfields which occurs at the base of the Lower Similis–Pulchra Biozone. *Anthraconaia pulchella* itself, however, no longer characterises the horizon and occurs in higher strata where the pale grey silty mudstone facies is present. Such a change of horizon has been shown to occur in the Ayrshire Coalfield (Brand, 1983). *Euestheria* is widespread in horizons above the Glasgow Upper Coal and the lowest of the Lower Similis–Pulchra Biozone marine bands also occurs in this part of the sequence. The Glasgow Upper Marine Band is only known in the whole of the Central Coalfield at Clyde Iron works [645 623] where *Lingula mytilloides* and indeterminate marine bivalves have been found. In general the nonmarine bivalve faunas below the Glasgow Upper Coal are best developed in eastern Glasgow, those above it, in Coatbridge and Airdrie.

The highest part of the sequence starts with the Carnbroe Marine Band and includes the Drumpark Marine Band and the recently discovered Dalziel Works *Lingula* Band near the top. The latter is known only in the Airdrie area in this district. *Euestheria* is rare and the few nonmarine bivalves are mostly species of *Naiadites*. The Carnbroe Marine Band is absent in the west, whilst in the east it contains foraminifera, *Lingula mytilloides* and *Planolites ophthalmoides*. The Drumpark Marine Band is now thought to be the marine band originally described by Skipsey (Forsyth and Brand, 1986). It has a richer fauna at his original locality at Drumpark between Glasgow and Coatbridge where it includes *Paraconularia* sp., *Orbiculoidea* cf. *nitida* and *Pustula* cf. *rimberti*, than elsewhere in this district where only *Lingula* sp., and locally foraminifera occur; the band is absent in places.

* Selected Westphalian fossils are illustrated in Plate 6.

Plate 6 Selected Westphalian fossils.

a. *Dunbarella papyraceus* mut δ (GSE 13313) ×1. Westphalian B, Vanderbeckei (Queenslie) Marine Band, Dalmacoulter Quarry [7685 6771].

b. *Anthracoceratites* cf. *vanderbeckei* (GSE 13707) ×2. Westphalian B, Vanderbeckei Marine Band, Moffat Mills Water Borehole at 37 m [7898 6499].

c. *Anthracosia planitumida* (GSE 13601) ×1.5. Westphalian B, Cambuslang Marble, Greenfield No. 7 Borehole at 13 m [6482 6464].

d. *Anthracosia* cf. *atra* (GSE 13894) ×1. Westphalian B, Cambusland Marble, Corsewall Street, Coatbridge No. 15 Borehole at 21.59 m [7261 6493].

e. *Anthraconauta* cf. *phillipsii* (GSE 13597) ×1.5. Westphalian C, 157 m above Bothwell Bridge Marine Band, Hallside Survey Borehole at 39.71 m [6694 5975].

f. *Pustula* cf. *rimberti* (Royal Museum of Scotland 1911.62. 3154e) ×1.5. Westphalian B, Drumpark Marine Band, Drumpark Sinking at c.55 m [705 643]. From Skipsey's original collection.

g. *Anthracosia* cf. *disjuncta* (GSE 13589) ×1. Wetphalian B, Cambuslang Marble, Blairhill No. 2 Borehole at 22.10 m [7238 6504].

h. *Anthraconaia salteri* (GSE 15100) ×1. Westphalian B, Coatbridge Musselband Coal roof, Darngavil Opencast Site [7870 6916].

Upper Coal Measures

The Aegiranum Marine Band (Forsyth and Brand, 1986) exhibits three different facies within the Airdrie district. In the east it occurs in shale with a black limestone near the base, reminiscent of the development of the band in much of the Pennine area of England, but with a less varied fauna. The latter includes foraminifera, sponge spicules, *Cancrinella* and *Rugosochonetes*, bivalves, cephalopods including *Donetzoceras aegiranum*, conodonts and *Planolites ophthalmoides*. In the west the fauna is reduced to foraminifera, sponge spicules, *Lingula mytilloides*, rare conodonts and abundant *Planolites ophthalmoides*. In an intermediate zone, which includes the sites of the Hallside [6694 5975] and Craighead [7008 5735] boreholes, a few bivalves also occur in the fauna which otherwise is similar to that of the western zone.

The only other marine horizon recognised in the Upper Coal Measures is the Bothwell Bridge Marine Band, now known to extend from the type locality westwards to the Prospecthill Borehole in the Glasgow district (Sheet 30E). The fauna includes *Lingula mytilloides*, *Euphemites* sp., *Myalina*?, *Posidonia* sp. and *Planolites ophthalmoides*. *Euestheria* is present at the base of the cycle. A nonmarine bivalve band is closely associated above the marine band at the type locality and contains species of *Anthraconaia* including *A. persulcata* and *Naiadites* sp. The association has led to this band being correlated with the Shafton Marine Band of the Pennine coalfields of northern England. Near the top of the sequence *Anthraconaia* and variants of *Anthraconauta phillipsii* and *A. tenuis* occur. *Euestheria* sp, *Leaia* sp. and *Carbonita* sp. have also been recorded.

SEVEN

Late- or post-Carboniferous intrusive igneous rocks

ALKALI-DOLERITE SILLS

A sill complex of teschenitic olivine-dolerite, up to 38 m thick in several leaves, occurs in eastern Glasgow from the western margin of the Airdrie district as far east as Easterhouse [682 652]. The thickest leaf is usually the highest and may be over 100 m above the lowest one. Many of the thinner leaves are largely or completely carbonated and bleached to form 'white trap'. The horizon of intrusion rises eastwards from low in the Coal Measures to above the Glasgow Main Coal in the Middle Coal Measures. In places the change of horizon occurs at or very close to faults, suggesting that the magma used pre-existing fractures as easy channels through which to climb. Three members of the sill complex in the adjacent Glasgow district (Sheet 30E) have been radiometrically dated (de Souza, 1979) at 270–273 Ma, suggesting that the complex is early to mid-Permian in age.

Some of the sills were formerly well exposed and extensively quarried, but working has ceased and many of the quarries are now filled in. Some exposures remain and some new ones have been created, but they are mostly in motorway cuttings and difficult of access. In the quarry beside Queenslie Bridge [663 661], now filled in, the sill was clearly seen to be composed of numerous lenses up to 7.6 m thick with bands and pockets of baked sedimentary rocks between them. Even where country rock was absent, chilled contacts revealed the presence of two leaves. Nearby, in Cardowan Quarry [664 664], on the other hand, only a single 15 m-thick leaf was exposed.

These rocks have traditionally been known as 'teschenites' but they contain fairly abundant olivine, now pseudomorphed by serpentine, bowlingite and chlorite, hence the preference for the term teschenitic olivine-dolerite. Purplish brown titaniferous augite and calcic plagioclase are the main primary minerals. Biotite, titaniferous magnetite, apatite and rare hornblende occur as accessories. Analcime occurs interstitially. In the coarser varieties it is commonly conspicuous and is regarded as a late-stage primary mineral. A picritic facies has been reported from the lower part of one of the sills in the Milncroft Quarry [646 659], which is now obscured.

QUARTZ-DOLERITE DYKES

Several quartz-dolerite dykes with a generally west–east trend traverse the central and northern parts of the district. The dykes are conspicuously exposed at intervals along their length and most have also been proved in mine workings. They cut strata up to Westphalian A in age (Lower Coal Measures). Their thicknesses range up to 45 m and they are commonly 20–30 m thick. Some were quarried in the past but their narrowness compared to the thickness of quartz-dolerite sills (see below) makes them a less attractive resource. The dykes are generally regarded as feeders of the sills although they continue much farther west than any known sill and the thickest sills occur in Fife where dykes are absent. Their age is assumed to be the same as that of the sills, namely 290–295 Ma, that is late-Westphalian or early Stephanian.

The Campsie Dyke enters the district near Campsie Glen and extends east for almost 4 km. South of Meikle Bin it reappears, offset to the north by a kilometre, and crosses the Kilsyth Hills for 14 km to the sill at Myothill [781 825]. East of Myothill a continuation of the dyke cuts Namurian strata and extends into the Falkirk district (Sheet 31E). The Queenzieburn Dyke extends from Queenzieburn [693 775] to Kilsyth, east of which it may continue as the Dullatur Dyke. The latter continues eastwards into the Falkirk district. The Croy Dyke is intruded through the quartz-dolerite sill at Croy and extends through Cumbernauld into the Falkirk district. The Milton Dyke has at its western end, the Kinkell tholeiite (see below). It extends eastwards as far as Twechar [700 758], where it is replaced en échelon by the East Board Dyke (proved in mine workings) for a further 3.5 km. The Greenfaulds Dyke is also about 3.5 km long. The Lenzie–Torphichen Dyke stretches for 40 km, across the whole width of the district, and has an offshoot 4 km long on its southern side at Auchengeich [685 715]. The Claddens Dyke in the west, dies out en échelon with the Bedlay–Greengairs Dyke, the most southerly of the swarm.

QUARTZ-DOLERITE SILL COMPLEX

The Midland Valley quartz-dolerite sill complex is regarded as late-Westphalian or early Stephenian, with a radiometric age of 290–295 Ma (de Souza, 1979). It extends into the Airdrie district from the north-east almost as far as Kirkintilloch and Coatbridge. Outcrops extend almost continuously from Dunipace to Kilsyth (Plate 7) and thence more intermittently to Glenboig and Airdrie. There is no outcrop in or around Cumbernauld, but the sill complex is present there at depth where it reaches its maximum thickness in the district of fully 90 m. In the north the main part of the sill complex is intruded into Lower Carboniferous strata. Southwards it rises stratigraphically through the Limestone Coal Formation at Kilsyth, the Upper Limestone Formation at Cumbernauld, the Passage Formation at Glenboig, reaching the Middle Coal Measures at Airdrie. Thin (up to 6 m) representatives occur at about the level of the Glasgow Splint Coal as far south as Newarthill. Many of

Plate 7 Columnar jointing in quartz-dolerite sill, Croy Quarry, Kilsyth [730 760] (D 4867).

the changes of horizon occur at or very close to faults, suggesting that the intrusion postdates the initiation of these faults.

Many of the quartz-dolerite sills are conspicuously exposed, for instance between Loch Coulter and Dunipace, and form prominent features such as Myot Hill [781 825], Cowden Hill [767 799] and Bar Hill [709 759]. The sills are also well displayed in numerous quarries although some previous quarry exposures are now obscured. The thicker sills, including most of those more than 10 m thick, generally include a very coarse central zone with a patchy appearance and elongate crystals of augite. This zone extends down from a fine-grained top to about one third of the total thickness and grades down to a fine-grained base (Robertson and Haldane, 1937, p.103). Late-stage quartz-calcite veins with pyrite and chlorite are usually confined to this zone. Quartz-feldspar veins which may be an acid differentiate from the main magma injected into irregular cracks in the rock during consolidation, are common towards the top, although present throughout; some pass up into quartz-calcite veins.

Petrography of quartz-dolerite intrusions

The quartz-dolerite intrusions are nonporphyritic, olivine-free, subophitic dolerites. They are predominantly composed of labradorite and augite, with abundant titaniferous magnetite, accessory apatite and a mesostasis which consists of micropegmatite of quartz and feldpar. Fine-grained tholeiites which occur as a marginal facies of some of the intrusions have much the same composition (Walker, 1935) and are distinguished only on textural grounds. Among the latter is the Kinkell tholeiite, which consists of bytownite crystals about 1 mm long, subordinate granular augite and octohedra of magnetite in an abundant base of clear brown glass (written communication, A Herriot, 1991).

OTHER BASIC INTRUSIONS

The famous Lennoxtown essexite is exposed on the hill slopes north of the town. It occurs as two separate plug-like intrusions at [623 793 and 626 795], both comprised of essexite and theralite. The more northerly plug intrudes the Clyde Plateau Volcanic Formation and the other, separated from it by the Campsie Fault, straddles a NE–SW fault between the Clyde Plateau Volcanic Formation and the Lower Limestone Formation. Field and geophysical evidence indicate that the margins of both bodies are steep. The essexite resembles a fine gabbro or coarse dolerite in appearance, with idiomorphic augite phenocrysts up to 12 mm across and, locally, conspicuous biotite flakes. Purple augite, mainly fresh olivine and basic plagioclase in almost equal proportions make up most of the rock, the rest being composed of biotite, titaniferous magnetite, apatite needles, and interstitial patches of orthoclase, analcime and nepheline. Overgrowths of orthoclase may form outer zones round the plagioclase crystals.

The northern intrusion is of particular interest in that the host tuffisites and lavas are hornfelsed in a narrow zone 10–15 m wide round the intrusive margin, though the essexite shows no evidence of chilling. The tuffisites have been mainly converted to cordierite-magnetite rocks, sometimes with mullite, while new clino- and orthopyroxenes, biotite and garnet have been developed in the lavas (written communication, A Herriot, 1991).

Biotite crystals from the Lennoxtown essexite have been dated radiometrically at 270 Ma (de Souza, 1979) suggesting an early or mid-Permian age, the same as the alkali-dolerite sills.

Two narrow NW-trending dykes occur about 150 m to the north-west of the northern intrusion [624 796]. The more northerly dyke has an extraordinary concentration of cobble-like quartzose and granitic xenoliths in a teschenitic matrix. The inclusions are notably similar to those found in Lower Devonian conglomerates along the Highland Boundary Fault. In thin section the quartzose rocks show evidence of severe thermal and possibly metasomatic effects with the production of glass, now devitrified, and tridymite, now inverted. The southerly dyke encloses a large subrounded block of baked sandstone (written communication, A Herriot, 1991).

Olivine-dolerite dykes with a WNW–ESE trend occur in late-Dinantian and Namurian strata at the surface in the Lennoxtown area, underground near Torrance [620 742] and both above and below ground between Glasgow and Coatbridge. They may be of Tertiary age.

EIGHT

Structure

REGIONAL CONTEXT

The Airdrie district lies in the centre of the Midland Valley of Scotland, an ancient rift valley bounded in the north by the Highland Boundary Fault and in the south by the Southern Upland Fault (Figure 16). The graben structure was developed in the early Devonian (Bluck, 1978) in a zone of crustal weakness inherited from the Lower Palaeozoic. Analyses of plate movements, structural patterns, facies distribution of the sediments, and the presence of volcanism, have led to proposals of a wide variety of stress systems and their origins, which are thought to have affected the Devonian and Carboniferous of the Midland Valley. More recent suggestions include east–west extension (Russell, 1971; Haszeldine, 1988; Stedman, 1988), north-south extension (Leeder, 1982; Leeder and McMahon, 1988) and NW–SE extension with superimposed right-lateral strike slip (Dewey, 1982; Read, 1988). However, several authors such as Kennedy (1958) and Read (1988), have pointed out that different stress

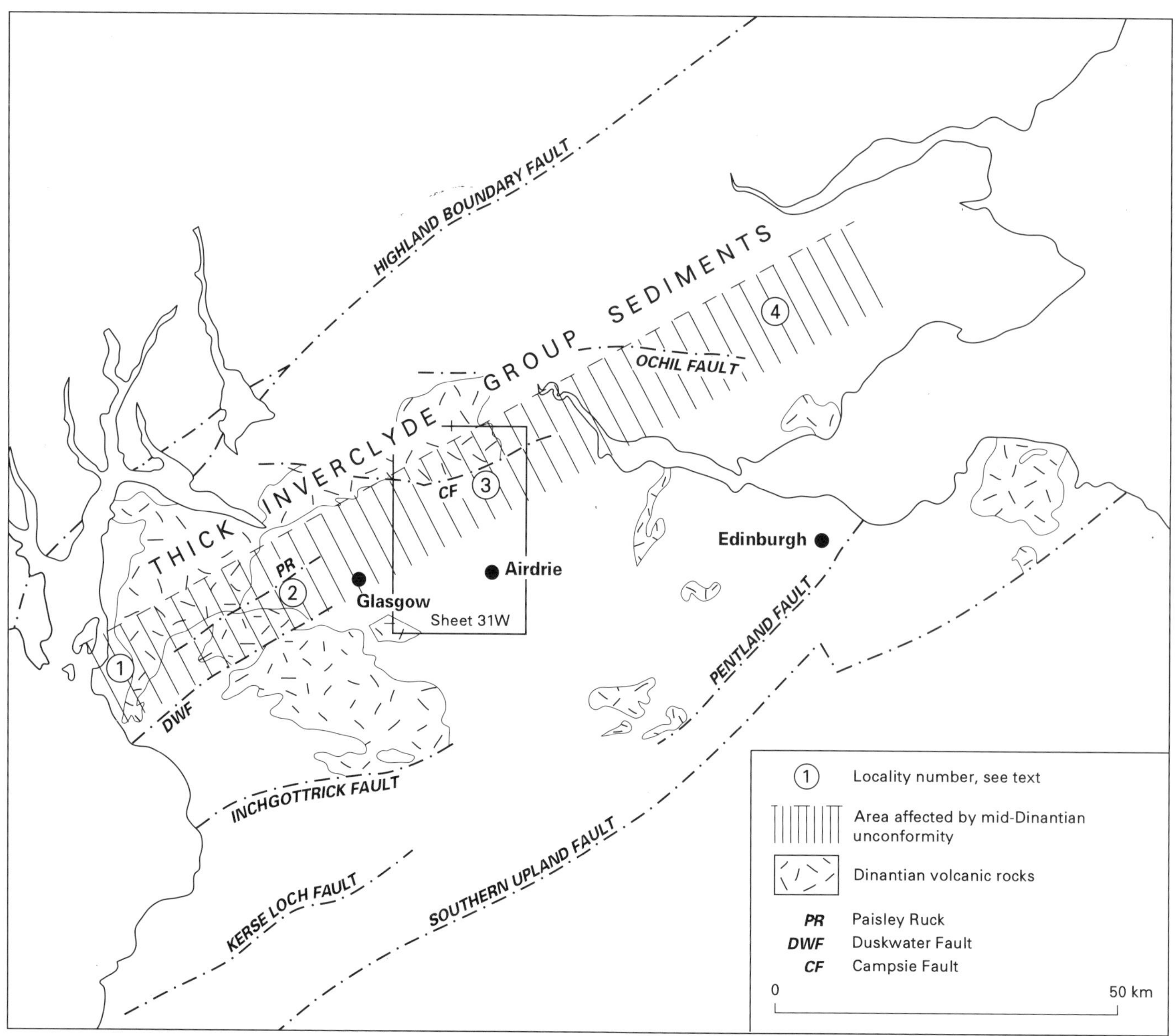

Figure 16 Location of the mid-Dinantian unconformity.

systems appear to have been operative at different times during the late Devonian and Carboniferous.

The oldest sedimentary rocks seen at the surface in the Airdrie district, the Inverclyde Group of late Devonian-early Carboniferous age, were deposited under quiet tectonic conditions on an alluvial plain which became marginally marine and subject to fluctuating salinity and periodic desiccation. The end of this period is marked by a return to fluvial sedimentation, indicating rejuvenation and uplift of the source area. Shortly after, during the mid-Dinantian, a major unconformity occurred along the south margin of the Kilsyth Hills (Chapter 4) (Locality 3, Figure 16), to the south of the South Campsie Linear Vent System. The amount of missing strata decreases away from the South Campsie Linear Vent System, until at Carron Valley Reservoir, 5 km to the north, there is no evidence for an unconformity and a full sequence is preserved. This implies that the break may be due to magmatic updoming prior to eruption of the Clyde Plateau Volcanic Formation lavas. This phase of uplift and erosion can also be recognised along the north margin of the Gleniffer Braes (Locality 2, Figure 16); and in north Ayrshire (Locality 1, Figure 16) which Monro (1975) suggests is caused by magmatic updoming. The Lomond Hills (Locality 4, Figure 16) lie on a projection of the Caledonoid trend of the other sites. Here one or more major mid-Dinantian disconformities have been postulated (Browne, 1980a). The absence of volcanic rocks in a very attenuated Lower Carboniferous sequence in the Lomond Hills does not preclude magmatic updoming as a controlling mechanism. In the western part of the Midland Valley the mid-Dinantian unconformity was followed by the eruption of several hundred metres of lavas belonging to the Clyde Plateau Volcanic Formation. These are alkali basalts typical of intra-plate rift systems associated with tensional stress regimes. The eruption of some of these volcanics from a series of linear vent systems aligned ENE–WSW (Craig, 1980) is thought to be strongly suggestive of NNW–SSE tension or possibly transtension (Read, 1989). However, in the apparent absence of a hot-spot trail in the Midland Valley, Smedley (1986) suggests that passive rifting with gentle upwelling of magma occurred in a region already weakened by Caledonian tectonism. If this is the case, it seems possible that the trend of the linear vent systems may have been inherited and consequently the apparent orientation of the regional tensional stress system at this time may be misleading.

After volcanism ceased, erosion of the lava blocks took place and detritus was deposited locally along the margins while terruginous sediments were being laid down elsewhere. Cyclic sedimentation became established and continued throughout the late Dinantian and Silesian. The development of widespread limestones and coals which can be used as marker bands allows facies analyses of smaller stratigraphical intervals. During the late Dinantian the cyclic sediments of the Lower Limestone Formation indicate repeated subsidence of a fluviodeltaic environment below a shallow sea. The strata are thickest in the middle of the present district where an ENE–WSW basin, the Kilsyth Trough, was developed (Browne et al., 1985, fig. 13). A similar pattern is seen in Ayrshire but to the east, the Kincardine, the east and the west Fife basins are developed with a north–south trend. During the Namurian the Limestone Coal Formation strata of the present district were deposited in a similar pattern in river-dominated deltas with occasional marine influxes. The sediments also thin towards the north–south-trending margin of the Bathgate Hills which acted as a positive area at this time. On the basis of facies and thickness distribution of the Limestone Coal Formation strata Stedman (1988) suggests that the stress regime at the time of their deposition was one of east–west tension which in the south-west of the Midland Valley reactivated a Caledonoid grain. Read (1988) on the other hand, proposes that dextral shear was operating during this period. In the Airdrie district the succeeding fluviodeltaic and marine sediments of the Upper Limestone Formation are thickest in an ENE–WSW basin which developed under what is thought to be transtensional conditions near the centre of the area. The dominantly fluvial conditions with short-lived marine incursions which followed during the deposition of the Passage Formation show a marked change in facies and sediment thickness. Many minor unconformities occur reflecting tectonic instability and the overall thickness gradually increases to the north-east of the district. In the central part of the Midland Valley north–south folds which replaced ENE–WSW lineaments as the dominant controls on sedimentation are interpreted as a return to a transpressional regime (Read, 1989). The overlying fluviodeltaic Lower and Middle Coal measures of Westphalian age are thickest in the east of the present district and thin gradually westwards reflecting a continuing north-east control. The east–west-trending quartz-dolerite dykes are now generally accepted to be of late Westphalian-early Stephanian age. They are commonly intruded along early faults with a similar trend. This is thought to indicate an apparent north–south tensional or transtensional phase during the late Carboniferous (Read, 1988). Read concluded that all these Silesian structural features are compatible with dextral strike slip superimposed on thermal subsidence. Although the amount of lateral movement may be relatively small up to the end of the Namurian, it may have been greater at the end of the Carboniferous (Read, 1989).

Most of the Airdrie district lies on the western limb of the major Central Coalfield Syncline, a complex and much faulted structure with a north–south axis that can be traced from the Ochil Fault in the Alloa district (Sheet 39E) through the whole of the Falkirk district (Sheet 31E) (Francis et al., 1970). The Salsburgh Anticline, also in the Falkirk district, separates this part of the syncline from the deeper western part that forms the Lanarkshire Basin and occupies the southern part of the district. The minor structures are briefly described below; fold axes and faults are shown in Figure 17. Dips are generally low (mostly less than 10°) except on the Riggin Anticline.

FOLDS

The Clyde Plateau Volcanic Formation north of the Campsie Fault is very gently tilted to the east but shows no sign of folding. To the south of the Campsie Fault younger strata are folded into a number of synclines and anticlines, whose axes are displaced laterally by faulting (Figure 17). It is probable that the faults functioned as planes of separation between fault blocks which penecontemporaneously or subsequently folded independently. For instance, at St Flanan [688 747], a basin and a half-dome occur on the opposite sides of the Hilton–St Flanan Fault implying an apparent lateral shift. However, that displacement decreases very markedly in both directions and the fault dies out 3 km to the east, indicating that the two blocks must have responded to west–east compression in different ways, rather than pre-existing fold axes having been displaced horizontally.

In the western part of the district the Kirkintilloch Syncline can be traced NNE–SSW from east of Milton of Campsie [652 767] to Stepps [658 685] through the ill-defined Passage Group outcrop east of Torrance [620 742]. Towards the north, where it becomes a very shallow, open fold, an ill-defined anticline separates it from a NNE–SSW syncline that runs from Balmalloch [704 782] to Shirva [691 755], where it ends in the basin

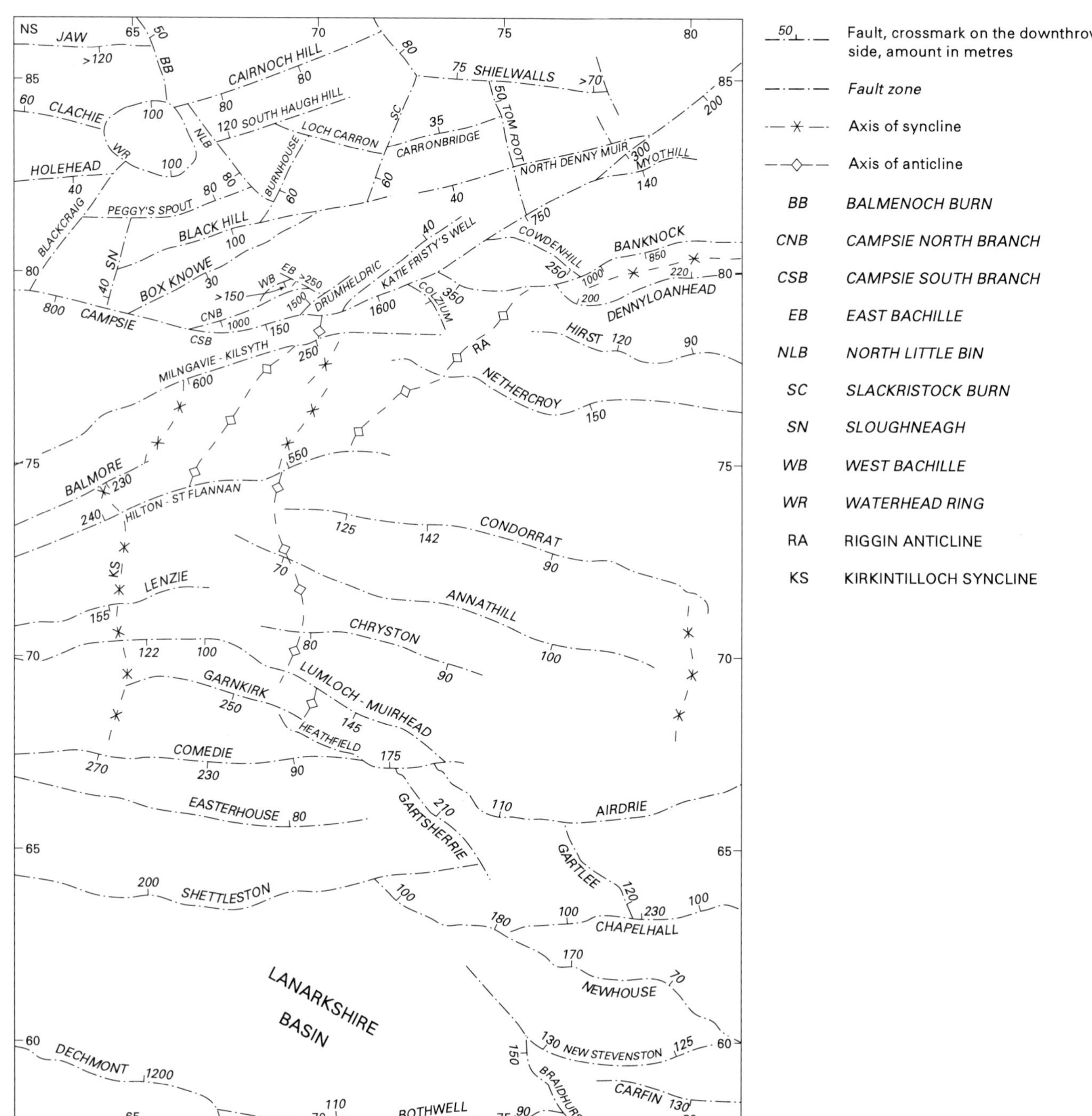

Figure 17 Generalised structure showing the principal faults and folds.

with Passage Formation strata on the north side of the Hilton–St Flanans Fault (Figure 17). From the half-dome with Limestone Coal Group strata south of the fault, a diffuse, ill-defined NNE–SSW anticline can be traced as far south as Gartcosh [699 681] (Figure 17).

The Riggin Anticline of Kilsyth is a narrow fold with steep dips throughout, becoming vertical in places. It extends for 7.5 km NE–SW from the Banton Fault at Banton [750 792] to the Hilton–St Flanans Fault at Twechar [700 752]. The Coal Measures in the Banknock Coalfield are bounded by two large faults and quite steeply folded into a west–east syncline with a small deep basin at each end, in which are found the youngest strata. Northwards to Dunipace, the general easterly dip is only slightly interrupted by minor flexures. In the Cumbernauld area, between Greengairs and Airdrie, a broad shallow north–south basin contains Middle Coal Measures.

The southern part of the district is dominated by the northern part of the Lanarkshire Basin, a broad, open structure largely free of faults, and occupied by Upper Coal Measures (Figure 17). To the south-west the northerly dipping southern limb of the basin is cut off to the south by the major lineament, the Dechmont Fault, south of which the rocks of the Clyde Plateau Volcanic Formation are almost horizontal.

FAULTS

The more important of the many faults are shown in Figure 17, together with selected throws. They are all normal faults (Plate 8) and in the coalfield most have been proved underground. Hades are usually between 45° and 60°, but a few are more gently inclined, such as the Colzium Flat Fault [72 79]. Re-examination of the available mining evidence suggests, however, that it is not necessary to postulate such an undulating fault plane as that shown by Robertson and Haldane (1937, p.125).

The most important structure is the Campsie Fault which trends west–east and then WSW–ENE as it traverses the sheet area from west to east. In general it separates the Clyde Plateau Volcanic Formation to the north from younger rocks to the south. The southerly downthrow reaches a maximum of about 1600 m but decreases markedly towards the east. The fault splits into northern and southern branches [663 783] that extend for over 3 km and are up to 600 m apart. In the western part of the split zone the northern branch has much the bigger throw (1000 m) but this is largely cancelled out by the northerly downthrow of the Drumheldric Fault with which the northern branch converges. The southern branch in turn cancels out the Drumheldric Fault as its throw increases eastwards and it continues in that direction but with decreasing downthrow as the single Campsie Fault. The rapid changes in downthrow seen along its length could also be explained by an element of lateral movement.

North of the Campsie Fault, fractures are numerous in the Clyde Plateau Volcanic Formation and can mostly be divided into three types (Figure 17). Firstly, there are those with WSW–ENE trend, which are the most numerous type. Secondly, there are several that radiate out from the Waterhead Central Volcanic Complex and thirdly there is the Waterhead Ring Fault that bounds the complex itself (see Chapter 4). Some NW–SE and NNE–SSW faults also occur.

South of the Campsie Fault, faults are equally numerous and some (Figure 17) have much bigger throws than those to the north. The dominant faults trend between WSW–ENE and WNW–ESE, with a subordinate but quite numerous NW-trending fault set. The faulting is not equally distributed, the Lanarkshire Basin especially and the Cumbernauld area being relatively fault-free.

Plate 8 Normal fault cutting Middle Coal Measures strata in opencast site at Mossend [755 597] (C 2868).

NINE

Quaternary

The Scottish landmass was glaciated on several occasions during the Quaternary period. Evidence from ocean floor sediments indicates that there have been at least 16 major cold events during the last 1.6 million years (Bowen, 1978; Price, 1983). Whether each of these events produced ice sheets and till deposits in Scotland is not known. Because of the erosive action of successive ice sheets only the very latest events, about 30 000 years before present (BP), are known with some certainty and in any detail for the Airdrie district. Even during this period, the record is incomplete but from an assessment of evidence from central Scotland the glacial and post-glacial history may be constructed.

SUMMARY OF LATE QUATERNARY HISTORY

According to Price (1983) the most recent cold events took place from about 28 000 to 14 000 years BP and 11 000 to 10 000 years BP. Both events were associated with the build-up of glaciers in the mountains of the Highlands of Scotland. The combination of increasing precipitation and cooling climate resulted in the generation of the Dimlington ice sheet which, at its maximum some 18 000 years ago, extended over most of the Scottish landmass and much of England. It is estimated that at this time the ice sheet was over 1 km thick in central Scotland. Till deposited from the ice covers a wide area and locally conceals deposits of clay, sand and gravel and earlier accumulations of till which were laid down some time prior to the Dimlington Stade. The Dimlington sheet receded slowly over a period of several thousand years. That arctic conditions still prevailed in newly deglaciated areas between 15 000 and 13 500 years ago, is indicated by the presence of faunas in the glacimarine Errol Beds which were deposited in the fjordic valleys of eastern Scotland and offshore (Peacock, 1975; 1981).

The final stages of recession of the Dimlington ice sheet were probably accompanied by the climatic amelioration which heralded the Windermere Interstade (13 500 to 11 000 years BP). By about 13 500 years BP the Airdrie district was probably largely ice-free. During deglaciation, rivers nourished by meltwaters transported and deposited sand and gravel either under or adjacent to bodies of melting ice. Associated terraced landforms and kame and kettle topography developed at this time especially in parts of the Clyde and Kelvin valleys. In the valley of the Kelvin meltwaters initially drained eastwards via the valleys of the Bonny Water and River Carron into the Forth Estuary (Figure 18). In the valley of the River Clyde meltwaters were initially ponded by north-westward-retreating glacier ice occupying the Glasgow area. Deltaic sands and lacustrine clays and silts were deposited within the valley upstream as far south as Lanark [880 440]. With further ice recession and down-wasting, the barrier in the Clyde valley collapsed and the sea flooded the lower ground of the Airdrie district up to an elevation of about 45 m above OD. Associated marine clays of the Paisley and Linwood formations (the Clyde Beds of Peacock, 1981) are preserved in parts of the Clyde valley. In the district there is little evidence that the sediments are fossiliferous but elsewhere, in the Firth of Clyde and the Forth estuary (Browne et al., 1984), equivalent facies contain a fauna indicative of the cold temperate (boreal) conditions pertaining to the Windermere Interstade. By 11 000 years BP local sea level in the Clyde valley had probably fallen from the late-Devensian maximum to present OD or lower.

With the return of arctic climatic conditions during the Loch Lomond Stade between 11 000 and 10 000 years BP, valley glaciers again developed in the western Highlands. Although the glaciers did not reach the Airdrie district, evidence for periglacial activity includes gelifluction particularly on the flanks of steep drumlin slopes. Landslips on the south-facing slopes of the Campsie Fells probably also developed during this period.

The climate started to improve about 10 000 years BP and following initial fluctuations in relative sea level (as illustrated by the buried beaches of the Forth valley, Sissons (1966; 1969)), the major Flandrian (Postglacial) marine transgression commenced about 8000 years ago. The maximum of the transgression in the Forth valley is placed at about 6500 years BP (cf. Sissons and Brooks, 1971). Thereafter sea levels fell by stages to present OD. These changes in relative Flandrian sea level may be seen in the Glasgow area where the upper limits of a series of terrace surfaces are recorded at 12 m above OD, at less than 7.5 m above OD and less than 5 m above OD (Browne and McMillan, 1989a, fig. 5). Estuarine sands and gravels with clays and silts, associated with these levels, are present in eastern Glasgow, on the west margin of the Airdrie district. Most of the deposits flooring the floodplains of the principal valleys including those of the River Clyde upstream of eastern Glasgow, and the rivers Kelvin, Carron and Bonny Water, are of Recent age. During the Flandrian basin peat and lake clays developed in interdrumlin areas and in hollows on higher ground. Hill peat also developed in the Campsie Fells. Locally, Flandrian peat may bury similar pre-existing late-Devensian deposits.

The following account of the Quaternary sediments and associated landforms is structured to reflect their relative ages and utilises the stratigraphical framework established by Browne and McMillan (1989a; 1989b) for the Clyde valley with the addition of one newly defined unit, the Kelvin Formation. The formations are defined

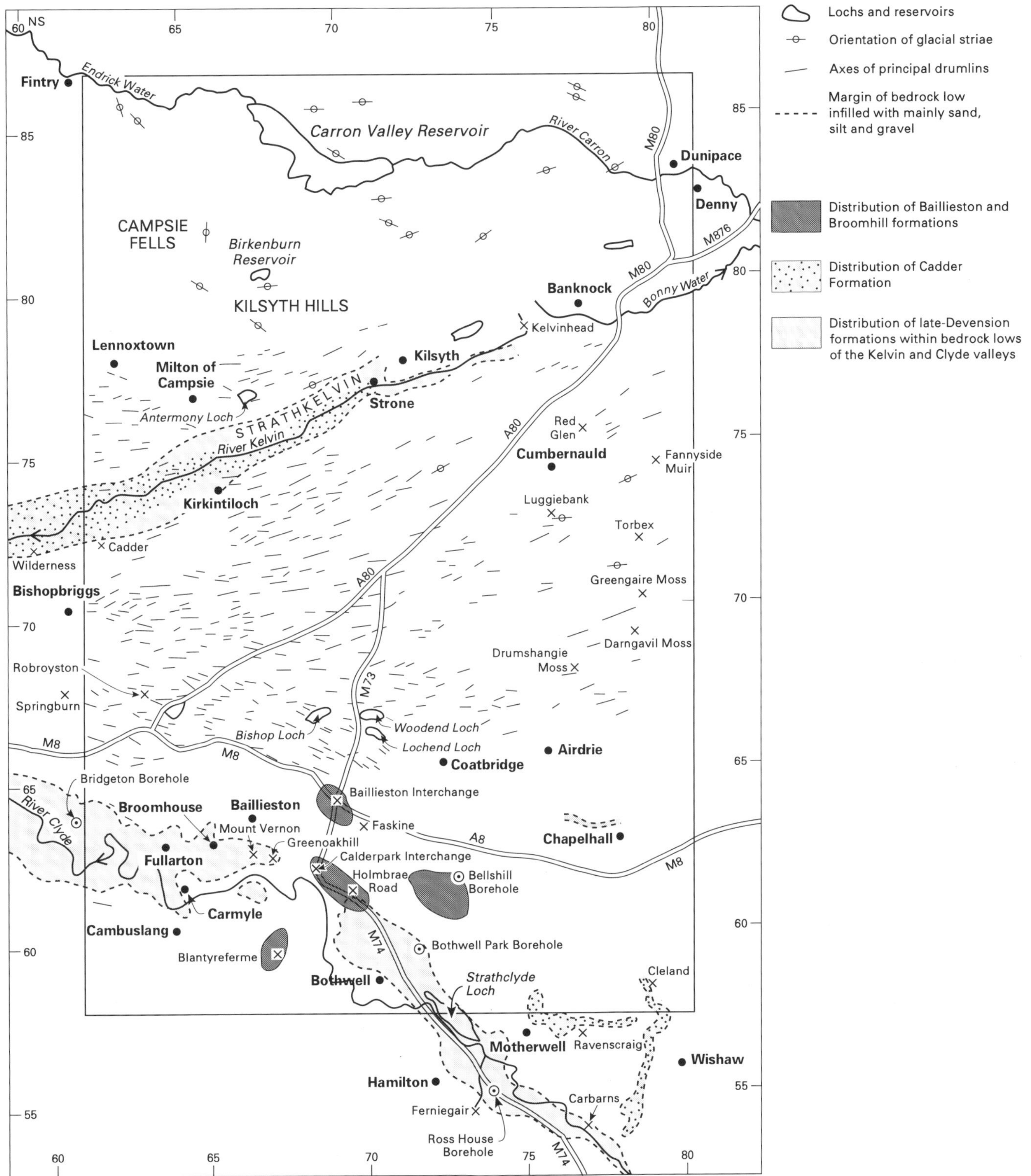

Figure 18 Location map showing orientation of drumlin axes, glacial striae, 'buried channels' and the main distribution of pre-Dimlington and late-Devensian deposits.

on the basis of sediment lithology and are classified according to principal provenance. Glacial, lacustrine, fluvial, marine and organic origins are identified (Table 4). Principal localities are shown on Figure 18.

DEVENSIAN TOPOGRAPHY

There is little doubt that major rockhead depressions under the valleys of the River Clyde and River Kelvin

Table 4 Quaternary lithostratigraphy and chronostratigraphy of the Airdrie district.

Main lithology	Clay and silt		Sand and gravel		Diamicton	Peat	Approximate age in years before present (BP)		
Provenance	Marine	Lacustrine and fluvial	Marine	Lacustrine and fluvial	Glacial	Organic			
Formations	Erskine	Kelvin Kilmaronock	Gourock	Law Endrick		Clippens[1]	10 000	Flandrian Stage	
	No mappable deposits identified in the Airdrie district						Loch Lomond Stade 11 000	Late Devensian	Devensian Stage
	Linwood Paisley	Bellshill	Killearn Bridgeton	Ross Broomhouse			Windermere Interstade 13 500	Late Devensian	Devensian Stage
					Wilderness Till		Dimlington Stade 27 500	Late Devensian	Devensian Stage
		Broomhill		Cadder	Baillieston Till[1]		Pre-Dimlington Stade		Devensian Stage

1 Earlier deposits exist locally.

(Figure 18) represent a generally pre-Dimlington Stade topography which may have been initiated in the Pliocene (cf. George, 1974, fig. 2.1) or earlier (cf. Linton, 1951). Carruthers (in Clough et al., 1911) noted the coincidence of both bedrock depressions with broadly synclinal structural axes in the underlying Carboniferous strata. However, he indicated that drainage may have been initiated on younger rocks which were subsequently eroded. Recent opinions on the origin of the depressions include those of Jardine (1977, pp.104–106) who proposed river action at a time of lower global sea level, and Menzies (1981) who favoured excavation by subglacial streams. Jardine (1986, p.32) concluded that the rockhead depressions were probably composite both in origin and age.

Whatever the sequence of events, it seems likely that erosive processes at work beneath ice sheets during the Quaternary have overdeepened these drainage systems. During late-Devensian and Flandrian times the bedrock depressions have been filled principally with water-laid sediments. In the Kelvin valley, the records of many site investigation boreholes illustrate that beneath the alluvial cover thick sequences of unfossiliferous sand and gravel are interbedded with or underlain by silt with clay. The coarse-grained sediments are of glacifluvial and deltaic origin associated with the melting of the Dimlington ice sheet. The silts and clays are glacilacustrine. Pre-Dimlington Stade sand and gravel of the Cadder Formation is also present locally, underlying the Dimlington till of the Wilderness Till Formation.

In the Airdrie district, borehole records indicate thicknesses of the infilling sediments to range from about 30 m west of Kilsyth [700 770] to 87 m at Torrance [620 735]. Corresponding topographic levels for the bedrock surface range from 11 m above OD to 49 m below OD, illustrating a generally westwardly deepening depression. This trend is confirmed by rockhead levels of 50 to 75 m below OD recorded farther west in the Glasgow district (Sheet 30E), notably in the Bearsden [540 720] and Drumry [500 710] areas, and may indicate that erosion was initiated during a period of relatively low sea level. However, such levels are lower than the minimum rockhead values recorded in the

Firth of Clyde, for example in the channel between Toward Point [135 670] and Skelmorlie [195 675] where Deegan et al. (1973, fig. 9) recorded levels of 40 to 60 m below OD. Such evidence points to overdeepening of the Kelvin bedrock depression by glacier ice or subglacial meltwaters under a high hydraulic head. In the Clyde valley, rockhead surface descends below OD downstream of Cambuslang [640 600]. At Bridgeton [610 640], boreholes show rockhead levels lower than 40 m below OD. Here, most of the infilling sediments are generally younger than the till of the Dimlington ice sheet. In the Clyde valley east of Bothwell, rockhead level is at 6 m below OD and rises upstream.

Other smaller 'buried channels' which were probably excavated prior to or during the Dimlington glaciation include those at Chapelhall [780 630] (Geikie, 1863; Clough et al., 1926) and Cleland [796 580] (Dron, 1914; Clough et al., 1920; Cummings, 1962) (Figure 18). At Chapelhall Geikie (1863) reported up to 9 m of laminated clay on sand with clay laminae and thin peat layers. These sediments were concealed by hard, stony till and underlain by a lower till up to 9 m thick. The clay succession locally showed evidence of compressional deformation by the overriding ice. East of Motherwell [750 570], on the southern margin of the Airdrie district, evidence from boreholes in the Ravenscraig area confirms the existence and extends the known area of drift-filled depressions described by Dron (1914), Clough et al. (1920) and Cummings (1962). At the Ravenscraig Steelworks [770 570], up to 50 m of mainly sand and gravel locally overlie till in a westerly deepening channel. The thalweg deepens from 62 m above OD at the eastern end of the Ravenscraig Steelworks site to 35 m above OD north of Motherwell.

In the Clyde valley parts of the present river's course are not coincident with the axis of the earlier bedrock depression. Between Bothwell [700 580] and Cambuslang [640 600] the river bed is cut mainly in rock and is therefore likely to be mainly of Flandrian age. Any narrow pre-Dimlington Stade channel, although locally coincident with the present course of the river, mainly trends parallel to it. The gorges through which the South Calder Water, the Rotten Calder and North Calder Water flow, were also probably cut during postglacial times.

On the high ground of the Airdrie district, the Devensian topography was probably similar to that of today. The effect of the last ice sheet was to modify pre-existing glaciated landforms and alluvial tracts and redistribute till deposits over a wide area. Over the western part of the district predominantly easterly moving ice sculptured well-formed drumlins, with generally west–east aligned axes (Figure 18). On high ground north of Airdrie [760 650] and around Cumbernauld [770 745], where drift thicknesses generally do not exceed a few metres, easterly aligned crag and tail landforms are developed on resistant bedrock including Upper Carboniferous sandstones and Permo-Carboniferous dolerite sills and dykes. North of the Kelvin valley, in the Campsie Fells, till is thickest on the valley floors with exposed rock and upland blanket peat predominating on the flanks and summits of hills.

PRE-DIMLINGTON DEPOSITS

In general, pre-Dimlington Stade deposits are concealed beneath younger sediments. Information from sections and subsurface data from BGS and commercial boreholes have revealed the existence of glacial, glacifluvial and glacilacustrine deposits beneath the Dimlington till. The limited areal extent of these deposits (Figure 18) may be an indication of the erosive power of the Dimlington ice sheet. Deposits of possible marine origin interbedded with till were reported in the 19th century from the Chapelhall area, south of Airdrie, although it is not now possible to locate them precisely.

Glacial deposits

Known only from site investigation boreholes, the oldest sediments in the Airdrie district are considered to be muds which formed in ice-dammed lakes. These deposits, which are preserved only in a limited area around Baillieston [670 640] in eastern Glasgow, are overlain by the Baillieston Till Formation. This formation is named from temporary sections exposed during the construction of the M8 Baillieston Motorway Interchange [693 641] (Figure 19). It is also present in the BGS Bellshill Borehole [7304 6161]. The till lies stratigraphically below the Wilderness Till Formation (see below) and, despite the absence of definitive age data, is considered to be the product of a glacial event earlier than the late-Devensian. The typical lithology is a glacially organised diamicton, composed of boulders, pebbles and gravel in a matrix of sandy silty clay. Elongate clasts are preferentially oriented and the deposit is systematically jointed. Examined samples have proved unfossiliferous. The deposit is of a stiff to hard consistency and low plasticity. In general the colour of the clay matrix is greyish brown reflecting that of the local Coal Measures bedrock. Possible ancient surface weathering, in the form of oxidation, results in a reddish brown hue to the upper surface of the Baillieston Till as seen in the M8 sections.

Glacifluvial outwash deposits

Outwash deposits related to the advance of the Dimlington ice sheet occur on the south side of the Kelvin valley in the parish of Cadder. Here sand and gravel of the Cadder Formation rests on the Baillieston Till Formation and is in turn overlain by the Wilderness Till Formation. The poorly known subsurface sands and gravels and interbedded diamicton beds under the floodplain of the River Kelvin are also assigned to the Cadder Formation. Within the area of the Kelvin's bedrock depression, the formation may be at least 40 m thick as illustrated by the Cadder No. 16 borehole record [6002 7326] in the Glasgow district. The stratigraphical relationships are diagrammatically shown in Figure 20. Between Torrance [620 740] and Kirkintilloch [655 740] most available borehole logs record only the top part of the Quaternary sequence through the Flandrian and late-Devensian sediments. However, records of boreholes south of Redbog Farm at

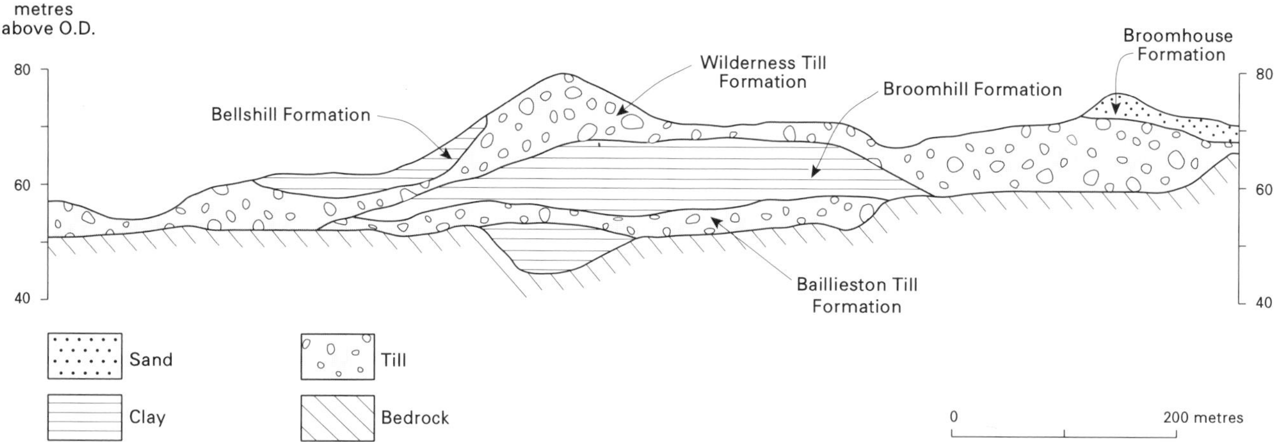

Figure 19 Horizontal section at the Ballieston Interchange.

Torrance [615 736] and Crofthead [622 727] penetrated the top few metres of sand and silt (Cadder Formation) lying below the Wilderness Till.

Sand and gravel within the small 'buried channels' of Chapelhall [780 630], Cleland [796 580] and Ravenscraig [770 570] are tentatively assigned to the Cadder Formation. At the former Nether Johnstone Sand Pit, Ravenscraig in the Hamilton district (Sheet 23W), over 40 m of sand, gravel and clay capped by thin till deposits were proved in sections and boreholes (Clough et al., 1920).

In the Cadder area, although exposures were formerly plentiful in workings for sand and gravel, there are now only two sections remaining where the Cadder Formation can be seen. Both are in the in the Glasgow district at the Wilderness [594 725, 615 722]. Field notes and BGS photographs of former exposures establish the stratigraphical position of the formation (Figure 20). The typical lithological assemblages consist of mainly framework-supported bouldery gravel and sand, and coarse- to fine-grained, sometimes pebbly, sand with silt. Locally a thin clay and silt bed of possible lacustrine origin (?Broomhill Formation, see below) lies between the sand and gravel and the Baillieston Till. Geotechnically, the deposits are usually dense to very dense. Based on observations from sections in the top 30 m of the formation much of the gravel is thickly bedded and displays trough cross-bedding in sets up to 3 m thick. These interfinger with sands. The sands are trough cross-bedded, ripple-laminated and horizontally laminated.

Observed faulting of the sediments may be due in part to glacial overriding by the ice-sheet that deposited the overlying Wilderness Till Formation. The contact between the two formations is disconformable and locally complex. The faulting may also partly reflect the presence of buried masses of ice which have subsequently melted. Clay-filled fissures penetrating the top of the formation in the Wilderness Sand Pit [6006 7230] were observed by Rolfe (1966). These features were said by Galloway (1961) to be common in this area and were regarded as ice-wedge casts which formed under periglacial conditions.

Mammalian remains have been found in the Cadder Formation at several localities. Swinton (1927, p.395) describes the finding near Bishopbriggs of a single toe bone of the woolly rhinoceros *Coelodonta antiquitatis* (Blumenbach) and Flett (1927, pp.396–397) mentions the discovery in 1925 of a left second metacarpal in Bishopbriggs No.2 sand pit [623 732]. Other occurrences of the woolly rhinoceros in the form of an upper molar and a left tibia both from Crofthead Sand Pit c. [617 725] near Bishopbriggs are reported by Rolfe (1966, pp.253–258) who also figures bones from the Wilderness Sand Pit. The latter locality lies about 2 km west of Bishopbriggs No. 2 Sand Pit and is significant in that one of the bones collected provided a radiocarbon date of 27 550 (+ 1370, − 1680) years BP. This date is compatible with recently reported dates from a stratigraphically similar position from Sourlie [338 414] near Irvine (Sheet 22W; Jardine et al., 1988). An arctic environment is indicated by the flora and fauna.

The sedimentological and faunal evidence both point to deposition of the unit in a periglacial environment with the possibility that some of the sediments are ice-contact deposits. Based on the scale of the trough cross-bedded units, the sediments appear to be fluvial or more likely fluvideltaic in origin. Overall the deposits appear to form a major outwash system laid down in front of the advancing Dimlington ice sheet about 27 000 years ago. The outwash deposits were subsequently overridden by the ice which deposited the overlying Wilderness Till Formation.

Glacilacustrine deposits

Pre-Dimlington Stade lacustrine deposits are found in various areas around Glasgow. Subsurface data and temporary sections reveal laminated muds resting discontinuously upon the Baillieston Till. Accorded the name

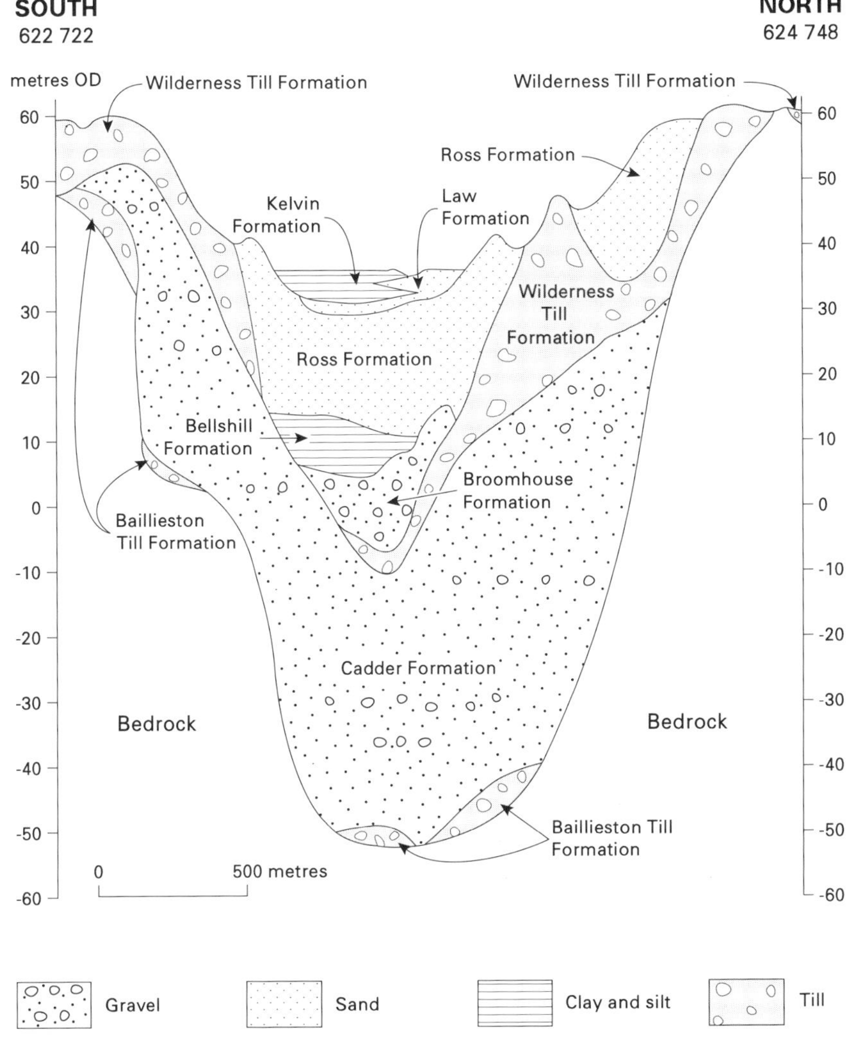

Figure 20 Generalised section across the buried valley of the River Kelvin near Torrance.

Broomhill Formation from the type sections of the Broomhill Park Borehole No. 2 [5985 6650] in the Glasgow district, these sediments have also been observed on the eastern fringes of the city at Baillieston and in the BGS Bellshill Borehole. The latter proved 1.45 m of banded dark brownish grey and reddish brown clay with graded units and diamicton layers up to 12 cm thick. The clay is probably in faulted contact with tills above and below. In sections at the Baillieston M8 Motorway Interchange up to 14 m of stiff to hard, dark brownish grey and grey clay and silt with reddish brown laminae and bands contain isolated clasts and rafts of diamicton. The clay was observed to be in thrust contact with the underlying Baillieston Till and overlying Wilderness Till. Evidence including overfolds facing to the east, westward-dipping reverse faults, shearing and polished surfaces points to glacitectonic deformation.

Evidence from sections and boreholes together with the mapped extent (Figure 18) of the Broomhill Formation points to the deposition of the laminated muds in the form of varves representing seasonally controlled sedimentation in a temporary lake occupying part of the Clyde valley. Lake shorelines are estimated to have been in excess of 70 m above OD. Isolated clasts, interpreted as dropstones and rafts of diamicton testify to the proximity of ice and it appears likely that the lake developed at some stage during the build-up of the Dimlington ice sheet. An estimate of the duration of lake sedimentation has been made from the cores of the Broomhill Park No. 2 Borehole and the Erskine Bridge Borehole [4634 7251] in the Greenock district (Sheet 30W). Varved laminae have been considered to represent between 600 and 1500 years of sedimentation (Browne and McMillan, 1989a, p.20). The Broomhill Formation, as previously noted, may also be present in the Kelvin valley but the data are equivocal.

Marine deposits, in situ or ice-rafted?

Possible marine deposits at an elevation of 155 m near the former Monkland Ironworks at Chapelhall [783 625] were reported by James Smith of Jordanhill (1862, pp.17, 139–141) and Archibald Geikie (1863, pp.58–59). They described a section of up to 0.6 m of stoneless shelly clay lying between beds of till. The fauna, including broken and intact shells of *Macoma calcarea*, is indicative of cold marine waters. Investigations in the district by Horne et al. (1894) failed to reveal any further evidence of the presence of the shelly clay and the indications are that the deposit is a small raft of glacially transported marine sediment (cf. Browne et al., 1983a) caught up in the Dimlington till. The alternative view, that it is in situ and is a remnant of a high-level marine inundation (described by Sutherland, 1981) which occurred prior to the build-up of the last Scottish ice sheet seems unlikely.

DIMLINGTON ICE SHEET

Glacial deposits

Evidence from the Cadder area indicates that the build-up of the Dimlington ice sheet began at about 27 500 years BP. At its maximum, around 18 000 years BP, the ice sheet was probably over 1 km thick in central Scotland. The direction of ice movement is recorded by moulded landforms including drumlins, some of which are rock-cored, by crag and tail features and by striae. Between Strathkelvin and the Clyde valley movement is generally from west to east with local variations from a north-westerly direction (Figure 18). In Strathkelvin the easterly to east-north-easterly movement of ice is confirmed by the distribution cone of erratic blocks of the distinctive Lennoxtown essexite (Peach, 1909; Shakesby, 1976).

The principal deposit of the Dimlington ice sheet is the Wilderness Till Formation. Following the classification of Rose et al. (1988), the formation is named after the Wilderness Plantation north of Bishopbriggs [605 720] in the Glasgow district. In the Airdrie district the formation comprises a hard, reddish brown, sandy, silty diamicton which rests with stepped but low-angle disconformity on the Cadder Formation.

The Wilderness Till Formation was proved, amongst others, in the BGS Bellshill [7304 6161] and Bothwell Park [7159 5956] boreholes. The typical lithology is a massive, glacially organised diamicton composed of isolated boulders, gravel and pebbles in a matrix of sandy silty clay. The more elongate clasts are preferentially oriented and the deposit usually has systematic sets of joints. It is of a hard to stiff consistency and low plasticity. The colour of the matrix varies, depending upon that of the local bedrock and can be reddish brown from Devonian and Upper Coal Measures sources, brownish grey or black from Lower and Middle Coal Measures and Namurian strata and greenish grey from Highland metamorphic rocks.

Minor features noted in the Wilderness Till include pockets and bands of medium-grained sand and thin bands of laminated clay. In the Cadder area, temporary sections in the Wilderness Till revealed that locally the diamicton is graded, displaying both upward and downward coarsening of the dispersed pebble- to bouldersized clasts. Also recognised were zones within the formation in which the clasts become far less common. Locally, the diamicton also appeared to have a 'structurally stratified' top with discontinuous partings sometimes of sand but elsewhere with no obvious lithological association. In one case, a unit of apparently cross-bedded diamicton was seen above the junction with the underlying Cadder Formation.

Glacitectonics

The effects of the Dimlington ice sheet overriding pre-existing glacial, fluvial and lacustrine sediments may be seen at several localities including Bellshill, Baillieston and Cadder. Carruthers (notebook sketches dated 1906; Summary of Progress for 1906, 1907, p.105; and in Clough et al., 1911) described a section in a railway cutting [730 607] to the north of Bellshill in which contorted laminated clays (presumed to be the Broomhill Formation) were observed to be caught up in till. Other examples of glacitectonic disturbance in the Broomhill Formation were revealed in excavations for the Baillieston M8 Motorway Interchange [693 641] (Figure 19). Here the bedding of the lacustrine sediments was cut by high-angle, westward-dipping reverse faults. In the easternmost of the sections the clays and silts are sheared out so that the Wilderness Till Formation rests directly upon the Baillieston Till. In the temporary section low angle polished surfaces were noted as common particularly where the clay and silt pinched out. The Wilderness Till was observed to contain slices of laminated clay. One raft, measuring tens of metres long included near the base of the formation, lay between two discordant low-angle thrust planes. To the west of the Airdrie district, borehole cores at Broomhill and Erskine Bridge showed steeply dipping faults and polished surfaces in geotechnically overconsolidated clay, silt and diamicton.

A section at Holmbrae Road, Thorniewood [698 614] demonstrates the complexity of deposits lying below the Wilderness Till (Figure 21). Here, a sequence of till, sand, gravel and clay has been overridden by ice to produce a series of repeated thrust slices (McMillan and Browne, 1983). The overlying till (unit 1 in Figure 21), which is considered to be the Wilderness Till, is a red-brown, sandy, clayey diamicton. Its base truncates the underlying sequence of bedded and nonbedded sediments (units 2–11) along a sharp, undulating, sub-horizontal surface. The bedded sediments comprise brown and grey clay with silt laminae (units 2, 7 and 10) of the Broomhill Formation, and cross-laminated, yellow-brown, fine- to coarse-grained sand and gravel (units 3, 5, 6, 9 and 11), the last being of granule to boulder grade. The sand and gravel may be the southern equivalent of the Cadder Formation. Contacts between different bedded units are sharp and many are faulted. Locally sandwiched within the bedded units is a unit of stiff, red-brown till (units 4 and 8) (?the Baillieston Till

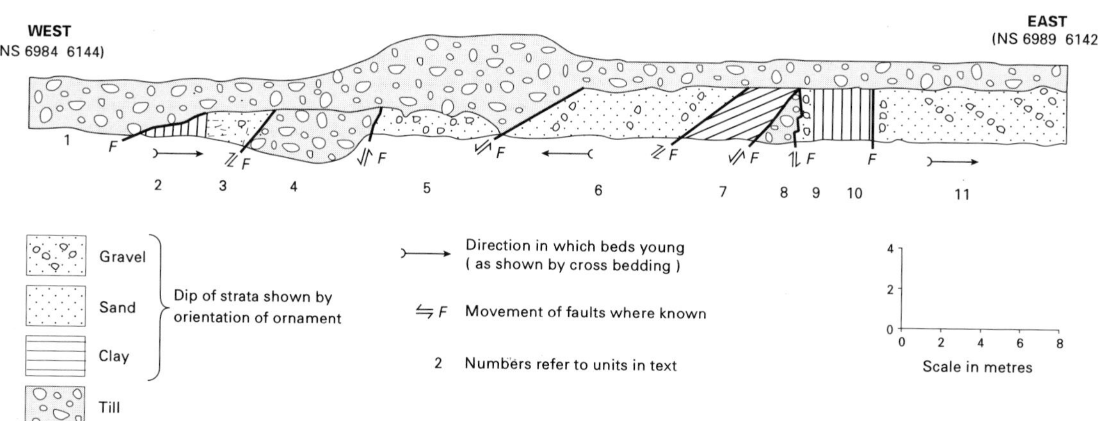

Figure 21 Horizontal section at Holmbrae Road, Thorniewood.

Formation) which in places is seen to be truncated by the Wilderness Till.

If the bedded sediments are the product of meltwater activity associated with the build-up of the Dimlington ice sheet (cf. Cadder and Broomhill formations) the present configuration of thrust slices shows that these sediments probably underwent deformation as the ice sheet overrode them (cf. Banham, 1975, pp.77–79). The origin of the lower till is less clear. The observed faulted blocks may represent a disturbed floor of the Baillieston Till Formation or may alternatively be isolated slices of the Wilderness Till broken off and incorporated into the bedded sediments by glacitectonic processes.

At Cadder, glacitectonic disturbance in the Cadder Formation, which underlies the Wilderness Till Formation, is restricted to minor faulting and small-scale folding. However, the sands and gravels are geotechnically dense indicating consolidation during the ensuing glaciation.

Organic deposits within the the Wilderness Till Formation

Early references to organic remains either caught up within or underlying the Wilderness Till Formation provide indications of boreal and subarctic climatic conditions before and during the build-up of the ice sheet. An early reference by Dunlop (1888, pp.312–315) mentions an exposure of 'Boulder-clay' at Burnhead Quarry, east of Airdrie [781 665] within which were sandwiched layers of peat. The latter contained glacially striated boulders and also seeds, berries and leaves of a number of plant species. These were identified by C Reid (personal communication) as: *Apium nodiflorum* Reich, *Betula nana* Linné, *Carduus* sp., *Carex dioica* Linné, *Carex rostrata* Stokes, *Empetrum nigrum* Linné, *Hippuris vulgaris* Linné, *Isoetes lacustris* Linné, *Menyanthes trifoliata* Linné, *Potamogeton* sp., *Potentilla comarum* Linné, *Prunus padus* Linné, *Ranunculus aquatilis* Linné.

Also found at this locality were parts of the carabid beetles *Pterostichus* and *Anchomenus*, together with a weevil identified (Fowler *in* Dunlop, 1888, p.314) as *Otiorhynchus maurus* = *Onodusus* Müller. Fowler also noted that, within Britain, the last-named species is confined to Scotland. Although no vertebrate remains have been recorded, Dunlop (1888) suggested that the presence of vivianite above the lower peat layer was indicative of the former presence of bones. More recently Coope (1962) was able to examine a small quantity('little more than a cubic inch') of this peaty material. This comprised half of a sample held by the Hunterian Museum, Glasgow. From this he identified five coleopteran species, namely *Boreaphilus henningianus* Sahlberg, *Nebria gyllenhali* (Schönherr) *Olophrum rotundicolle* Sahlberg, *Otiorhynchus nodosus* (Müller) and *Patrobus septonrionus* Dejean. All were claimed by Coope (1962, p.283) to have boreo-alpine distributions, but two, *B. henningianus* and *O. rotundicolle*, are shown (Coope, 1962, figs. 1 and 2) to have been recorded in Britain only as fossils. Their absence from southern and western Europe indicates a much colder and more continental climate than at present. Coope was unable to refer the deposit to a specific interstadial. Although all of the species recorded from Airdrie occur in Devensian interstadial faunas, no specific interstadial has been found to contain all five of the Airdrie taxa. This, he suggested, could have been due to inadequate sampling.

In a former brickworks at Faskine, near Coatbridge [706 633] an exposure of till also containing layers of peat was described by Bennie (1894, pp.148–152). He noted the presence of the arctic willow *Salix herbacea* Linné in these layers as evidence of significantly lower temperatures than those presently prevailing. Plant seeds, leaves and stems together with remains of beetles, water mites and a single ostracod were found in some layers of peat. From the distribution of these fossils within the layers, and the presence of overlying till, Bennie concluded that the fauna lived in a lake formed during a temporary withdrawal of the ice sheet, the plant remains being dropped into the lake before the ice returned to bury all the remains.

Material from a borehole at Monkland Colliery [7784 6510] was observed by Clough (1908, pp.98–100) to contain a moss layer of variable thickness (up to about 0.5 m) overlain by about 10 m of till and resting on a lower till. This organic layer contained eight species of mosses dominated by *Tomentipnum nitens* (Hedwig) Loeske and including *Helodium blandovii* (Weber & Mohr) Warnstorf. The latter is believed to be absent from Scotland today although found in Europe as far south as Central Germany. Also present were leaves and fragments of trees such as *Betula nana* Linné and *Salix* sp. together with *Carex* sp. and *Potentilla comarum* Linné. These plant remains indicate that the country was free of ice when the peat was deposited. The assemblage of mosses suggests a boreal to subarctic environment. On the available field evidence Clough was unable to determine whether this material was in situ or glacially transported.

A temporary excavation in a cutting for the Edinburgh to Glasgow road c. [6370 6545] revealed a peat layer up to 0.3 m thick overlain by about 3.5 m of till. The peat, which rested on greenish silt, contained plant seeds and insects including carabid beetles.

WINDERMERE INTERSTADE: DEGLACIATION

Deposits of ice wastage

The initial stages of deglaciation were marked by ice wastage on the high ground of the Campsie Fells and Renfrew Hills. At first, summits of hills reappeared from beneath the ice. Continuing wastage in high valleys resulted in the deposition of 'morainic drift deposits', ill-sorted sediments comprising boulders and gravel in a sandy clay matrix. These deposits are particularly extensive on the flanks of the valleys of the Carron and Endrick waters where hummocky morainic landforms are developed. Isolated high-level terraces of sandy and gravelly clay at elevations between 120 and 300 m above OD have been interpreted as deltaic flats. These formed in ice-marginal positions when meltwater streams flowed into temporary bodies of standing water (Robertson and Haldane, 1937, pp.111–112). As the ice sheet continued to melt the high ground between Airdrie and the Kelvin valley was exhumed. Here, local accumulations of melt-out till, comprising large blocks of locally derived sandstone in a sand matrix, were deposited as at Torbrex [790 720]. A belt of similar deposits can be traced eastwards for about 8 km as far as Bathgate [970 690] in the Falkirk district (Sheet 31E) and it is suggested that these represent the last active ice stand during early deglaciation. Lying to the west and possibly associated with the deposition of the melt-out till are small areas of ice-contact, water-laid sands and gravels (assigned to the Broomhouse Formation, see below) at Luggiebank [765 727].

Glacial meltwater deposits

In time, ice became restricted to the principal valleys and meltwaters issuing from glaciers transported and deposited large volumes of sediment. Based upon sedimentological and palaeocurrent data for meltwater deposits in the Clyde and Kelvin valleys, it is clear that in west-central Scotland the direction of retreat was northwestwards towards the main Highlands ice-source. As a result, in the Clyde valley, ice receded progressively down-valley and seaward towards the inner Firth of Clyde and the fjords of the western Highlands. Likewise in the Kelvin valley, west of the watershed at Kelvinhead [757 785] between the westerly flowing River Kelvin and the easterly draining Bonny Water, the valley glacier receded westwards and down-valley. Sand and gravel transported and deposited by meltwaters in both valleys are referred to the Broomhouse Formation, named after the Broomhouse area of eastern Glasgow, where the deposits directly overlie the Wilderness Till Formation.

Glacifluvial deposits of the Clyde valley in eastern Glasgow

The landforms associated with deposits of the Broomhouse Formation indicate an ice contact environment. In the Broomhouse–Tollcross area esker ridges, mounds and isolated flat-topped kames are commonly found. The lithological associations are, rarely, matrix-supported bouldery gravel with sand, common framework-supported bouldery gravel with sand, and pebbly coarse- to fine-grained sand and silt. Overall, the most abundant deposit is sand except where esker ridges are present. Geotechnically, the deposits vary from loose to very dense. They are up to 25 m thick. Much of the gravel is massive to crudely bedded but planar beds and trough cross-bedded units are also present. The sands are planar and trough cross-bedded, ripple-laminated and horizontally laminated. Deformed bedding, including reverse faults and folds, probably marks the former contacts between dead-ice masses and the sediments (Plates 9, 10). Deformation is most common in the esker ridge deposits. The fine-grained sands and silts commonly exhibit minor load casts. Flame structures are present locally.

In a major section at the Greenoakhill Pit just north of Wester Daldowie Farm [665 626], over 12 m of succession was observed beneath clay and silt belonging to the Paisley Formation (see below). In general the sequence showed upward-fining grain size. The lower 8 m consisted of fine- to coarse-grained sand with layers rich in coal debris, particularly at bases of cross-bedded units. Beds of sandy, fine to coarse gravel were present displaying cross-bedding including metre-scale planar foresets. Climbing ripples rose eastwards, a direction of transport confirmed by measurement of cross-stratal dips. The upper 4 m was of fine-grained sand which was mainly flat and ripple-laminated. Near the top of the succession thin units of brownish grey diamicton up to 20 cm thick were

Plate 9 Laminated silt and sand of the Paisley Formation showing folding and small-scale thrust faulting, Foxley Pit, Lanark [651 631] (C 4233).

Plate 10 Folded beds of laminated silt and sand of the Paisley Formation on sand and gravel of the Broomhouse Formation, Greenoakhill Pit, Lanark [6650 6275] (C 4236).

composed of sandy clay with pebbles up to 3 cm. The contact with the overlying Paisley Formation was disconformable.

The sedimentological features of the Broomhouse Formation point to the operation of fluvial and deltaic processes. The coarsest gravel deposits are associated with esker ridges (encased and exposed). The eskers display most evidence of contemporaneous faulting and were deposited by glacial meltwaters flowing through tunnels in the wasting icesheet. The massive deposits may have been laid down in the full-pipe sliding bed phase described by Saunderson (1977) but most show cross-bedding features consistent with fluvideltaic processes and transport eastwards. The presence of sandy clay diamicton units may also point to the presence of decaying glacial ice but these might also have formed as debris flows in a fluvial context.

Lake Clydesdale: glacilacustrine deposits

In the Clyde valley, south-east of Hallside [665 600] a north-westward direction of deglaciation has been associated with the concept of an ice-dammed 'Lake Clydesdale' (Bell, 1874). Some authors, however, (e.g. Sissons, 1976, p.128) have preferred an up-valley, south-eastward direction of ice retreat in the Clyde valley. The present survey has identified proglacial lake deposits, the Bellshill Formation, in the lower Clyde valley, the distribution of which appears to confirm the existence of such a lake (or series of lakes), as Bell envisaged. The elevation of the deposits ranges from less than 60 m above OD in the north-west (by Hamilton and Bothwell) to over 165 m above OD in the south-east near Law [820 525] in the Lanark district (Sheet 23E) (Browne and McMillan, 1989a, pp.22, 59). To the south of the Clyde valley, south-east of Strathaven [700 445], laminated silt and clay recorded at altitudes ranging from 165 to 215 m above OD (Nickless et al., 1978, pp.5–7, resource map) represent earlier stages in the development of a glacial lake.

In the Clyde valley, the lake deposits are generally thin indicating that the lake (or series of lakes) was transitory in existence. Further lines of evidence to support this belief are the lack of identifiable lake shorelines and lake outlets cut into the landscape. As Browne (in Jardine, 1980, p.6) has noted, lake spillways are problematical; one possible drainage route was through the ice sheet via the Glen of the Red Burn [777 760] at Cumbernauld eastwards to the valley of the Forth. Evidence for the final drainage of ponded waters may be provided by the sands of the Bridgeton Formation (see below), which are believed to have been deposited in the lower Clyde when the ice dam in eastern Glasgow collapsed.

The Bellshill Formation is named from the Bellshill area where the unit is widely distributed at surface and is usually underlain by the Wilderness Till. The typical lithological association is of silty clay incorporating wisps, laminae and bands of silt and sand. The deposit is dark brownish grey to brownish grey in colour. It may be varved with multiple silt units. Isolated clasts up to 1–2 cm are interpreted as dropstones, and load structures and distinct traces of grading are present. In the Bellshill Borehole the clay and silt are in the soil profile (1.0 to 1.65 m depth) at the feather-edge of the deposit.

In the Ross House Borehole [7390 5504], sited immediately west of the River Clyde to the south in the Hamilton district (Sheet 23W), the clays and silts occur between 19.53 and 22.19 m depth. They are well laminated, commonly with isolated clasts believed to be dropstones. Sand laminae and thin bands are present together with bands of sandy clayey diamicton up to 9 cm thick.

All the sedimentological features point to the Bellshill Formation being a glacial lake bed deposit. The presence of clay-silt varve couplets, ice-rafted debris and diamicton units indicate deposition close to an ice-margin in a proglacial lake environment. Turbidity currents flowing along the lake floor are indicated by the occurrence of graded beds. The distribution of this deposit in the lower Clyde valley between east Glasgow and Lanark suggests that the ice margin retreated north-westwards through the area, the sediments at the highest altitude being preserved farthest up the valley system. The succession as preserved is consistent with the existence of one such lake ('Lake Clydesdale') rather than a series. However it is suggested that the areal extent and volume of the lake must have varied with time. Its size was affected by partial draining events associated with changes in the retaining ice dam and the availability of spillways.

Lake Clydesdale: deltaic sands and gravels

The presence of deltas building out laterally into the lake from tributary valleys of the Clyde is indicated by the occurrence of the sand and gravel bodies which have been assigned to the Ross Formation (defined in sections of BGS boreholes at Ross House, Crossford and Carluke to the south in the Hamilton and Lanark districts.

Sediments deposited in a proximal position to the ice dam at the north-west end of the proglacial lake are interpreted as a complex of ice-contact and deltaic sands and gravels, assigned respectively to the Broomhouse and Ross formations. Although the transport direction of the Ross Formation is ambivalent in temporary sections exposed at Bothwell [708 589], there are clear indications of easterly current directions in the Broomhouse formation at Greenoakhill Pit [675 625]. Here, evidence of the ice-contact association is indicated by the presence in these sediments of high-angle reverse and normal faults associated with folding of the deposits. Similar structures also affect the overlying marine Paisley Formation clays.

The presence, in close association, of deltaic and ice-contact sediments points to an ice position represented by a terminal moraine in eastern Glasgow. Such a moraine was proposed by Clough et al. (1911) on the basis of a major cross-valley ridge at Hallside which, although poorly exposed is known to comprise a range of lithologies including till, sand and gravel, laminated clay and silt.

Glacifluvial and glacilacustrine deposits of the Kelvin valley

Moundy deposits of sand and gravel, assigned to the Broomhouse Formation, occupy mainly the northern slopes of the Kelvin and Bonny Water valley, between Kilsyth [720 780] and Bonnybridge [824 800]. Marginal drainage channels cut both within the sands and gravels and in till at higher levels indicate easterly drainage. A series of channels extends north-eastwards to Denny [810 830] where moundy meltwater sand and gravel flank the valley sides of the River Carron. These deposits form an integral part of the complex series of sediments which comprise the glacifluvial and glacimarine delta of the River Carron in the Forth valley (Browne et al., 1984).

The nature and thickness of the deposits can be demonstrated from a number of former sections and records of site investigation boreholes. The sediments are often interbedded with till-like material (Browne, 1977) and were probably laid down in contact with ice which still filled the Kelvin valley (Robertson and Haldane, 1937). A section at Kelvinhead [7590 7852] revealed about 3 m of poorly bedded, locally clayey gravel. At Coneypark [7725 7910], at least 6 m of mainly massive, dense sand with scattered boulders (diameters between 0.5 and 1 m) was formerly seen. Beds of fine to coarse gravel were also present. East of Banknock at Knowehead [8045 7936] up to 2 m of coarse gravel were present. Boreholes put down on the northern valley side show deposits to range from 2 to 4 m in thickness and to rest on Wilderness Till. The till surface may be drumlinised. On the south side of the valley at Easter Dullatur [747 772] boreholes sited on the moundy terrain proved between 1 and 6 m of sand and gravel assigned to the Broomhouse Formation. Thicker deposits of gravel, locally in excess of 8 m, may be present beneath the alluvium of the River Kelvin. South of Longcroft a borehole [7971 7903] indicates in excess of 12 m of gravel, of which the lower 8 m or so may be of glacifluvial origin.

South-west of Kilsyth a complex sequence of sediments flanks the valley sides and infills the bedrock depression of the Kelvin. On the valley sides the sediments are disposed principally in the form of dissected terrace surfaces which are predominantly composed of sand with finely laminated silt beds and locally with gravel. The deposits which were once extensively worked at Torrance, Birdston and Cadder (Robertson and Haldane, 1937, Cameron et al., 1977) were considered by previous surveyors to represent the margin of a glacial lake formed during a late phase of deglaciation as the valley glacier continued to retreat westwards (Clough et al., 1911). Recently acquired borehole data tends to confirm the presence of both deltaic and lake bottom sediments which can be referred to the Ross and Bellshill Formations respectively. Locally ice-contact deposits of sand and gravel of the Broomhouse Formation are probably also present.

Successions through the glacilacustrine sediments can be illustrated from the records of several boreholes. Figure 23 shows the stratigraphical relationship of these deposits in the Kilsyth to Kirkintilloch area. Generally the sequence coarsens upwards from laminated lake silt and clay into fine-grained deltaic sand as shown by a borehole record at Strone [7033 7665] which proved at least

13.2 m of such deposits beneath 16.8 m of Flandrian sediments:

Made ground to 3.0 m	
Peat to 9.0 m	Clippens Formation
Sand to 14.0 m	Law Formation
Dark grey silt to 16.8 m	Kelvin Formation
Fine- to medium-grained sand to 26 m	Ross Formation
Dark grey, laminated silt to 30 m	Bellshill Formation

Other records show similar sequences. For example, a borehole at Wester Shirva [6864 7540], sited on the floodplain, proved 3 m of sand (Ross Formation) overlying 8 m of dark grey sandy silt with clay laminae (Bellshill Formation) beneath the Flandrian deposits. On the valley sides, boreholes at Shirva [6914 7571] and Netherinch [6894 7637] proved respectively 10 m and 14 m of laminated silt (Bellshill Formation) overlain by glacideltaic sand (Ross Formation). West of Queenzieburn [693 774] terraced deposits of sand and gravel are present on either side of the Kelvin valley. On the north side boreholes prove between 3 and 26 m of sand and gravel (probably Ross Formation) usually resting on Wilderness Till. On the south side around Kirkintilloch [655 738] 4 to 6 m of Ross Formation sand and gravel are present.

Downstream, between Kirkintilloch and Cadder [615 722] concealed fine-grained deposits of the Bellshill Formation were proved at Bogton [6168 7298]. Here in a site investigation borehole, at least 7.5 m of laminated silt containing what were described as shell fragments (?derived shells or possibly kaolinite) underlie 22.5 m of sand and gravel of the Ross Formation. Boreholes sited on the floodplain at Birdston Farm [6572 7563], Springfield [6490 7443] and Sandy Knowes [6318 7357] all prove deposits of sand and gravel, assigned to the Ross Formation, beneath alluvial silt of the Kelvin Formation.

Records of deep boreholes illustrate deposits below the Bellshill Formation. Sited near the axis of the Kelvin valley bedrock depression, Torrance No. 2 Borehole [6408 7391] proved about 14 m of silty sand and clay (Bellshill Formation) beneath 6.7 m of alluvial clay, sand and gravel. The Bellshill deposits rest on some 28 m of sand and gravel, presumed to be the Broomhouse Formation, which in turn overlie about 10 m of Wilderness Till.

Drainage of Lake Clydesdale: ice-clearance deposits

The final clearance of glacier ice from the lower Clyde valley is unlikely to have been associated with the highest levels of 'Lake Clydesdale'. The deposition of lacustrine clay and silt in the Strathaven area in the Hamilton district at elevations in excess of 165 m above OD (Nickless et al., 1978, resource map) resulted from the ponding of meltwaters by ice at similar elevations in the Clyde valley and Firth of Clyde. From the distribution of the identified lake sediments of the Bellshill and Ross formations around Hamilton, Bellshill and Bothwell the latest level of the lake immediately prior to final drainage was about 70 m above OD. At about the same time as Highland glacier ice in the Firth of Clyde had wasted sufficiently to allow the lake to drain, the sea gained access to the Clyde estuary. As the ice front continued to retreat northwards as independent glaciers in the fjords and valleys of the south-western Highlands, any remaining ice in the Glasgow area is considered to have become detached. Relative sea-level in the inner Firth of Clyde was probably about 35 m above OD at this time, some 13 500 years BP (Browne et al., 1983b; Browne and McMillan, 1989a, pp.13–14).

In central and western Glasgow outwash deposits which formed in a submarine environment have been defined as the Bridgeton Formation (Browne and McMillan, 1989). They are interpreted as being material which was eroded from the sand and gravel of the Broomhouse and Ross formations and redeposited farther downstream. If observations and deductions about the altitudinal limits of marine (greater than 35 m above OD) and lacustrine (greater than 70 m above OD) deposits are reasonably accurate for the lower Clyde valley either side of Glasgow, failure of the ice dam at the terminal moraine at Hallside is likely to have released lakewaters under a considerable hydraulic head which are considered to be responsible for this event.

The Bridgeton Borehole [6121 6367], sited just in the Glasgow district to the west, contains the standard but incomplete section for this formation between 29.31 and 40.38 m depth, the base of the borehole. The two typical lithologies recognised are beds of very fine- to medium-grained (sometimes coarse-grained) sand, and fine to coarse gravel and boulders with a sandy matrix. Some of the sand was seen to be flat bedded but no other sedimentological features were identifiable. This deposit is loose to dense in a geotechnical sense. In a nearby site investigation borehole the base of the formation was recorded at 50.29 m, resting on the Wilderness Till. The formation is apparently unfossiliferous.

Sections in the formation at Shieldhall [536 664] also in the Glasgow district have been recorded by McMillan and Browne (1989) who noted that the deposits were transported by westward-flowing currents. They also commented on evidence for former buried dead ice masses, and compared sedimentological features of the deposits with those described by Rust and Romanelli (1975) and Cheel and Rust (1982) for subaqueous outwash fans forming at an ice front.

Dead ice must also have remained to cap some of the remnant mounds of sand and gravel of the Broomhouse Formation. Locally the mounds were situated at elevations low enough to allow burial by the marine clays and silts of the Paisley Formation. As at Shieldhall, the Greenoakhill sections reveal evidence for burial of ice which survived perhaps for many hundreds of years in or under deposits of sand and gravel sealed under a thick cap of marine clay and silt of the Paisley Formation. The bedding of the overlying muds is disrupted by normal and reverse, high-angle faults, and by low-angle thrusts with folding. These structures developed when the ice buried in the underlying Broomhouse and Ross formations melted.

Windermere Interstade: marine inundation

Peacock (1971) suggested that the route of entry of the late-Devensian sea to the Paisley–Glasgow basin was not via the Clyde estuary but by a more southerly route, through the Lochwinnoch Gap between Johnstone [43 63] and Dalry [29 49]. There is no stratigraphical evidence to support this suggestion despite two attempts to find the linking marine deposits by drilling, by Dickson et al. (1976) at North Kerse [339 556] and by the BGS at Lochwinnoch [352 581] (Browne and McMillan, 1989a, pp.44 & 61). In the absence of either stratigraphical or geomorphological evidence to the contrary, it is currently accepted that dead ice is likely to have blocked the Lochwinnoch Gap until after deglaciation of the Glasgow area.

Once water levels of 'Lake Clydesdale' and the sea had reached equilibrium in the Clyde valley, high-energy environments were restricted to the beach zone and to the mouths of tributary valleys where lateral deltas built out. Initially, meltwater plumes dominated and the Paisley Formation clay and silt reflects this influence. Laminated brownish grey clay and silt were proved on this sheet in the Bothwell Park Borehole [7159 5956]. The stratigraphical relationships of the Paisley Formation to the late-Devensian glacial and glacilacustrine deposits at Bothwell are shown on Figure 22.

The presence in the Paisley Formation sediments of primary current lineation suggests relatively high-energy depositional conditions. Graded bedding suggests that turbidity currents played a part. Well-layered clay units within the formation have previously been interpreted in terms of lacustrine seasonal banding but both clay turbidites and tidal flocculation layering are known to produce such features in the marine environment (Mackiewicz et al., 1984).

The marine fauna is substantial in the more seaward parts of the region (Peacock et al., 1978; Browne et al., 1983b; Browne and McMillan, 1989a, pp.23–26) but sparse farther inland, in the Glasgow–Hamilton area, where sediment supply was greater. In the Clyde valley upstream of Bothwell, the sediments rarely contain any fossils. At Carbarns [774 540] in the Hamilton district a sparse marine fauna was recovered at an elevation of 45 m above OD. The maximum altitudes to which clays assigned to the Paisley Formation are known to occur are generally over 40 m above OD in eastern Glasgow and 45 m above OD at Ross House, Hamilton.

In the Glasgow and Paisley areas the Paisley Formation is commonly overlain by thickly bedded muds of the Linwood Formation (Browne and McMillan, 1989a, pp.26–27) which contain a rich mid- to high-boreal fauna. There is no definitive evidence for the existence of the Linwood Formation in the Airdrie district although an occurrence of shells was recorded in 'blue' clays in the former Polmadie Brick Pit [600 628], just to the west in the Glasgow district, at a depth of 8 m. Such evidence may indicate the presence locally of small outliers of marine clays of the Linwood Formation farther east.

The sea-level curve for the Clyde area following deglaciation is poorly known compared with that for the eastern coast firths (Sissons, 1976, fig. 9d; Armstrong et al., 1985, figs. 13, 15). In the Fullarton [640 630], Mount Vernon [650 630] and Carmyle [640 620] areas, deltaic sand and gravel deposits of the Killearn Formation occur. Elsewhere in Glasgow, the Firth of Clyde and Strathblane raised shorelines, raised beach and delta deposits are present but no clear assessment of relative sea level changes can be reconstructed in the absence of systematic levelling. It is likely that during the Windermere Interstade and by early in the Loch Lomond Stade,

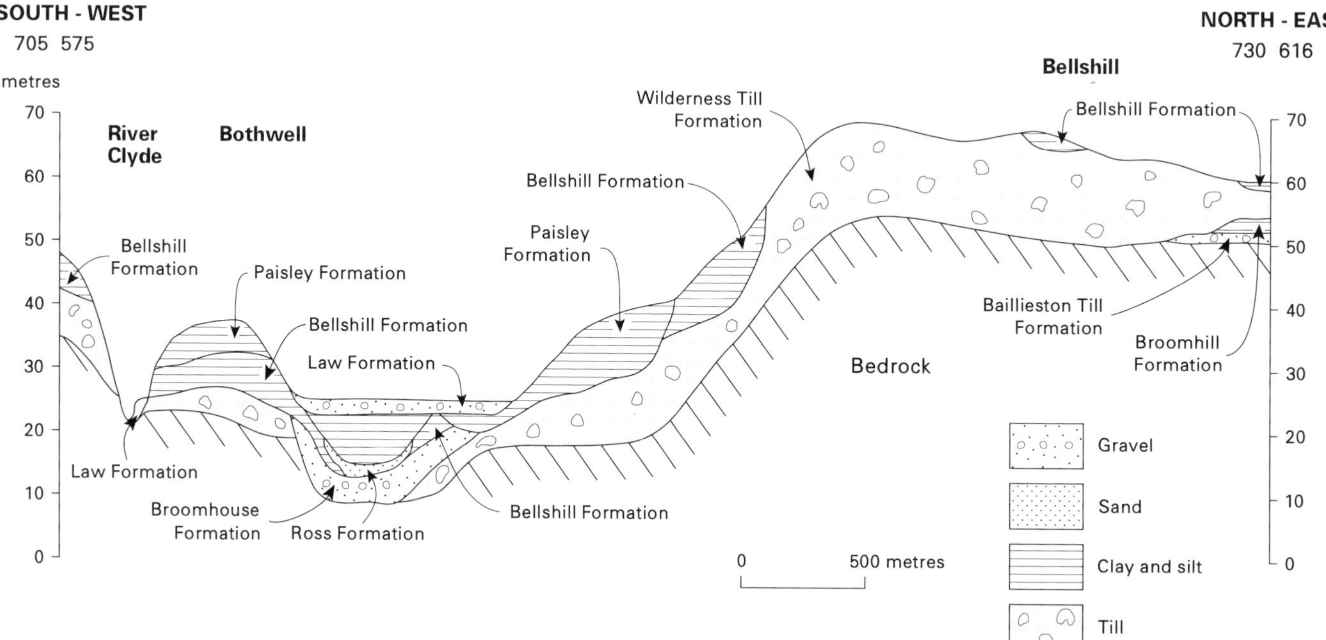

Figure 22 Generalised section across the valley of the River Clyde at Bothwell.

the relative sea-level fell to OD or below, due to the local dominance of isostatic uplift of the land over the generally rising world sea level.

LOCH LOMOND STADE

The Loch Lomond Readvance (Simpson, 1933) occurred about 11 000 to 10 000 years ago. Glacial deposits are confined to the lochs of the western Highlands adjacent to the Firth of Clyde. Glacier ice extended as far south as Finnich Glen [49 84] in Strathblane, some 12 km to the west of the Airdrie district.

Sea levels

Movements of relative sea level during the stade are not well known. At, or just before, the time of the maximum extent of the ice, sea level may have been as high as 11 m above OD, based upon the presence of former intertidal platforms and clifflines at about this height in the Firth of Clyde and around the shores of Loch Lomond (Rose *in* Jardine, 1980, pp.29–31). On the east coast of Scotland sea level may have fallen below that of the present at some period during the Loch Lomond Stade (Browne, 1985 *in* discussion of Sutherland, 1984; Armstrong et al., 1985, pp.87–89). The implications are that on the west coast sea level was also lower than OD. This is a possibility in the Clyde, as implied by McGown and Miller (1984, fig. 7) for central Glasgow, where they recognise a channel incised to over 40 m below OD, aligned close to the course of the River Clyde, backfilled with river sands and gravels. However, dating of the supposed incision is open to doubt because of the problem of correlating largely unfossiliferous superimposed successions of sands and gravels which could include the late-Devensian Broomhouse and Bridgeton formations. It may therefore, as previously suggested, be related to much earlier erosional events (see above, Devensian topography).

Landslip, soliflucted deposits and peat

Landslips are common on the south-facing slopes of the Kilsyth Hills, north of Lennoxtown [630 780] and Milton of Campsie [652 766]. They were probably initiated during the Loch Lomond Stade. They consist principally of rotated blocks of basaltic lavas and tuffs. Adjacent areas of thin gelifluctced drift (head) are also present. The largest landslips which cover an area of up to 1 km^2 occur beneath basalt lava scarps between Jamie Wright's Well [617 803] and Meikle Reive [640 790]. Other extensive areas are found south of Brown Hill [665 785] and between West Corrie Reservoir [674 790] and Laird's Hill [700 800].

In Glasgow unusual subsoil profiles observed on the flanks of drumlins may also be the product of large-scale solifluction (Dickson et al., 1976). At Robroyston [633 676] peat dated between 11 210 ± 150 years BP and 11 653 ± 190 years BP rests under gelifluctced till. At Springburn [609 678] in the Glasgow district, gelifluctced

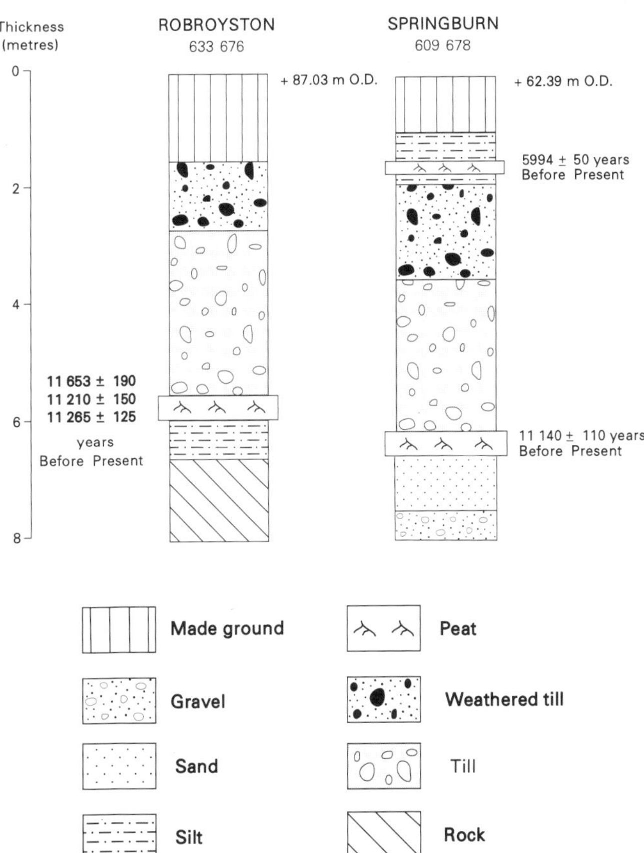

Figure 23 Graphic sections and radiocarbon dates for sequences of gelifluctced till at Robroyston and Springburn.

till overlies peat dated at 11 140 ± 110 years BP. Here the till is overlain by a thin Flandrian peat dated at 5994 ± 50 years BP (Figure 23). Because these sites lie well beyond the limit of the Loch Lomond Stade ice, the tills seem most likely to be the products of the Dimlington glaciation. The available evidence therefore suggests that till has moved over the organic materials probably by gelifluction processes which were thought to be a major feature of periglacial activity in west-central Scotland during the Loch Lomond Stade.

Other examples occur in the Airdrie district of late-Devensian peat and associated fine-grained lake sediments which formed immediately prior to the cold episode of the Loch Lomond Stade. At North Mount Vernon [6630 6378], a sample of a fibrous peat bed, overlain by 0.6 m of sand and resting on at least 0.6 m of laminated silt and clay, yielded a radiometric date of 11 040 ± 60 years BP (Scottish Universities Research and Reactor Centre 1526, unpublished).

FLANDRIAN

The Loch Lomond Stade ended about 10 000 years ago and the glacier ice in and around Loch Lomond and adjacent sea-lochs seems to have disappeared quickly.

The succeeding warm phase, the Flandrian Stage, is marked by marine and nonmarine deposits and landforms in the Clyde area but, despite their wide geographical distribution, these are not well understood.

The pioneering, open, treeless, heathland vegetation typical of the Windermere Interstade was re-established after the Loch Lomond Stade glaciation. This was replaced by landscapes dominated by woodlands of birch (*Betula*) and hazel (*Corylus*) from about 9700 years ago, and by a major increase in alder (*Alnus*) around 7000 years ago. Subsequently a major decrease in elm (*Ulmus*) occurred (possibly as a result of anthropogenic activity) about 5000 years ago (see Price, 1983, pp.165–170 for summary).

Between about 8400 and 5000 years BP, the main Flandrian marine transgression led to the inundation of ground on either side of the River Clyde as far upstream as Cambuslang. Evidence for changes in sea level is seen in the presence of three series of Flandrian to Recent levels in the lower Clyde valley. In east Glasgow two of these series are recognised: early to mid-Flandrian levels of up to 12 m above OD, and late-Flandrian to Recent surfaces of 3 to 6 m above OD. Associated with these surfaces in the Clyde valley are estuarine sediments of the Erskine and Gourock formations (Browne and McMillan, 1989a, pp.17–18, fig. 5). Although mapped as river alluvium, estuarine deposits may be present in the Clyde valley as far upstream as Carmyle [650 615].

Although some late-Devensian peat beds occur, the principal deposits of peat found in the Airdrie district are of Flandrian age. During the early Flandrian, as the Scottish climate became warmer and wetter *Sphagnum* peat began to develop in hollows on former lake floors and on poorly drained flat areas. Blanket bogs also started to form on sloping ground in the Campsie Fells in response to high rainfall. Peat, which in the Glasgow area has been assigned to the Clippens Peat Formation (Browne and McMillan, 1989a, pp.35–36), formed in low-lying ground particularly to the north of Coatbridge. Here, extensive deposits accumulated in interdrumlin hollows and other poorly drained ground at Bishop Loch [690 670], Woodend Loch [705 667] and Lochend Loch [705 663]. At Lochend up to 7 m of basin peat was proved in borehole sections. At Drumshangie Moss [770 680], north of Airdrie, thicknesses of 6 m have been recorded. At the eastern margin of the Airdrie district an extensive area of peat is present at Fannyside Muir [800 745]. Much of the Greengairs [795 705] and Darngavil [795 690] mosses have been removed during opencast coal operations, although peat thicknesses up to 3 m are locally present.

Thick accumulations of peat are present locally on and under the valley floor of the River Kelvin. Surface peat was probably extensive prior to improvements made to the drainage of the floodplain at the end of the 18th century. South-west of Kilsyth excavations for the Kilsyth Sewage Works [710 773] revealed at least 1 m of peat interbedded with alluvial clay (Robertson and Haldane 1937, p.116). Recently drilled boreholes at Garrel Burn [7086 7697] and Strone [7033 7665] indicate between 5 and 6 m of basin peat beneath made ground. The peat rests on earlier Flandrian alluvial sediments. West of the town a borehole record at Twechar Station [6994 7672] showed 1 m of peat interbedded with alluvial silt. This record serves to indicate that peat accumulated intermittently on the valley floor during the Flandrian.

Fluvial and lacustrine sand and gravel

Coarse-grained Flandrian sediments deposited in fluvial environments, including present-day river courses, were assigned by Browne and McMillan (1989a, pp.39–40) to the Law Formation. Older Flandrian sand and gravel which may have been partly associated with deltaic and lacustrine environments were referred to the Endrick Formation. The latter was defined by Browne and McMillan (1989a, pp.36–37) from deposits in the valley of the Endrick Water, by Loch Lomond, which are considered to have been laid down in either a slow meandering river or as part of a lacustrine delta.

The Law Formation is named from the Law Borehole in the Hamilton district, which contains the standard section. The formation includes much of the Recent sand and gravel alluvium of the River Clyde together with that of the Rotten Calder, the South Calder Water and North Calder Water. Up to 6 m of Law Formation sand and gravel is proved in records of boreholes on the alluvial plain of the River Clyde south-east of Bothwell [700 580] (Figure 22). The lithology is of loose, grey, fine- to coarse-grained sand with some silt and beds of fine to coarse gravel. Plant remains are present and dark sulphide patches occur. The deposit may be partly massive, sometimes flat-laminated but is probably mainly cross-bedded.

In the northern part of the district, alluvial gravels of the Law Formation are present in the valleys of the River Kelvin, Bonny Water, Luggie Water, River Carron and Glazert Water. Records from boreholes in the Kelvin valley illustrate the thickness and lithology of these deposits. East of Kilsyth, at Craigmarloch Drawbridge [7372 7745] some 2.5 m of sand and gravel ascribed to the Law Formation rests on late-Devensian gravels. Between Kilsyth and Kirkintilloch up to 5 m of sand and gravel, commonly overlain by fine-grained deposits of the Kelvin Formation (see below) are present (Figure 24). In the valley of the Glazert Water at Lennoxtown [630 780] up to 10 m of coarse gravel, boulders and sand are present. The deposits are likely to have been derived from Strathblane to the north-west via the wide dry valley of the Pow Burn. The whole sequence has been ascribed to the Law Formation but the basal part could have been deposited by glacial meltwaters during either of the late-Devensian glaciations.

Deposits of the deltaic Endrick Formation may be present under alluvial terraces of the Kelvin lying above the general level of the floodplain at elevations of 35 to 50 m above OD. East of Kilsyth, boreholes sited south of Longcroft and at Hirst [7602 7798] illustrate the sequence. At Longcroft, about 4 m of gravels of the Endrick Formation overlie late-Devensian glacifluvial gravels of the Broomhouse Formation, the latter probably having been transported along the Red Glen

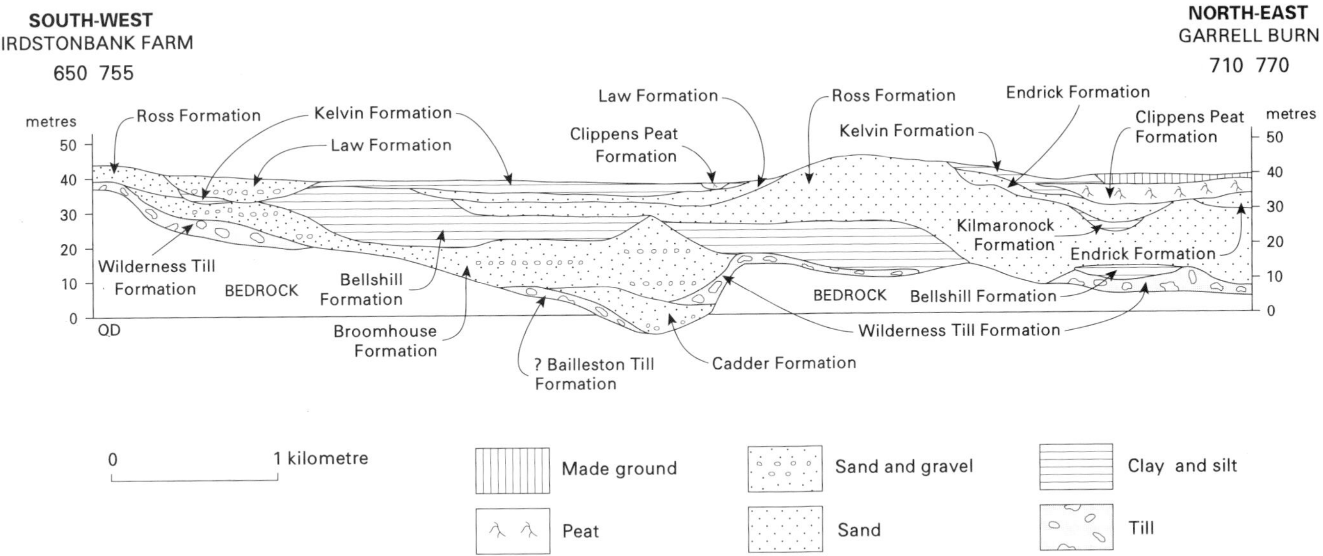

Figure 24 Generalised section along the valley of the River Kelvin between Kirkintilloch and Kilsyth.

[777 760].The glacifluvial gravels overlie Wilderness Till. At Hirst 2.2 m of sandy gravel, of possible deltaic origin, rest directly on Wilderness Till. South-west of Kilsyth, boreholes sited on the valley floor at Garrel Burn and Strone prove thick sands lying between peat and earlier glacilacustrine and deltaic deposits. These sands may be early Flandrian fluvial deposits and as such are best referred to the Endrick Formation (Figure 23).

Fluvial and lacustrine clay and silt

The Kelvin Formation includes the recent fine-grained sediments of the valley floor of the River Kelvin, Bonny Water and other rivers and streams. Lake alluvium of Flandrian age present north-east of Glasgow and east of Bisphopbriggs at elevations between about 60 and 90 m above OD is also referred to this formation. The sediments are silty clays and silts, commonly with organic remains, interbedded with peat, generally formed either on the floodplain or in lacustrine environments such as interdrumlin hollows. Clay and silt of the Kelvin Formation forms much of the valley floor of the River Kelvin (Figure 24). Borehole records show the thickness of these sediments to range from about 2 to 9 m and to be locally interbedded with peat as at Twechar Station.

In the Kelvin valley lacustrine clay and silt deposits concealed by younger Flandrian sediments are locally present. These deposits probably belong to the Kilmaronock Formation defined by Browne and McMillan (1989a, pp.35–36) from the Mains of Kilmaronock Borehole by Loch Lomond. Typically, the sediments comprise thinly bedded silt with clay laminae and some sand layers. Plant remains are common. At Strone a borehole record proved 2.8 m of dark grey clayey silt below sand of the Endrick Formation (Figure 24).

Man-made deposits

Extensive areas of man-made deposits are present in and around the urban areas of the Airdrie district. Wherever construction for houses, factories and roads has taken place, there are likely to be areas where the natural ground surface has been covered by redistributed, geotechnically variable, natural and man-made materials. Typically made ground of this nature is only a few metres thick but in areas close to former excavations thicker deposits may be present. Examples of major ground disturbance include the M8 and M80 motorways and interchanges such as those at Baillieston and Calderpark. Former pit bings and slag tips also constitute made ground. At the Ravenscraig Steelworks [770 570] boreholes exceptionally show that made ground can be in excess of 15 m thick.

The area has been extensively quarried for minerals including sand and gravel, brick clay, fireclay, sandstone and coal. Many former excavations are infilled or partially infilled with variably compacted materials and these deposits, classified as Fill or Disturbed ground on the Airdrie Sheet, are generally thicker than other made ground and may be in the order of tens of metres.

TEN

Economic geology

The rocks of the Airdrie district have in the past been extensively exploited for several minerals. Now the only rock to be extracted to any extent at the present time (1993) is the quartz-dolerite sill complex for use as aggregate and roadstone.

Coal

The Limestone Coal Formation and the Coal Measures contain most of the economic coals. At least 12 seams in the former and 20 in the latter have been mined, some of them very extensively. The Hurlet Coal in the Lawmuir Formation and the Chapelgreen, Upper Hirst coals plus one or two other minor seams in the Upper Limestone Formation have also been worked. Mining ceased in 1983 when the last colliery finally became uneconomic.

Ironstone

The Limestone Coal Formation was the main source of both blackband and clayband ironstones in the Airdrie district: at least six seams of the former and four of the latter were exploited. In the Middle Coal Measures the Airdrie Blackband Ironstone was mined extensively, and the Palacecraig Blackband Ironstone was worked to some extent. The Cambuslang Marble, a limy ironstone packed with nonmarine shells, was worked at Cambuslang [646 597] as an ornamental stone. An example of its use is seen in a decorative fireplace at Chatelherault, near Hamilton.

The Lower Coal Measures are deficient in ironstone, but four seams were locally extracted. Mining has long since ceased having become uneconomic when thick, lower-grade deposits, such as the Mesozoic ironstones of England became available.

Limestone

The Hurlet, Index, Calmy and Castlecary limestones have all been quarried and all but the Index were also mined, the Hurlet around Lennoxtown, the Calmy around Muirhead [683 695] and Cumbernauld and the Castlecary at Castlecary. The Hurlet limestone was extracted together with the Alum Shale and the Hurlet Coal. All extraction ceased more than 50 years ago when the more accessible resources were worked out.

Fireclay

Mining of fireclays, mostly from the Passage Formation, began in the Garnkirk and Glenboig areas over 100 years ago and later spread along the outcrop of the formation westwards to Glasgow and north-eastwards to Castlecary. At Chapelhall, two seams in the Lower Coal Measures were extracted. The Glenboig Lower Fireclay provided the bulk of the material. In recent years the industry has declined and no extraction is now taking place within the district.

Brickclay

The mudstones above the Calmy Limestone have been quarried quite extensively for brick manufacture, mainly around Cumbernauld. The National Coal Board used Blantyreferme Nos. 4 and 5 mines for about 10 years to obtain a terracotta clay from the Upper Coal Measures but this operation ceased 20 years ago. Materials from colliery tips have been and are still being used, for instance in the Kilsyth area.

Hard rock

Lavas in the Clyde Plateau Volcanic Formation at Cathkin Quarry [622 583], alkaki olivine-dolerite sills in eastern Glasgow, quartz-dolerite dykes in several places and quartz-dolerite sills almost wherever they occur, have all been used for concrete aggregate, roadstone and kerbstones. Only the quartz-dolerite sills, being generally better quality and easier to work than the dykes, are still exploited, at Boards [794 854], Northfield [800 854], Croy [730 759], Beltmoss [720 790], Riskend [728 792] and Madrox [726 699]. Reserves are enormous at the first three: at the others they are limited.

Building sandstone and moulding sand

Numerous quarries were formerly operated in the Airdrie district to supply Glasgow and surrounding towns with building sandstone and sandstone for moulding purposes. A detailed account of the quarries and the composition and properties of sandstones is given in Clough et al. (1911, pp.236–50). Quarries at Bredisholm [702 624] north of Uddingston, Bothwell Park [713 603], Bells [713 605] near Bellshill and Eastfield [631 610] west of Cambuslang supplied pink, fine-grained sandstone from the Upper Coal Measures. Middle Coal Measures sandstones were worked at Budhill [653 641] in Shettleston, Holmhills (Kirkburn) [645 597] south of Cambuslang and Braehead [703 637] east of Baillieston. In Strathkelvin, sandstone of the Limestone Coal Formation was worked at Queenzieburn [691 775] north-east of Kirkintilloch. Although none of these quarries has been worked for many decades and most are now filled in, a limited resource of good building stone may still be present in the district. Although the resource has, in the main, been sterilised by development, there are instances of recent quarrying, for example, Deer Park Quarry [735 539] in the Upper Coal Measures in the Hamilton district (Sheet 23W) was reopened to provide a source of stone for the renovation of Chatelherault Hunting Lodge (Stone Industries, 9, 1987, p.23).

Sand and gravel

A summary of resources of sand and gravel on the sheet is given in Cameron et al. (1977) and Browne (1977). Principal resources are confined to the valley floors and sides of the rivers Clyde and Kelvin. In eastern Glasgow, north of the Clyde moundy glacial sand and gravel has been worked extensively above the water table notably at Greenoakhill [668 627], Kenmuirhill [665 621] and Broomhouse [676 625]. Deposits of moundy sand and gravel are also present in the Easterhouse area between the M8 and the A8 Edinburgh–Glasgow roads. South of the River Clyde and east of Cambuslang deposits averaging some 10 m in thickness are estimated. Extensive terrace deposits are present under Uddingston and Bothwell and although the sequence, overall, is mainly clay, the upper part to a depth of about 6 m may be predominantly composed of sand. Alluvial sand and gravel, mainly below the water table, is present east of Bothwell and north of Cambuslang.

In Strathkelvin south-west of Kilsyth [720 780] dissected terraces of sands of mainly deltaic origin are present and were extensively worked at Torrance, Birdston and Cadder. Between Kilsyth and Bonnybridge [824 800] moundy deposits of sand and gravel occur on the northern flanks of the Rivers Kelvin and Bonny Water valleys. At Denny [810 830] moundy meltwater sand and gravel deposits are present on the valley sides of the River Carron. Below the water table alluvial sands interbedded with silt and clay are extensively developed on the valley floor of the River Kelvin.

Methane

The hazards associated with the build-up of methane gas (CH_4) concentrations in landfill sites are now well appreciated (Campbell, 1988). Examples where domestic waste infill have subsequently been sealed by fine-grained cohesive soils are numerous. In the Airdrie district the site at Morriston Park, Cambuslang [644 608], is a case where modern housing development was suspended following the detection of excessive methane gas levels. Plans to extract gas commercially to heat greenhouses from landfill sites at Summerston, Wilderness and Mavis Valley were in hand during 1991.

Hydrogeology

The Carboniferous strata which appear at, or near surface, in this district offer a wide range of hydraulic properties. Most of the strata are at least moderately permeable (hydraulic conductivity ranging from 10^{-2} to 1 m/d) with intergranular permeability, commonly subsidiary to secondary permeability, the latter derived from fissures and joints. There are also mudstones, particularly in the Limestone Coal Formation which are weakly permeable and act as barriers to vertical groundwater movement. In places perched water can occur over low permeability horizons. Nevertheless, groundwater has been a valuable resource for industry in the past, with abstraction notably from the Coal Measures, Passage Formation and Upper Limestone Formation. Few groundwater supplies remain in operation due to the decline in recent years of water-intensive industry and to the generally poor quality of available groundwater. Spring discharges above Lennoxtown are best known from this district today, as these are bottled and sold as a leading brand of Natural Mineral Water.

The regional shallow groundwater flow patterns in the Midland Valley were described by Robins (1990). The Forth–Clyde axis forms a focus towards which groundwater flows, ultimately to discharge within one or other river catchment. It follows that the predominant regional flow direction in the Airdrie district is from the Campsie Fells in the north through the sequence of Carboniferous rocks into the Central Coalfield in the south. Topographic influences, including the Carron valley, as well as induced drainage via minor adits, may locally alter or even reverse this direction of flow.

Mean average annual rainfall ranges from some 1800 mm on top of the Campsie Fells to only 850 mm in the Clyde valley. Effective rainfall (the amount left after removing actual evaporation) may range upwards from 450 mm, but about two thirds of this is lost in runoff, leaving, in general, not less than 150 mm as potential infiltration and consequent recharge to groundwater. Supplementary recharge may occur via surface water courses which enhance the theoretical value derived from infiltration alone. This is particularly the case where granular superficial deposits are present in the Kelvin and Clyde valleys and where till, with its characteristic low permeability, is absent. A likely minimum theoretical renewable resource of some 150 Ml/a/km^2 area of aquifer is sufficient to sustain a single source of not less than 5 l/s capacity/km^2 of groundwater.

Large-capacity supplies are available wherever boreholes intercept abandoned mine workings which drain very large areas of the rock. Mine drainage records in the Limestone Coal Formation and the Coal Measures bear this out. The wettest pits were the Bothwell Colliery [686 588], where a discharge of 230 l/s was constantly removed from a depth of 396 m, and the Kilsyth Colliery [715 779] where 150 l/s were removed from a depth of 206 m. The driest workings were at the Twechar Colliery [701 762] where 13 l/s were pumped from 317 m depth but only for 12 hours in any 24 hours.

Mine dewatering rarely affected total drainage of the ground above the workings. Weakly permeable horizons enabled perched waters to be retained in many places and local domestic and small rural supplies continued unaffected by the dewatering at deeper levels. Clearly, lateral flow at deep levels was a significant contribution to the mine sumps.

Borehole yields in the Coal Measures and the older strata are, for the most part, relatively modest. Intersection of flooded workings supports bigger yields at Parkhead [624 647] (25 l/s) and Netherfield [618 647]

(25 l/s) and a sustainable borehole yield of 14 l/s near Coatbridge [752 642]. Elsewhere sustainable yields of 0.5 to 4 l/s are common. Specific capacity which is discharge divided by a drawdown, ranges from 0.1 to 1.0 l/s/m, and no particular formation is apparently higher yielding than any other. This contrasts with the situation in the Lothians where, for example, the Passage Formation would normally offer the highest groundwater potential.

Borehole depths which range from 20 m to over 450 m do not appear to influence yield. Many boreholes naturally overflow at rates up to 0.5 l/s. This is due to the discrete horizontal layering which occurs in some areas and which allows groundwater to attain artesian head in selected horizons.

The volcanic rocks of the Campsie Fells offer little groundwater resource. However, a group of springs issue from favourable fissures and joints in the face of the volcanic escarpment above Lennoxtown at yields of up to 2 l/s. Seven of these are the sources of a thriving bottled water industry. These sources offer weakly mineralised calcium bicarbonate-type water from small protected upland catchments free from obvious sources of surface pollution. The groundwaters are young and derive from rainfall which fell perhaps some weeks or months earlier, there being very little storage in these rocks.

Little groundwater is present within the superficial rocks of this district. Small pockets of groundwater are available, but there is little storage and they are in any case vulnerable to surface pollutants. However the water contained within these deposits may have the potential to threaten opencast pits and other excavations. For example, at a proposed pit near Easterhouse [696 670], exploratory drilling revealed up to 8 m of sand and gravel concealed beneath peat and sandy clay. Test pumping of exploratory boreholes demonstrated that the transmissivity of the granular material, although relatively low, ranged from 0.7 to 8.0 $m^3/d/m$. Interestingly, the specific capacity of these shallow boreholes ranged from 0.04 to 0.2 l/s/m, values which are of a similar order to that found in some of the deeper boreholes in the Carboniferous sedimentary rocks (excluding those boreholes that intercept coal workings).

With the exception of groundwater in the volcanic rocks and small pockets of perched or hydraulically isolated rock in the sedimentary rocks, water quality is generally poor (Table 5). The abundance of pyrite in the sedimentary rock promotes reducing conditions whereby the groundwater is depleted in oxygen to such an extent that it becomes a reducing agent. This, combined with the acid which derives from the oxidation and solution of pyrite, allows iron and manganese to be taken up in solution. Typical groundwaters are moderately to highly mineralised with bicarbonate concentrations in the range 130 to 635 mg/l, rich in iron and manganese and aggressively reducing (that is, very low redox potential).

Because so much of the groundwater is barely potable, demand for the resource has declined in recent years. Current major uses of groundwater are coal washing and make-up water for an acid generation plant. By the same token, little attempt has been made to protect these poor quality groundwaters from surface pollutants, such as leaking urban sewers or leachates derived from domestic landfill sites. Indeed encouragement has been given in places to discharge landfill leachates into old mine adits. At Cleland [797 598] disposal of organic effluent to an old mine working has been licensed for some years. Up to 770 m^3/d of effluent is discharged with a high biological oxygen demand and a pH which may range as high as 10. Exactly where this effluent goes and what happens to it underground is not known.

At the former British Steel Works at Ravenscraig just to the south of the district, licensed discharge of oil-rich, coke-oven effluent and pickling wastes to boreholes eventually emerged in the South Calder Water. The licence to discharge these wastes underground was revoked in 1983 with provision for emergency disposal only thereafter.

Landfill disposal of domestic, industrial and inert wastes is practised throughout the district. Exhausted opencast coal pits provide the main potential for landfill, although care is required in leachate disposal particularly where old adits exist and where secondary permeability has been enhanced by the action of past mining. Several serious leachate breakouts have occurred in the past, for example at Dalmacoulter [76 67] north of Airdrie where leachate emerged on the fifth tee of the Airdrie Golf Club during 1985. New landfill sites are now being engineered to a much higher standard utilising the containment principle.

Table 5 Groundwater quality (mg/l).

Source	NGR	Ph	Eh (mV)	Ca	Mg	Na	K	HCO_3	SO_4	Cl	NO_3-N	Fe	Mn
Netherfield[1]	618 647	6.3	− 4.0	107	55	31	12	634	186	42	0	1.6	0.6
Airdrie[1]	788 697	6.2	− 330	39	20	11	5	137	76	13	0	3.0	0.3
Kilsyth[2]	723 796	7.3	nd	nd	nd	8	8	90	14	12	0	nd	nd
Bellshill[3]	724 612	7.9	nd	157	107	80	18	nd	nd	nd	0	0.2	0.1
Lennoxtown[4]	638 793	nd	nd	36	7	7	1	120	5	7	2	0	0

1 minewater intercepted by borehole;
2 borehole in Limestone Coal Formation;
3 borehole in Upper and Middle Coal Measures;
4 spring from Clyde Plateau Volcanic Formation.

ELEVEN
Geophysical investigations

Evidence for the deeper geological structure of the Airdrie district is provided by interpretation of geophysical surveys. The most comprehensive sources of information are the Bouguer gravity and aeromagnetic anomaly data, but these may be complemented by seismic reflection and refraction surveys.

Bouguer gravity and aeromagnetic anomaly data for the district are shown as contour maps in Figures 25a, b. These are based on published 1:250 000 scale maps. Many of the anomalies extend beyond the margins of the district and have been examined during regional assessments of geophysical data for the Midland Valley (Davidson et al., 1984; Rollin, 1987; Evans et al., 1988). Some of the major geophysical features are summarised in Figure 26.

PHYSICAL PROPERTIES OF THE ROCKS

The physical properties of the main rock units based on sample measurements and shallow surveys are summarised in Table 6. Generally, density and velocity increase significantly with depth.

There are no local exposures of crystalline basement from which its properties can be determined, but it can be expected to have a significant contrast with the overlying Palaeozoic sequence. Above the basement the first principal density (and probably velocity) contrast is taken as being between Lower Palaeozoic and Lower Devonian rocks, the second between Lower Devonian rocks and the overlying Upper Devonian and Lower Carboniferous sedimentary rocks taken together. The Lower Carboniferous lavas of the Clyde Plateau Volcanic Formation also have a marked contrast with the underlying and overlying sedimentary sequences (Upper Devonian/Lower Carboniferous and Upper Carboniferous respectively). However, average values for the Devonian and Carboniferous successions are variable, depending particularly upon the poorly known proportions of igneous material present in the sequences, and also on the sandstone to mudstone ratios.

The magnetic properties and the palaeomagnetic significance of igneous rocks in the district and elsewhere in the Midland Valley have been the subject of many studies, which have concentrated on the Carboniferous and Permian igneous rocks. These rocks generally retain a reversed natural remanent magnetisation (NRM) with a declination of about 180° and inclinations varying between 0° and 30° (upwards). These inclinations are consistent with movement of the Midland Valley Terrane during Carboniferous times from low southerly latitudes to the equator. The intensity of the NRM is commonly greater than the induced magnetisation, suggesting that this could determine the form of any related magnetic anomalies. In a detailed study of the Lenzie–Torphichen dykes Powell (1963) described how the differing types of magnetisation, indicated by changes in the ratio of the remanent to the induced magnetisations, occur along

Table 6 Representative experimental physical properties of saturated rocks.

Formation	Saturated density, mg m^{-3}	Total magnetic intensity, A m^{-1}	P-wave velocity, km s^{-1}
Drift (clays and sands)	1.72–2.24	—	—
CARBONIFEROUS:			
Westphalian	2.50	—	2.0–4.5
Namurian	2.55	—	3.2–3.6
Dinantian	2.55	—	2.0–3.8
Clyde Plateau Volcanic Formation,	2.74	1.4–4.6	2.8–4.8
DEVONIAN:			
Upper Devonian	2.40	—	2.0–4.0
Lower Devonian { sedimentary rocks	2.60	—	3.0–4.0
{ lavas	2.66	1.0	4.0–6.0
LOWER PALAEOZOIC:			
Ordovician–Silurian	2.72	—	3.7–4.3
IGNEOUS INTRUSIONS:			
Late Carboniferous–Early Permian quartz-dolerite intrusions	2.80	1.0	5.6
Carboniferous and Permian alkali dolerite intrusion	2.83	1.0	6.0

Sedimentary rocks unless otherwise stated.
— = not determined. Principally after Bullerwell et al. *in* Anderson (1963); Busbridge (1968); Cotton (1968); Evans et al. (1988); Everitt (1961); Forster (1976); Goswami (1968); Hall (1970; 1974); McLean (1961); Milton (1972); Powell (1960; 1963); Rolph and Shaw (1985); Samsudin (1981); Smith (1968); Wattananikorn (1978); Xu (1984).

strike in the same intrusion. The sedimentary rocks in the district are essentially nonmagnetic.

GEOPHYSICAL SURVEYS

Gravity surveys

The regional gravity map of the district (Figure 25a) is based on data from BGS surveys with a distribution of about one station per two square kilometres. The Bouguer anomaly values were referred to the 1973 National Gravity Reference Net, calculated against the 1967 International Gravity Formula and reduced to sea level using a density of 2.70 Mg m^{-3} for the Bouguer correction.

The map is dominated by a Bouguer anomaly low in the southern part of the area, and two highs to the north and east (Figure 25a). The Hamilton Low corresponds to an area of Westphalian and older Carboniferous sedimentary rocks. The Waterhead Farm High in the northwest of the district occurs over lavas in the Campsie Fells. The eastern margin of the map is dominated by the flank of the large Bathgate gravity high which is centred east of the Airdrie district [944 730]. The source of the Bathgate gravity high (and the associated aeromagnetic high) is believed to be deep-seated.

Although the Waterhead Farm anomaly occurs over the Clyde Plateau Volcanic Formation, the thickness of the lavas in this area is insufficient to explain its amplitude. Gravity and magnetic interpretations suggest that this anomaly must be due partly to basic igneous rocks present beneath the lavas (Cotton, 1968; Evans et al., 1988). Evans et al. (1988) interpret the Waterhead Farm feature as

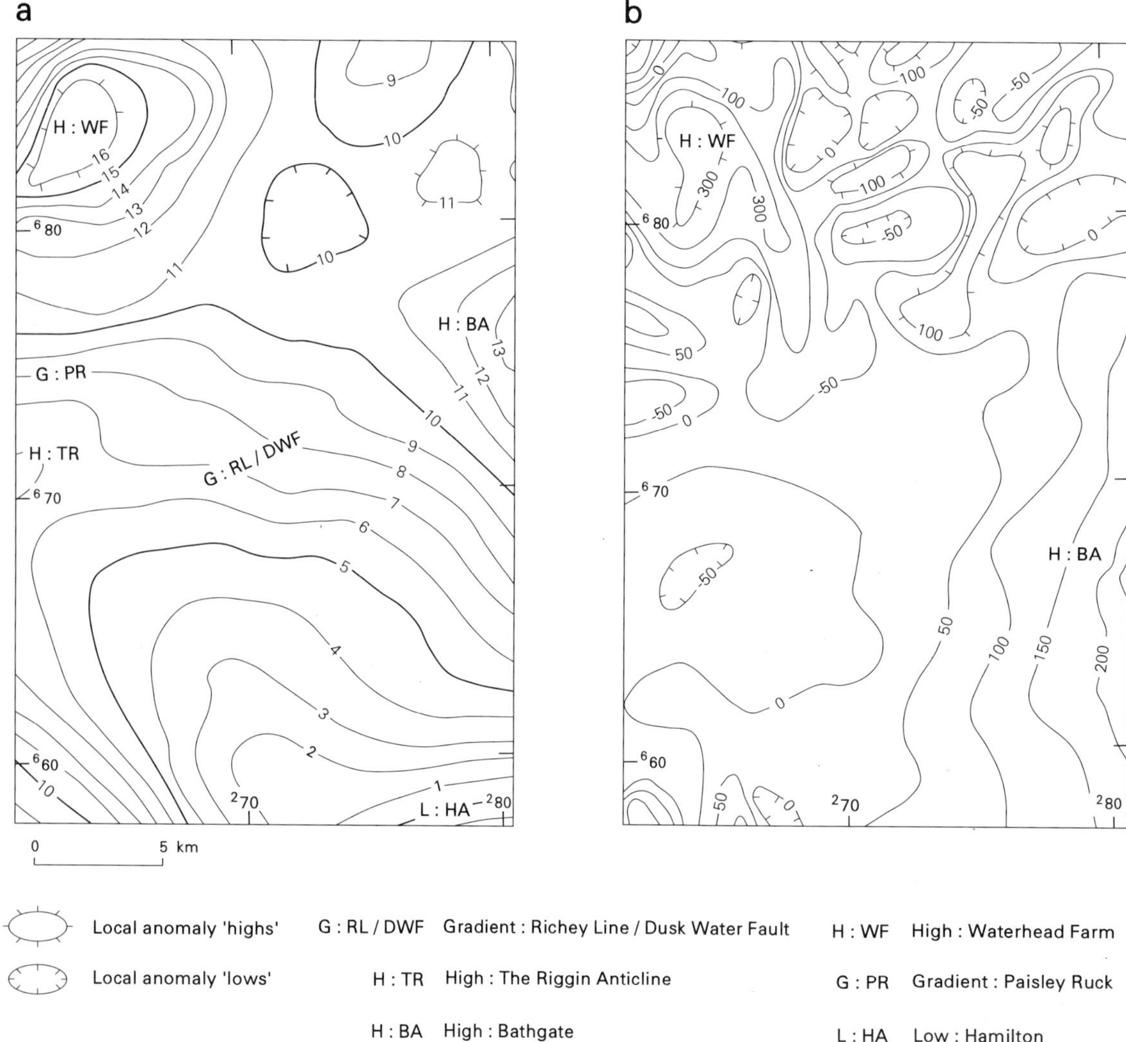

Figure 25 a. Bouguer gravity anomaly map of the Airdrie district, with contours at 1 mGal intervals. Density of 2.70 Mg m^{-3} used for the Bouguer correction.

b. Aeromagnetic total field anomaly map of the Airdrie district with contours generally at 50 nT intervals, otherwise 100 nT.

BA = Bathgate; DWF = Dusk Water Fault; G = Gradient; H = High; HA = Hamilton; L = Low; PR = Paisley Ruck; RL = Richey Line; RA = Riggin Anticline; WF = Waterhead Farm.

being due to about 600 m of Clyde Plateau Volcanic Formation (density 2.72 Mg m^{-3}, magnetisation 2.3 A m^{-1}) underlain by an about 1.8 km thick penecontemporaneous basic intrusion (2.82 Mg m^{-3}, about 1.2 A m^{-1}).

South of the Waterhead Farm High a gradient trends south-west from near Lennoxtown [686 764] towards the Paisley Ruck. Cotton (1968) inferred from the gradient that it marks a fault downthrowing the top of the Clyde Plateau Volcanic Formation and overlying sedimentary rocks about 140 m to the north-west. Its location suggests that the Paisley Ruck may continue north-east at depth to join the Campsie Fault and form the north-west boundary of a gravity high associated with the Riggin Anticline. Stedman (1988) suggested the latter may link with the Dusk Water Fault of Ayrshire. However, a weaker parallel gradient projecting from the Dusk Water Fault to near Cumbernauld [746 728] may mark the continuation of that fault across the district. This gradient coincides with the Richey Line (see Read, 1988), suggesting that this structure is the faulted south-east boundary of the Riggin Anticline and associated gravity high and that the Riggin Anticline is an upfaulted area lying between the extensions of the Dusk Water Fault (the Richey Line) and the Paisley Ruck.

Bouguer gravity anomaly values decrease southwards across the southerly downthrowing Campsie and Milngavie faults, reaching a minimum in the Hamilton Low, south of the Airdrie district (Figure 25a). Rollin (1987) and Evans et al. (1988) attribute this low to a 2.5 km-thick sequence of upper Palaeozoic rocks. This basin is defined to the west by the large Dechmont Fault (Figure 26), considered by Evans et al. (1988) on geophysical grounds to be one of the major basement structures in the Midland Valley. An alternative interpretation by Alomari (1980), discussed by Davidson et al. (1984), ascribes the Hamilton Low to a concealed granite or an 8 km-thick Lower Devonian basin.

Although the Bathgate gravity high, and its associated magnetic high, are centred outside the area of Figure 25a, their source has relevance in understanding the deep geology of the Airdrie district. The exposed Carboniferous igneous rocks in the area cannot account for the anomalies and therefore the source must underlie these rocks. There are two main current geophysical interpretations: 1) a shallow body with properties similar to those of the Clyde Plateau Volcanic Formation (believed to be present under the sedimentary cover) extending from their base (~ 2 km) to ~ 6 km deep (Shadid, 1970; Hossain, 1976; Powell, 1978; Alomari, 1980; Conway et al., 1987; Evans et al., 1988); 2) a deep body within the crystalline basement, extending from 8 to 17 km, with either the properties of an ultrabasic body (Hossain, 1976; Powell, 1970, 1975, 1978), or possibly a Caledonian granodiorite (Gunn, 1975). However, recent seismic refraction results have been interpreted in terms of crystalline basement across much of the Midland Valley at depths of only 3–6 km. To a depth of 12 km, the results show no velocity anomaly that could be associated with a possible causative body. Since the depth range from gravity and magnetic interpretations probably place the body near the top of the crystalline basement, that is above 12 km, its seismic properties appear to be indistinguishable from those of the basement (Davidson et al., 1984). The causative bodies in the above interpretations are generally regarded as intrusions of Carboniferous and/or Devonian age. However, Powell (1970; 1978) has also considered the possibility that dense magnetic Lewisian granulitic basement might be responsible for the Bathgate anomaly.

The minor Bouguer anomaly lows and highs occurring between the Bathgate and Waterhead Farm anomalies are probably due to thickness variations within the igneous rocks.

Magnetic surveys

The regional total field aeromagnetic map (Figure 25b) is based on data recorded at 305 m above ground level. Flights were made along east–west survey lines 2 km apart with north–south tie lines at a spacing of 10 km. A first order regional field has been removed from the observed data. The anomaly pattern comprises high-frequency, high-amplitude anomalies over the outcrop of the Clyde Plateau Volcanic Formation, and lower-frequency, low-amplitude anomalies over the areas of sedimentary rocks.

Regional magnetic studies suggest that the crystalline basement of the Midland Valley is of Lewisian type (Powell, 1970; 1978).

Many known dykes and sills intruded into the sedimentary rocks are not associated with marked aeromagnetic anomalies, showing that they have little volume or low magnetisation values. However, anomalies may not have been recorded effectively over the dykes because of the coincidence between their strike and the flight line direction. Ground level traverses across the approximately 30 m-wide, east–west, Late Carboniferous quartz-dolerite dykes yielded dipolar anomalies with amplitudes of 1000–5000 nT (Powell, 1963; Cotton, 1968; Maxwell, 1971). The forms of the anomalies generally indicated reversed total magnetisation, suggesting that their directions of NRM are closely grouped and consequently potentially reliable for making palaeogeographical inferences.

The lavas of the Clyde Plateau Volcanic Formation are associated with a dipolar anomaly at their boundary with the sedimentary rocks, with a trough to the north and peak to the south. This indicates that in bulk the lavas have a normal total magnetisation (McQuillin *in* Francis et al., 1970) and suggest that the NRM directions are highly scattered and consequently are probably less reliable than Carboniferous intrusions for making palaeogeographical deductions.

In those parts of the district where sedimentary rocks dominate at outcrop the magnetic anomalies have the appearance of being a smoothed version of those over the lavas. This suggests that the sedimentary rocks may be underlain by the Clyde Plateau Volcanic Formation.

Seismic surveys

The sonic velocity of the Clyde Plateau Volcanic Formation is generally so much higher than that of the

Figure 26 Main geophysical features and seismic lines in the Airdrie district and surrounding areas.

QB = Quarry blast, other abbreviations in Figure 25.

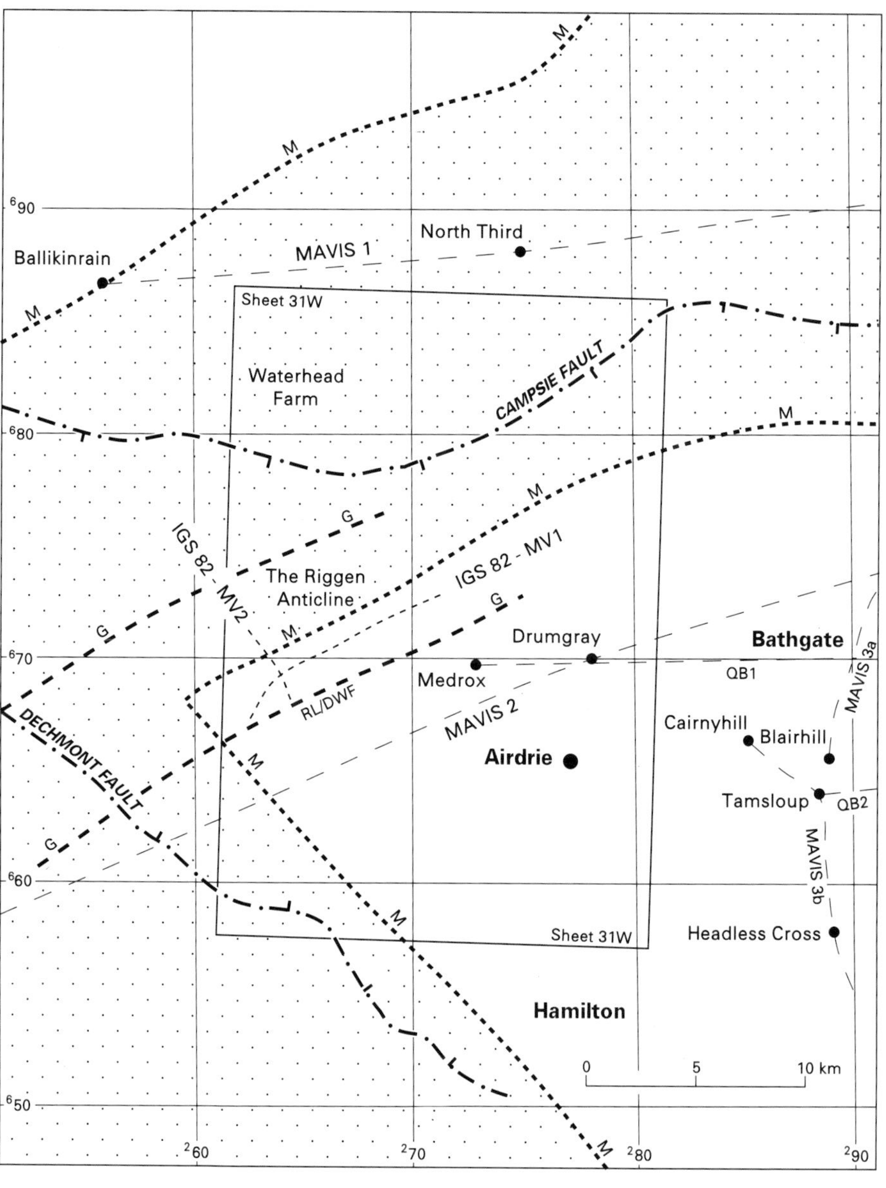

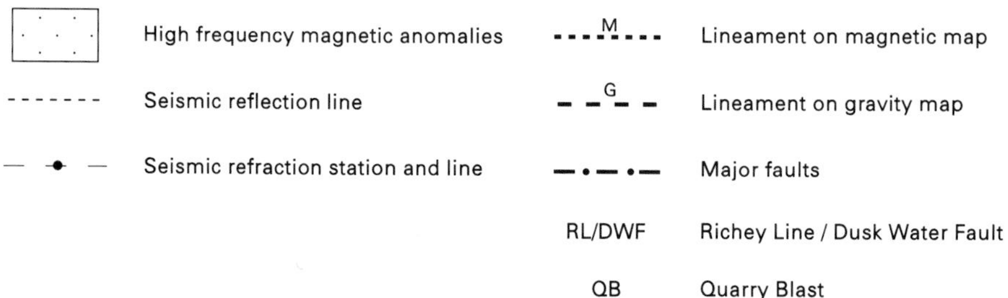

sedimentary rocks that its boundaries have high reflection coefficients, which prevents much energy from penetrating to greater depths. The usual velocity inversion at its base prevents detection of that surface in conventional refraction exploration.

Reflection surveys

A reflection survey in the region of the Geological Survey Rashiehill Borehole defined the top and bottom of the quartz-dolerite Torphichen Sill (Hall, 1971). The 800 m deep top of the underlying Clyde Plateau Volcanic Formation was also detected. The borehole proved at least 380 m of lavas but their base was not intersected. Hall (1971) suggested that a reflector occurring at 1.26 km was due to the base of the Clyde Plateau Volcanic Formation and that the lavas thin to the east.

The IGS82-MV1 and IGS82-MV2 lines (Figure 26) were recorded to 6 s two-way time (equivalent to 12–15 km depth) but showed coherent reflectors only in the upper 1 s (Penn et al., 1984). Among the reflectors were the top and bottom of about 600 m of the Clyde Plateau Volcanic Formation, showing an interval velocity of 4.2 km s^{-1} (Penn et al., 1984) and horizons in the Inverclyde Group and the Upper Devonian. The deepest identifiable reflector, at 1 s two-way time (2.05 km depth), was interpreted as the top of Lower Devonian and possibly older rocks.

Commercial seismic reflection surveys have been carried out in the district but the data are generally not available.

Refraction surveys

The deep structure of the Midland Valley has been investigated by several major refraction studies (Davidson et al., 1984; Conway et al., 1987; Dentith and Hall, 1989; 1990) including LISPB and LOWNET. Of these, only quarry blast Line 1 and MAVIS 2 occur in the district (Figure 26).

Four main refractors are generally recognised in the Midland Valley:

LAYER 1 0.5–3.0 km thick Carboniferous and Upper Devonian strata, (velocities in the range 3–5 km s^{-1}),

LAYER 2 1–5 km thick Lower Devonian and Lower Palaeozoic strata, (4.8–5.4 km s^{-1}),

LAYER 3 LISPB layer a 0, 3–4 km thick, top at 3–6 km, gneissose crystalline basement, (5.8–6.2 km s^{-1}),

LAYER 4 LISPB layer a1, top 7–9 km deep. An intrabasement refractor, possibly due to a downward increase in metamorphic grade from amphibole to pyroxene granulite facies, (6.4 km s^{-1}).

There is probably a décollement at the top of the basement and, locally, at least one higher level — in Layer 1 (Dentith and Hall, 1989; 1990). In the Airdrie district the tops of layers 2, 3 and 4 are at depths of about 2.0–2.5, 3.5–4.0, and 8.0 km respectively.

Resistivity surveys

Resistivity surveys have been used in the area in the search for abandoned coal workings (Jeffrey, 1969; Maxwell, 1971) and, in combination with seismic refraction surveys, for assessing rock masses for quarrying (Wattananikorn, 1978).

Geothermal surveys

The geothermal potential of Midland Valley is summarised in Browne et al. (1985, 1987), Downing and Gray (1986), Rollin (1987) and Evans et al. (1988). The average geothermal gradient is 22.5° C km^{-1} and the mean heat flow is 54.5 mW m^{-2}, but significantly higher values for both parameters also occur (Browne et al., 1987).

Only two formations above the basement possibly have geothermal potential as 'warm wet rock' (low enthalpy) sources: 1) sandstones of the Namurian Passage Formation, 2) sandstones at the top of the Devonian (Knox Pulpit Formation) and at the base of the Carboniferous (Kinnesswood Formation). In the Airdrie district both would be deepest in the south, where the former may reach a depth of at least 0.6 km (estimated temperature 20°C), and the latter 1.5 km (60–80°C). The Midland Valley appears generally unsuited for hot dry rock geothermal development (Evans et al., 1988), although concealed rocks in the Wishaw and Bathgate areas may have some potential.

REFERENCES

Most of the references listed below are held in the Libraries of the British Geological Survey at Edinburgh and Keyworth, Nottingham. Copies of the references can be purchased subject to the current copyright legislation.

ALOMARI, M I. 1980. Geological interpretations of the gravity field of the western Midland Valley of Scotland. Unpublished PhD thesis, University of Glasgow.

ANDERSON, F W. 1963. The Geological Survey Bore at Rashiehill, Stirlingshire (1951). *Bulletin of the Geological Survey of Great Britain*, No. 20, 43–106.

ANDREW, E M. 1978. Geothermal exploration in the Midland Valley of Scotland: some seismic reflection tests. *Report of the Applied Geophysics Unit, Institute of Geological Sciences*, No. 64.

ARMSTRONG, M, PATERSON, I B, and BROWNE, M A E. 1985. Geology of the Perth and Dundee district. *Memoir of the British Geological Survey*, Sheets 48W, 48E, 49 (Scotland).

BANHAM, P H. 1975. Glaciotectonic structures: a general discussion with particular reference to the contorted drift of Norfolk. 69–94 in *Ice ages: ancient and modern*. WRIGHT, A E, and MOSELEY, F (editors). (Liverpool: Seel House Press.)

BELL, D. 1874. On the aspects of Clydesdale during the Glacial Period. *Transactions of the Geological Society of Glasgow*, Vol. 4, 63–69.

BENNIE, J. 1894. On the occurrence of peat with arctic plants in boulder clay at Faskine, near Airdrie, Lanarkshire. *Transactions of the Geological Society of Glasgow*, Vol. 10, 148–152.

BISAT, W S. 1950. The junction faunas of the Visean and Namurian. *Transactions of the Leeds Geological Association*, Vol. 6, 151–181.

BLUCK, B J. 1978. Sedimentation in a late orogenic basin: the Old Red Sandstone of the Midland Valley of Scotland. 249–278 *in* Crustal evolution in northwestern Britain and adjacent regions. BOWES, D R, and LEAKE, B E (editors). *Special Issue of Geological Journal*, No. 10.

BOWEN, D Q. 1978. *Quaternary geology*. (Oxford: Pergamon.)

BRAND, P J. 1977. The fauna and distribution of the Queenslie Marine Band (Westphalian) in Scotland. *Report of the Institute of Geological Sciences*, No. 77/18.

— 1983. Stratigraphic palaeontology of the Westphalian of the Ayrshire Coalfield, Scotland. *Transactions of the Royal Society of Edinburgh, Earth Sciences*, Vol. 73, 173–180.

BROWNE, M A E. 1977. The sand and gravel resources of the Central Region, Scotland. *Report of the Institute of Geological Sciences*, No. 77/9.

— 1980a. Stratigraphy of the lower Calciferous Sandstone Measures in Fife. *Scottish Journal of Geology*, Vol. 16, 321–328.

— 1980b. Erskine Bridge. 10–13 in *Glasgow region: field guide*. JARDINE, W G (editor). (Quaternary Research Association.)

— 1985. Comments on the Quaternary deposits and landforms of Scotland and the neighbouring shelves: a review (by D G Sutherland). *Quaternary Science Reviews*, Vol. 4, I–III.

— 1986. The classification of the Lower Carboniferous in Fife and Lothian. *Scottish Journal of Geology*, Vol. 22, 422–425.

— GRAHAM, D K, and GREGORY, D M. 1984. Quaternary estuarine sediments in the Grangemouth area, Scotland. *British Geological Survey Report*, Vol. 16, No. 3.

— MCMILLAN, A A, and HALL, I H S. 1983a. Blocks of marine clay in till near Helensburgh, Strathclyde. *Scottish Journal of Geology*, Vol. 19, 321–325.

— — and GRAHAM, D K. 1983b. A late-Devensian marine and non-marine sequence near Dumbarton, Strathclyde. *Scottish Journal of Geology*, Vol. 19, 229–234.

— HARGREAVES, R L, and SMITH, I F. 1985. *The Upper Palaeozoic basins of the Midland Valley of Scotland. Investigation of the geothermal potential of the UK.* (Keyworth, Nottingham: British Geological Survey.)

— ROBINS, N S, EVANS, R B, MONRO, S K, ROBSON, P G, ELLIOT, R W, LAXTON, J L, ROLLIN, K E, and SMITH, E P. 1987. *The Upper Devonian and Carboniferous sandstones of the Midland Valley of Scotland. Investigation of the geothermal potential of the UK.* (Keyworth, Nottingham: British Geological Survey.)

— and MCMILLAN, A A. 1989a. Quaternary geology of the Clyde valley. *British Geological Survey Research Report*, SA/89/1.

— — 1989b. Geology for land use planning: Drift deposits of the Clyde valley. Volume 1 Planning report; Volume 2 Details of procedures and technical details; Volume 3 Thematic maps. *British Geological Survey Technical Report*, WA/89/78.

BUSBRIDGE, J R. 1968. In-situ geotechnical characteristics of glacial till in the Glasgow area. Unpublished MSc thesis, University of Strathclyde.

CAMERON, I B, FORSYTH, I H, HALL, I H S, and PEACOCK, J D. 1977. The sand and gravel resources of the Strathclyde Region, Scotland. *Report of the Institute of Geological Sciences*, No. 77/8.

CAMPBELL, D. 1988. Detecting the dangers. *Surveyor*, October 1988, 14–15.

CARRUTHERS, R G. 1907. Bellshill. 105 in *Summary of progress of the Geological Survey of Great Britain for 1906*.

CHEEL, R J, and RUST, B R. 1982. Coarse-grained facies of glacio-marine deposits near Ottawa, Canada. 279–294 in *Research in glacial, glacio-fluvial and glacio-lacustrine systems*. DAVIDSON-ARNOTT, R, NICKLING, W, and FAHEY, B D (editors). (Norwich: Geo Books.)

CHISHOLM, J I, MCADAM, A D, and BRAND, P J. 1989. Lithostratigraphic classification of Upper Devonian and Lower Carboniferous rocks in the Lothians. *British Geological Survey Technical Report*, WA/89/26.

CLARKE, W J. 1960. Scottish Carboniferous Conodonts. *Transactions of the Edinburgh Geological Society*, Vol. 18, 1–31.

CLOUGH, C T, WRIGHT, W B, and BAILEY, E B. 1908. Airdrie and Shotts District. 93–101 in *Summary of progress of the Geological Survey of Great Britain for 1907*.

— HINXMAN, L W, GRANT WILSON, J S, CRAMPTON, C B, WRIGHT, W B, BAILEY, E B, ANDERSON, E M, and CARRUTHERS, R G. 1911.

The geology of the Glasgow district. *Memoir of the Geological Survey of Great Britain*, Sheets (parts of) 30, 31, 22 and 23 (Scotland).

— WILSON, J S G, ANDERSON, E M, and MACGREGOR, M. 1920. The economic geology of the Central Coalfield of Scotland, description of area VII, Rutherglen, Hamilton and Wishaw. *Memoir of the Geological Survey of Scotland.*

— HINXMAN, L W, WRIGHT, W B, ANDERSON, E M, and CARRUTHERS, R G. 1926. The economic geology of the Central Coalfield of Scotland, description of area V, Glasgow East, Coatbridge and Airdrie. *Memoir of the Geological Survey of Scotland.*

CONWAY, A, DENTITH, M C, DOODY, J J, and HALL, J. 1987. Preliminary interpretation of upper crustal structure across the Midland Valley of Scotland from two east–west seismic refraction profiles. *Journal of the Geological Society of London*, Vol. 144, 867–870.

COOMBS, D S, and WILKINSON, J F G. 1969. Lineages and fractionation trends in undersaturated volcanic rocks from the East Otago volcanic province (New Zealand) and related rocks. *Journal of Petrology*, Vol. 10, 440–501.

COOPE, G R. 1962. *Coleoptera* from a peat interbedded between two boulder clays at Burnhead near Airdrie. *Transactions of the Geological Society of Glasgow*, Vol. 24, 279–286.

COTTON, W R. 1968. A geophysical survey of the Campsie and Kilpatrick Hills. Unpublished PhD thesis, University of Glasgow.

CRAIG, P M. 1980. The volcanic geology of the Campsie Fells area Stirlingshire. Unpublished PhD thesis, University of Lancaster.

— and HALL, I H S. 1975. The Lower Carboniferous rocks of the Campsie–Kilpatrick area. *Scottish Journal of Geology*, Vol. 11, 171–174.

CUMMINGS, R H. 1962. Note on the geology of the Ravenscraig district, Motherwell. *Transactions of the Geological Society of Glasgow*, Vol. 24, 8–13.

CURRIE, E D. 1954. Scottish Carboniferous Goniatites. *Transactions of the Royal Society of Edinburgh*, Vol. 62, 527–602.

DAVIDSON, K A S, SOLA, M A, POWELL, D W, and HALL, J. 1984. Geophysical model for the Midland Valley of Scotland. *Transactions of the Royal Society of Edinburgh, Earth Sciences*, Vol. 75, 175–181.

DE SOUZA, H A F. 1979. The geochronology of the Scottish Carboniferous Volcanism. Unpublished PhD thesis, University of Edinburgh.

DEEGAN, C E, KIRBY, R, RAE, I, and FLOYD, R. 1973. The superficial deposits of the Firth of Clyde and its sea lochs. *Report of the Institute of Geological Sciences*, 73/9.

DENTITH, M C, and HALL, J. 1989. MAVIS — an upper crustal seismic refraction experiment in the Midland Valley of Scotland. *Geophysical Journal International*, Vol. 99, 627–643.

— — 1990. MAVIS: geophysical constraints on the structure of the Carboniferous basin of West Lothian, Scotland. *Transactions of the Royal Society of Edinburgh, Earth Sciences*, Vol. 81, 117–126.

DEWEY, J F. 1982. Plate tectonics and the evolution of the British Isles. *Journal of Geological Sciences*, Vol. 139, 371–412.

DICKSON, J H, JARDINE, W G, and PRICE, R J. 1976. Three late-Devensian sites in West-central Scotland. *Nature, London*, Vol. 262, 43–44.

DINHAM, C H, and HALDANE, D. 1932. The economic geology of the Stirling and Clackmannan Coalfield. *Memoir of the Geological Survey of Great Britain.*

DOWNING, R A, and GRAY, D A (editors). 1986. *Geothermal energy — the potential in the United Kingdom.* (London: HMSO.)

DRON, R W. 1914. Notes on a buried river channel at Motherwell. *Transactions of the Geological Society of Glasgow*, Vol. 15, 1–3.

DUNLOP, J. 1888. Note on a section of Boulder Clay containing a bed of peat. *Transactions of the Geological Society of Glasgow*, Vol. 8, 312–315.

EVANS, C J, KIMBELL, G S, and ROLLIN, K E. 1988. *Hot dry rock potential in urban areas. Investigation of the geothermal potential of the UK.* (Keyworth, Nottingham: British Geological Survey.)

EVERITT, C W F. 1961. The magnetic properties of three Carboniferous sills. *Philosophical Magazine*, Vol. 6, 689–699.

FLETT, W R. 1927. Description of the sand deposits at Hungryside, Torrance. *Transactions of the Geological Society of Glasgow*, Vol. 17, 396–397.

FORSTER, A. 1976. Density, porosity determinations on fifty samples from the Clachie Bridge Borehole. *Geophysical Report of the Engineering Geology Unit, Institute of Geological Sciences*, Vol. 87 (unpublished).

FORSYTH, I H. 1961. The succession between Plean No.1 Limestone and No. 2 Marine Band in the Carboniferous of the east Glasgow area. *Transactions of the Geological Society of Glasgow*, Vol. 24, 213–234.

— 1978a. The Balmoral Coal of Coatbridge. *Bulletin of the Geological Survey of Great Britain*, No. 60, 9–16.

— 1978b. The Glenboig Marine Band in the Upper Limestone Group of the Namurian of central Scotland. *Bulletin of the Geological Survey of Great Britain*, No. 60, 17–22.

— 1978c. The lower part of the Limestone Coal Group in the Glasgow district. *Report of the Institute of Geological Sciences*, No. 78/29.

— 1979. The Lower Coal Measures of central Glasgow. *Report of the Institute of Geological Sciences*, No. 79/4.

— 1980. The Lingula bands in the upper part of the Limestone Coal Group (E_1 Stage of the Namurian) in the Glasgow district. *Report of the Institute of Geological Sciences*, No. 79/16.

— 1982. The stratigraphy of the Upper Limestone Group (E_1 and E_2 stages of the Namurian) in the Glasgow district. *Report of the Institute of Geological Sciences*, No. 82/4.

— 1993. The stratigraphy of the Central Coalfield of Scotland. *British Geological Survey Technical Report*, WA/93/51R.

— and BRAND, P J. 1986. Stratigraphy and stratigraphical palaeontology of Westphalian B and C in the Central Coalfield of Scotland. *Report of the British Geological Survey*, No. 18/4.

— and READ, W A. 1962. The correlation of the Limestone Coal Group above the Kilsyth Coking Coal in the Glasgow–Stirling region. *Bulletin of the Geological Survey of Great Britain*, No. 19, 29–52.

— and WILSON, R B. 1965. Recent sections in the Lower Carboniferous of the Glasgow area. *Bulletin of the Geological Survey of Great Britain*, No. 22, 65–79.

FRANCIS, E H, FORSYTH, I H, Read, W A, and ARMSTRONG, M. 1970. The geology of the Stirling district. *Memoir of the Geological Survey of Great Britain*, Sheet 39 (Scotland).

GALLOWAY, R W. 1961. Ice wedges and involutions in Scotland. *Biuletyn Peryglacjalny*, Vol. 10, 169–193.

GEIKIE, A. 1863. On the phenomena of the glacial drift of Scotland. *Transactions of the Geological Society of Glasgow*, Vol. 1, 58–65.

GEORGE, T N. 1974. Prologue to a geomorphology of Britain. *Institute of British Geographers Special Publication*, Vol. 7, 113–125.

— JOHNSON, G A L, MITCHELL, M, PRENTICE, J E, RAMSBOTTOM, W H C, SEVASTOPULO, G D, and WILSON, R B. 1976. A correlation of Dinantian rocks in the British Isles. *Special Report of the Geological Society of London*, No. 7.

GOSWAMI, G. 1968. A magnetic and chemical study of the titanium-bearing ore minerals of Carboniferous igneous rocks of the Midland Valley of Scotland. Unpublished PhD thesis, University of Glasgow.

GUNN, P J. 1975. Interpretation of the Bathgate magnetic anomaly, Midland Valley, Scotland. *Scottish Journal of Geology*, Vol. 11, 263–266.

HALL, J. 1970. The correlation of seismic velocities with formations in the south-west of Scotland. *Geophysical Prospecting*, Vol. 18, 134–148.

— 1971. A preliminary seismic survey adjacent to the Rashiehill borehole near Slamannan, Stirlingshire. *Scottish Journal of Geology*, Vol. 7, 170–174.

— 1974. A seismic reflection survey of the Clyde Plateau Lavas in North Ayrshire and Renfrewshire. *Scottish Journal of Geology*, Vol. 9, 253–279.

HALL, I H S, FORSYTH, I H, and BROWNE, M A E. In press. Geology of the Glasgow district. *Memoir of the British Geological Survey*, Sheet 30E (Scotland).

HASZELDINE, R S. 1988. Crustal lineaments in the British Isles: their relationship to Carboniferous basins. 53–68 in *Sedimentation in a synorogenic basin complex. The Upper Carboniferous of northwest Europe.* BESLEY, B M, and KELLING, G (editors). (Glasgow: Blackie and Son.)

HIGGINS, A C. 1975. Conodont zonation of the late Visean–early Westphalian strata of the south and central Pennines of northern England. *Bulletin of the Geological Survey of Great Britain*, Vol. 53.

— 1985. Chapter 6 in *A stratigraphical index of Conodonts.* HIGGINS, A C, and AUSTIN, R L (editors). (Chichester: Ellis Horwood for the British Micropalaeontological Society.)

HIGHLEY, D E. 1982. Fireclay. *Mineral Dossier Mineral Resources Consultative Committee*, No. 24.

HORNE, J, ROBERTSON, D, JAMIESON, T F, FRASER, J, KENDALL, P F, and BELL, D. 1894. Character of the high-level shell-bearing deposits at Clava, Chapelhall and other localities (Chapelhall section). *Report of the British Association for the Advancement of Science*, 307–315.

HOSSIAN, M M A. 1976. Analysis of the major gravity and magneticanomalies centred about Bathgate, central Scotland. Unpublished MSc thesis, University of Glasgow.

HUTTON, A N. 1965. Foraminifera of the Upper Limestone Group of the Scottish Carboniferous. Unpublished PhD thesis, University of Glasgow.

JARDINE, W G. 1977. The Quaternary marine record in southwest Scotland and the Scottish Hebrides. 99–118 in *The Quaternary history of the Irish Sea.* KIDSON, C, and TOOLEY, M J (editors). (Liverpool: Seel House Press.)

— (editor). 1980. *Glasgow region: field guide.* (Quaternary Research Association.)

— 1986. The geological and geomorphological setting of the estuary and Firth of Clyde. *Proceedings of the Royal Society of Edinburgh*, Vol. 90B, 25–41.

— DICKSON, J H, HAUGHTON, P D W, HARKNESS, D D, BOWEN, D Q, and SYKES, G A. 1988. A late Middle Devensian interstadial site at Sourlie, near Irvine, Strathclyde. *Scottish Journal of Geology*, Vol. 24, 288–295.

JEFFREY, B M. 1969. Resistivity interpretation techniques used in problems in civil and mining engineering. Unpublished MSc thesis, Strathclyde University.

KENNEDY, W Q. 1958. Tectonic evolution of the Midland Valley of Scotland. *Transactions of the Geological Society of Glasgow*, Vol. 23, 107–133.

LEEDER, H R. 1982. Upper Palaeozoic basins of the British Isles, Caledonian inheritance versus Hercynian plate marginal processes. *Journal of the Geological Society of London*, Vol. 139, 481–494.

— and McMAHON, A H. 1988. Upper Carboniferous (Silesian) basin subsidence in northern Britain. 43–52 in *Sedimentation in a synorogenic basin complex. The Upper Carboniferous of Northwest Europe.* BESLEY, B M, and KELLING, G (editors). (Glasgow: Blackie and Son.)

LINTON, D L. 1951. Problems of Scottish scenery. *Scottish Geographical Magazine*, Vol. 67, 65–85.

MACDONALD, J G. 1973. Carbon-dioxide metasomatism in the Campsie lavas. *Mineralogy Magazine*, Vol. 39, 119–121.

— and WHYTE, F. 1981. Petrochemical evidence for the genesis of a Lower Carboniferous transitional basaltic suite in the Midland Valley of Scotland. *Transactions of the Royal Society of Edinburgh: Earth Sciences*, Vol. 72, 75–88.

MACDONALD, R. 1975. Petrochemistry of the Early Carboniferous (Dinantian) lavas of Scotland. *Scottish Journal of Geology*, Vol. 11, 269–314.

— THOMAS, J E, and RIZZELLO, S A. 1977. Variations in basalt chemistry with time in the Midland Valley province during the Carboniferous and Permian. *Scottish Journal of Geology*, Vol. 13, 11–22.

MACGREGOR, A G. 1928. The classification of Scottish Carboniferous olivine-basalts and mugearites. *Transactions of the Geological Society of Glasgow*, Vol. 18, 324–360.

— 1960. Divisions of the Carboniferous in the Geological Survey Scottish Maps. *Bulletin of the Geological Survey of Great Britain*, No. 16, 127–130.

MACGREGOR, M. 1930. Scottish Carboniferous Stratigraphy: an introduction to the study of the Carboniferous rocks of Scotland. *Transactions of the Geological Society of Glasgow*, Vol. 18, 442–558.

— 1937. On a boring to prove the Limestone Coal Group near Hamilton, Lanarkshire. *Summary of progress of the Geological Survey of Great Britain for 1936*, Part 2, 62–74.

— DINHAM, C H, BAILEY, E B, and ANDERSON, E M. 1925. The geology of the Glasgow district (2nd edition). *Memoir of the Geological Survey of Great Britain.*

MACKIEWICZ, N E, POWELL, R D, CARLSON, P R, and MOLNIA, B F. 1984. Interlaminated ice-proximal glacimarine sediments in Muir Inlet, Alaska. *Marine Geology*, Vol. 57, 113–147.

McGOWN, A, and MILLER, D. 1984. Stratigraphy and properties of the Clyde alluvium. *Quarterly Journal of Engineering Geology*, Vol. 17, 243–258.

McLean, A C. 1961. Density measurements of rocks in south-west Scotland. *Proceedings of the Royal Society of Edinburgh*, Vol. 68B, 103–111.

McMillan, A A, and Browne, M A E. 1983. Glaciotectonic structures at Bellshill, East of Glasgow. *Quaternary Newsletter*, Vol. 40, 1–6.

— — 1989. Fold basins in Late-Devensian glacimarine sediments at Shieldhall, Glasgow. *Scottish Journal of Geology*, Vol. 25, 295–305.

Manson, W. 1957. On the occurrence of a marine band in the Anthraconaia modiolaris Zone of the Scottish Coal Measures. *Bulletin of the Geological Survey of Great Britain*, No. 12, 66–86.

Maxwell, G M. 1971. The geophysical investigation of sub-surface hazards due to abandoned coal-mines. Unpublished PhD thesis, University of Strathclyde.

Menzies, J. 1981. Investigations into the Quaternary deposits and bedrock topography of central Glasgow. *Scottish Journal of Geology*, Vol. 17, 155–168.

Milton, J J W. 1972. A palaeomagnetic study of Permian and Carboniferous rocks from the Midland Valley of Scotland. Unpublished MSc dissertation, University of Newcastle.

Monro, S K. 1982. Sedimentation, stratigraphy and tectonics in the Dalry Basin, Ayrshire. Unpublished PhD thesis, University of Edinburgh.

Mykura, W. 1960. The replacement of coal by limestone and the reddening of Coal Measures in the Ayrshire Coalfield. *Bulletin of the Geological Survey of Great Britain*, No. 16, 69–109.

— 1967. The Upper Carboniferous rocks of south-west Ayrshire. *Bulletin of the Geological Survey of Great Britain*, Vol. 26, 23–98.

Neves, R, Read, W A, and Wilson, R B. 1965. Note on recent spore and goniatite evidence from the Passage Group of the Scottish Upper Carboniferous succession. *Scottish Journal of Geology*, Vol. 1, 185–188.

— Guienn, K J, Clayton, G, Ioannides, N S, and Neville, R S W. 1972. A scheme of miospore zones for the British Dinantian. *Compte Rendu 7me. Congrès international de Stratigraphie et de Géologie du Carbonifère, Krefeld 1971.*

Nickless, E F P, Aitken, A M, and McMillan, A A. 1978. The sand and gravel resources of the country around Darvel, Strathclyde. Description of 1:25 000 Resource Sheets NS 53, 63 and 64. *Mineral Assessment Report of the Institute of Geological Sciences*, No. 35.

North American Commission on Stratigraphic Nomenclature. 1983. North American Stratigraphic Code. *American Association of Petroleum Geologists Bulletin*, Vol. 67, 841–875.

Owens, B, Neves, R, Guienn, K J, Marshall, D C F, Sabry, H M S Z, and Williams, J E. 1977. Palynological division of the Namurian of northern England. *Proceedings of the Yorkshire Geological Society*, Vol. 41, 381–398.

Paterson, I B, and Hall, I H S. 1986. Lithostratigraphy of the late Devonian and early Carboniferous rocks in the Midland Valley of Scotland. *Report of the British Geological Survey*, No. 18/3.

Peach, A M. 1909. Boulder distribution from Lennoxtown, Scotland. *Geological Magazine*, Vol. 46, 26–31.

Peacock, J D. 1971. Marine shell radiocarbon dates and the chronology of deglaciation in western Scotland. *Nature, London*, Vol. 230, 43–45.

— 1975. Scottish late and post-glacial marine deposits. 45–48 in *Quaternary studies in North East Scotland.* Gemmell, A M D (editor). (Aberdeen: University of Aberdeen.)

— 1981. Scottish Late-Glacial marine deposits and their environmental significance. 222–236 in *The Quaternary in Britain.* Neale, J, and Flenley, J (editors). (Oxford and New York: Pergamon Press.)

— Graham, D K, and Wilkinson, I P. 1978. Late-Glacial and post-Glacial marine environments at Ardyne, Scotland and their significance in the interpretation of the history of the Clyde sea area. *Report of the Institute of Geological Sciences*, 78/17.

Penn, I E, Smith, I F, and Holloway, S. 1984. *Interpretation of a deep seismic reflection profile in the Glasgow area. Investigation of the geothermal potential of the UK, British Geological Survey* (Unpublished).

Powell, D W. 1960. Stress-dependent magnetization in some quartz-dolerites. *Nature, London*, Vol. 187, 225.

— 1963. Significance of differences in magnetization along certain dolerite dykes. *Nature, London*, Vol. 199, 674–676.

— 1970. Magnetised rocks within the Lewisian of Western Scotland and under the Southern Uplands. *Scottish Journal of Geology*, Vol. 6, 353–369.

— 1975. Interpretation of the Bathgate magnetic anomaly, Midland Valley, Scotland. *Scottish Journal of Geology*, Vol. 11, 266.

— 1978. Gravity and magnetic anomalies attributable to basement sources under northern Britain. 107–114 *in* Crustal evolution in northwestern Britain and adjacent regions. Bowes, D R, and Leake, B E (editors). *Geological Journal Special Issue*, Vol. 10.

Price, R J. 1983. *Scotland's environment during the last 30 000 years.* (Edinburgh: Scottish Academic Press.)

Ramsbottom, W H C. 1977. Correlation of the Scottish Upper Limestone Group (Namurian) with that of the north of England. *Scottish Journal of Geology*, Vol. 13, 327–330.

— Calver, M A, Eagar, R M C, Hodson, F, Holliday, D W, Stubblefield, C J, and Wilson, R B. 1978. A correlation of Silesian rocks in the British Isles. *Special Report of the Geological Society of London*, No. 10.

Read, W A. 1969. Fluviatile deposits in Namurian rocks of central Scotland. *Geological Magazine*, Vol. 106, 331–347.

—1988. Controls on Silesian sedimentation in the Midland Valley of Scotland. 222–241 in *Sedimentation in a synorogenic basin complex: the Upper Carboniferous of Northwest Europe.* Besly, B M, and Kelling, G (editors). (Glasgow and London: Blackie.)

— 1989. The interplay of sedimentation, volcanicity and tectonics in the Passage Group (Arnsbergian, E_2 to Westphalian A) in the Midland Valley of Scotland. 143–152 *in* The role of tectonics in Devonian and Carboniferous sedimentation in the British Isles. Arthurton, R J, Gutteridge, P, and Nolan, S C (editors). *Occasional Publication of the Yorkshire Geological Society*, No. 6.

Robertson, T, and Haldane, D. 1937. The economic geology of the Central Coalfield of Scotland, Area I. Kilsyth and Kirkintilloch. *Memoir of the Geological Survey of Great Britain.*

Robins, N S. 1990. *Hydrogeology of Scotland.* (London: HMSO for the British Geological Survey.)

Rolfe, W D I. 1966. Woolly rhinoceros from the Scottish Pleistocene. *Scottish Journal of Geology*, Vol. 2, 253–258.

Rollin, K E. 1987. The geothermal environment in Scotland. *Modern Geology*, Vol. 11, 235–250.

ROLPH, T C, and SHAW, J. 1985. A new method of paleaeofield magnitude correction for thermally altered samples and its application to Lower Carboniferous lavas. *Geophysical Journal of the Royal Astronomical Society*, Vol. 80, 773–781.

ROSE, J. 1980. Geilston. 29–31 in *Glasgow region: field guide.* JARDINE, W G (editor). (Quaternary Research Association.)

— LOWE, J J, and SWITSUR, R. 1988. A radiocarbon date on plant detritus beneath till from the type area of the Loch Lomond Readvance. *Scottish Journal of Geology*, Vol. 24, 113–124.

RUSSELL, M J. 1971. North–south geofractures in Scotland and Ireland. *Scottish Journal of Geology*, Vol. 8, 75–84.

RUST, B R, and ROMANELLI, R. 1975. Late Quaternary subaqueous outwash deposits near Ottawa, Canada. 177–192 in *Glaciofluvial and glaciolacustrine sedimentation.* JOPLING, A V, and McDONALD, B S (editors). *SEPM Special Publication*, No. 23.

SAMSUDIN, A R. 1981. Palaeomagnetism and magnetic properties of Permo-Carboniferous quartz dolerite dykes of Scotland. Unpublished PhD thesis, University of Aberdeen

SAUNDERSON, H C. 1977. The sliding bed facies in esker sands and gravels: a criterion for full-pipe (tunnel) flow? *Sedimentology*, Vol. 24, 623–638.

SCOTT, A C, GALTER, J, and CLAYTON, G. 1984. Distribution of anatomically preserved floras in the Lower Carboniferous in Western Europe. *Transactions of the Royal Society of Edinburgh, Earth Sciences*, Vol. 75, 311–340.

SHADID, M Z. 1970. An interpretation of certain aeromagnetic anomalies in the Midland Valley of Scotland. Unpublished MSc thesis, University of Strathclyde.

SHAKESBY, R A. 1976. The Lennoxtown essexite erratics train, central Scotland. Unpublished PhD thesis, University of Edinburgh.

SIMPSON, J B. 1933. The late-glacial readvance moraines of the Highland border west of the River Tay. *Transactions of the Royal Society of Edinburgh*, Vol. 57, 633–645.

SISSONS, J B. 1966. Relative sea-level changes between 10 300 and 8 300 BP in part of the Carse of Stirling. *Transactions of the Institute of British Geographers*, Vol. 39, 19–29.

— 1969. Drift stratigraphy and buried morphological features in the Grangemouth-Falkirk-Airth area, central Scotland. *Transactions of the Institute of British Geographers*, Vol. 48, 19–50.

— 1976. *The geomorphology of the British Isles: Scotland.* (London: Methuen.)

— and BROOKS, C L. 1971. Dating of early postglacial land and sea level changes in the western Forth valley. *Nature Physical Sciences*, Vol. 234, 124–127.

SMEDLEY, P L. 1986. The relationship between calc-alkaline volcanism and within-plate continental rift volcanism: evidence from Scottish Palaeozoic lavas. *Earth and Planetary Science Letters*, Vol. 77, 113–128.

— 1988. Trace element and isotope variations in Scottish and Irish Dinantian volcanism: evidence for an OIB-like mantle source. *Journal of Petrology*, Vol. 29, 413–443.

SMITH, A H V, and BUTTERWORTH, M A. 1967. Miospores in the coal seams of the Carboniferous of Great Britain. *Special Papers in Palaeontology*, 1.

SMITH, J. 1862. *Researches in newer Pliocene and post-Tertiary geology.* (Glasgow: John Gray.)

SMITH, P J. 1968. Estimates of the Devonian geomagnetic field intensity in Scotland. *Professional Paper, US Geological Survey*, 575-D, D164–D168.

STEDMAN, C. 1988. Namurian E1 tectonics and sedimentation in the Midland Valley of Scotland: rifting versus strike-slip influence. 242–255 in *Sedimentation in a synorogenic basin complex: the Upper Carboniferous of Northwest Europe.* BESLY, B M, and KELLING, G (editors). (Glasgow and London: Blackie.)

SUTHERLAND, D G. 1981. The high-level marine shell beds of Scotland and the build-up of the last Scottish ice sheet. *Boreas*, Vol. 10, 247–254.

— 1984. The Quaternary deposits and landforms of Scotland and the neighbouring shelves: a review. *Quaternary Science Review*, Vol. 3, 157–254.

SWINTON, W E. 1927. Note on a rhinoceros bone from the glacial sands at Cadder. *Transactions of the Geological Society of Glasgow*, Vol. 17, 395.

WATTANANIKORN, K. 1978. The determination of the nature of the reserves of typical igneous intrusive rock quarries by both field and laboratory geophysical measurements. Unpublished PhD thesis, University of Strathclyde.

WHYTE, F, and MACDONALD, J G. 1974. Lower Carboniferous vulcanicity in the northern part of the Clyde plateau. *Scottish Journal of Geology*, Vol. 10, 187–198.

WILSON, R B. 1958. A revision of the Carboniferous lamellibranchs *Edmondia punctatella* (Jones) and '*Estheria*' *youngii* Jones. *Bulletin of the Geological Survey of Great Britain*, No. 15, 21–28.

— 1966. A study of the Neilson Shell Bed, a Scottish Lower Carboniferous marine shale. *Bulletin of the Geological Survey of Great Britain*, No. 24, 105–130.

— 1967. A study of some Namurian marine faunas of central Scotland. *Transactions of the Royal Society of Edinburgh*, Vol. 66, 445–490.

— 1989. A study of the Dinantian marine macrofossils of central Scotland. *Transactions of the Royal Society of Edinburgh, Earth Sciences*, Vol. 80, 91–126.

XU, T C. 1984. Palaeomagnetic studies of Upper Palaeozoic rocks in Scotland. Unpublished PhD thesis, University of Newcastle upon Tyne.

YOUNG, J. 1875. On a bed of fine-grained indurated sandstone, enclosing rolled pebbles of quartzite, interstratified with the traps of the Campsie Fells. *Transactions of the Geological Society of Glasgow*, Vol. 5, 51–54.

OPEN-FILE REPORTS

CAMERON, I B, FORSYTH, I H, McMILLAN, A A, and BALL, D F. 1986. Report accompanying the thematic geology maps of the Airdrie and Coatbridge district (NS 76). *British Geological Survey Open-file Report.*

DAVIES, A, McADAM, A D, McMILLAN, A A, and MONRO, S K. 1982. Planning for development: Hamilton Project. *Report* SL 82/3.

ELLIOT, R W. 1985. Central Scotland Mineral Portfolio: Resources of clay and mudstone for brickmaking. *Report* IM 84/2.

FORSYTH, I H. 1977. The solid geology of the Glasgow East-end Renewal Project. *Report* NL 77/1.

— 1977. The 'drift' geology of the Glasgow East-end Renewal Project. *Report* NL 77/2.

— BROWNE, M A E, and JONES, S M. 1982. Planning for development: Falkirk and Grangemouth Project. *Report* NL 82/3.

— and MCMILLAN, A A. 1983. Geological report on the Parkhead–Camlachie Study Area. *Report* NL 83/6.

— BROWNE, M A E, and BALL, D F. 1983. Account accompanying environmental geology maps of Glasgow (National Grid Sheet NS66). *Report* NL 83/1.

— PATERSON, I B, and HALL, I S H. 1985. Account accompanying environmental geology maps of Glasgow (parts of National Grid Sheets NS 55, 57 and 65). *Report* A3 85/2.

MERRITT, J W. 1985. Central Scotland Mineral Portfolio: Fireclay resources. *Report* A3 85/2.

— and ELLIOT, R W. 1985. Central Scotland Mineral Portfolio: hard rock aggregate resources. *Report* IM 84/2.

MONRO, S K. 1980. Scottish limestone resources — an appraisal. *Report* SL 80/8.

PATERSON, I B, and HALL, I H S. 1983. Planning for development: Wishaw Project. *Report* NL 83/7.

APPENDIX 1

List of BGS boreholes in the Airdrie district and adjacent areas that are cited in the text

Name	Accession number in BGS files	Grid reference
Solid		
Alexandra Parade	NS 66 NW/408	NS 6177 6566
Drumpark	NS 76 SW/232	NS 7055 6426
Hallside	NS 65 NE/66	NS 6694 5975
Clachie Bridge	NS 68 SW/1	NS 6447 8368
Tak-ma-doon	NS 78 SW/5	NS 7291 8053
Lawmuir	NS 57 SW/161,2	NS 5183 7310
Abronhill†	NS 77 NE/208	NS 7881 7564
Rashiehill‡	NS 87 SW/22	NS 8386 7301
Shettleston*	NS 66 SW/548	NS 6307 6414
Craighead*	NS 75 NW/86	NS 7008 5735
Drift		
Bellshill**	NS 76 SW/451	NS 7304 6161
Bothwell Park**	NS 75 NW/87	NS 7159 5956
Erskine Bridge**	NS 47 SE/18	NS 4634 7251
Bridgeton**	NS 66 SW/826	NS 6121 6367
Ross House**	NS 75 NW/88	NS 7390 5504

† Not published

‡ published in full, *Bulletin of the Geological Survey*, No. 20

* outline stratigraphy published in *BGS Report*, No.18/4

** Published in *British Geological Survey Research Report*, SA/89/1.

Preliminary logs of the other boreholes are published in *IGS Report*, Nos. 76/10; 77/10; 78/21; 79/12.

APPENDIX 2

1:10 000 maps (Solid)

The maps at 1:10 000 covering, wholly or in part, the solid rocks in 1:50 000 Sheet 31W are listed below with the names of the surveyors (I B Cameron, J I Chisholm, P M Craig, I H Forsyth, I H S Hall, D N Halley, S M Jones, A A McMillan, and W A Read) and the date of survey.

The maps are available for consultation in the British Geological Survey office, Murchison House, Edinburgh where photocopies can be purchased.

National Grid sheets

NS 65 NW	Craig and Forsyth	1968–80
NS 65 NE	Craig and Forsyth	1968–76
NS 66 NW	Forsyth	1953–54
NS 66 NE	Forsyth	1953–74
NS 66 SW	Forsyth	1954–76
NS 66 SE	Forsyth	1954–76
NS 67 NW	Craig and Forsyth	1953–72
NS 67 NE	Craig and Forsyth	1953–72
NS 67 SW	Forsyth	1953–75
NS 67 SE	Forsyth	1953–74
NS 68 NW	Craig	1971–72
NS 68 NE	Craig	1971
NS 68 SW	Craig	1970–72
NS 68 SE	Craig	1970–73
NS 75 NW	Forsyth and Halley	1979–85
NS 75 NE	Forsyth and Halley	1979–85
NS 76 NW	Forsyth	1969–75
NS 76 NE	McMillan	1985–88
NS 76 SW	Cameron	1985–86
NS 76 SE	Cameron	1985–86
NS 77 NW	Craig and Forsyth	1967–73
NS 77 NE	Forsyth	1969–77
NS 77 SW	Forsyth	1953–74
NS 77 SE	Forsyth and Chisholm	1969–77
NS 78 NW	Read	1953–61
NS 78 NE	Read	1953–61
NS 78 SW	Craig and Forsyth	1968–72
NS 78 SE	Read, Craig and Forsyth	1953–78
NS 85 NW	Hall and Forsyth	1982–85
NS 86 NW	Jones and Forsyth	1977–85
NS 86 SW	Jones and Forsyth	1977–85
NS 87 NW	Jones and Forsyth	1979–81
NS 87 SW	Jones and Forsyth	1978–84
NS 88 NW	Read	1952–54
NS 88 SW	Read and Forsyth	1952–81

APPENDIX 3

1:10 000 maps (Drift)

The maps at 1:10 000 covering, wholly or in part, the superficial deposits in 1:50 000 Sheet 31W are listed below with the names of the surveyors (A M Aitken, M A E Browne, P M Craig, I H Forsyth, D N Halley, S M Jones, A A McMillan, I B Paterson and W A Read) and the date of survey.

The maps are available for consultation in the British Geological Survey office, Murchison House, Edinburgh where photocopies can be purchased.

NS 65 NW	Browne, Craig and Forsyth	1968–80
NS 65 NE	Browne, Craig and Forsyth	1968–80
NS 66 NW	Browne and McMillan	1975–83
NS 66 NE	Browne and McMillan	1975–83
NS 66 SW	Forsyth, Browne and McMillan	1954–83
NS 66 SE	Forsyth, Browne and McMillan	1954–83
NS 67 NW	Forsyth and Craig	1953–72
NS 67 NE	Forsyth and Craig	1953–73
NS 67 SW	Forsyth and McMillan	1953–80
NS 67 SE	Forsyth	1953–68
NS 68 NW	Craig	1971–72
NS 68 NE	Craig	1971–72
NS 68 SW	Craig	1970–72
NS 68 SE	Craig	1970–73
NS 75 NW	Halley, Forsyth, Browne and McMillan	1975–87
NS 75 NE	Halley, Forsyth, Browne and McMillan	1975–87
NS 76 NW	Forsyth	1969–86
NS 76 NE	McMillan	1985–88
NS 76 SW	Browne, Cameron and Forsyth	1975–86
NS 76 SE	Cameron	1985–86
NS 77 NW	Forsyth and Craig	1967–73
NS 77 NE	Forsyth	1969–77
NS 77 SW	Forsyth	1953–74
NS 77 SE	Forsyth	1969–77
NS 78 NW	Read	1953–61
NS 78 NE	Read	1953–61
NS 78 SW	Forsyth and Craig	1968–72
NS 78 SE	Craig, Forsyth and Read	1953–78
NS 85 NW	Paterson	1988
NS 86 NW	Jones and Aitken	1989
NS 86 SW	Jones and Aitken	1978–89
NS 87 NW	Jones and Aitken	1978–89
NS 87 SW	Jones and Aitken	1978–89
NS 88 NW	Read	1952–54
NS 88 SW	Browne, Jones and Aitken	1982–89

APPENDIX 4

List of Geological Survey photographs

Copies of these photographs are deposited for public reference in the Library of the British Geological Survey, Murchison House, West Mains Road, Edinburgh, EH9 3LA. The photographs belong to the Series C and D as indicated. Prints are available on application.

C2864–5 Stoop workings and old shaft in Splint Coal (Middle Coal Measures) in opencast site at Mossend.
C2866–8 Normal fault cutting Middle Coal Measures strata in opencast site at Mossend.
C3063 Loch in hollow enclosed by till, Loch Coulter, near Stirling.
C4032–5 Incompetent structures affecting Pyotshaw and Main coals (Middle Coal Measures) in opencast site at Holytown.
C4036–7 General view of working in opencast site at Holytown.
C4038 Pillar and collapsed stoop in Splint Coal in opencast site at Holytown.
C4077–8 Glacilacustrine deltaic sands of the Ross Formation, Bishopbriggs No. 2 Pit.
C4079–80 Glacial overflow channels near Kirkintilloch.
C4083 Quarry in east–west quartz-dolerite dyke, near Auchinairn.
C4084 Calmy Limestone and Blaes cut by quartz-dolerite dyke, near Chryston.
C4085–6 Sand of the Ross Formation overlying the Wilderness Till Formation which in turn overlies sand and gravel of the Cadder Formation, Bishopbriggs No. 1 Pit.
C4089–90 Sandstone cast of Lepidodendron, Kilsyth.
C4225 Lens of baked sediment in teschenite sill, quarry at Queenslie Bridge, Lanark.
C4226 Alternating bands of fine- and coarse-grained varieties of teschenite sill, quarry at Queenslie Bridge, Lanark.
C4227–8 General view of quarry in teschenite sill, Queenslie Bridge, Lanark.
C4229 General view of quarry in teschenite sill, Cardowan.
C4230–1 Glacial sand and gravel of the Broomhouse Formation, Broomhouse Pit, Lanark.
C4232–5 Laminated silt and sand of the Paisley Formation showing folding and small-scale thrust faulting, Foxley Pit, Lanark.
C4236–7 Folded beds of laminated silt and sand of the Paisley Formation on sand and gravel of the Broomhouse Formation, Greenoakhill Pit, Lanark.
C4238 Sand and gravel with lenses of coal fragments, Broomhill Formation, Greenoakhill Pit, Lanark.
C4239 General view of workings, Greenoakhill Pit, Lanark.
D836 North escarpment of the Campsie Hills showing trap features of the Clyde Plateau Volcanic Formation.
D1867–8 Accessory agglomerate forming part of a tephra cone in or close to a vent, Gonachan Glen near Fintry.
D1869 Accessory agglomerate cut by an irregular sheet of intrusive basalt with a chilled margin, Gonachan Glen near Fintry.
D2672 Dip slope of Clyde Plateau Volcanic Formation with morainic drift in foreground, Cringate Muir, Gargunnock Hills.
D4858–61 South scarp of the Campsie Fells showing trap features of the Clyde Plateau Volcanic Formation, near Lennoxtown.
D4862–3 Tephra cone developed on early lavas of the Clyde Plateau Volcanic Formation, Meikle Bin.
D4864–5 Upward-coarsening sequences in lower part of the Limestone Coal Formation, Corrie near Queenzieburn.
D4866–8 Columnar jointing in quartz-dolerite sill, Croy Quarry, Kilsyth.
D4869 Mudstone sequence with thin ironstone bands occurring above the Calmy Limestone (Upper Limestone Formation), Luggiebank Quarry, near Cumbernauld.
D4870 Sandstones of the Middle Coal Measures showing large-scale cross-bedding, Cambuslang.
D4871 Bothwell Castle built of reddened Upper Coal Measure sandstone on outcrop of same rock, Bothwell.
D4872 Reddened, cross-bedded Upper Coal Measure sandstone, Bothwell.

FOSSIL INDEX

To satisfy the rules and recommendations of the international codes of botanical and zoological nomenclature, authors of cited species are included in the index.

GENERAL INDEX

BRITISH GEOLOGICAL SURVEY

Keyworth, Nottingham NG12 5GG
0115-936 3100

Murchison House, West Mains Road, Edinburgh
EH9 3LA 0131-667 1000

London Information Office, Natural History Museum
Earth Galleries, Exhibition Road, London SW7 2DE
0171-589 4090

The full range of Survey publications is available through the Sales Desks at Keyworth and at Murchison House, Edinburgh, and in the BGS London Information Office in the Natural History Museum (Earth Galleries). The adjacent bookshop stocks the more popular books for sale over the counter. Most BGS books and reports can be bought from HMSO and through HMSO agents and retailers. Maps are listed in the BGS Map Catalogue, and can be bought together with books and reports through BGS-approved stockists and agents as well as direct from BGS.

The British Geological Survey carries out the geological survey of Great Britain and Northern Ireland (the latter as an agency service for the government of Northern Ireland), and of the surrounding continental shelf, as well as its basic research projects. It also undertakes programmes of British technical aid in geology in developing countries as arranged by the Overseas Development Administration.

The British Geological Survey is a component body of the Natural Environment Research Council.

HMSO publications are available from:

HMSO Publications Centre
(Mail, fax and telephone orders only)
PO Box 276, London SW8 5DT
Telephone orders 0171-873 9090
General enquiries 0171-873 0011
Queuing system in operation for both numbers
Fax orders 0171-873 8200

HMSO Bookshops
49 High Holborn, London WC1V 6HB
(counter service only)
0171-873 0011 Fax 0171-831 1326
68–69 Bull Street, Birmingham B4 6AD
0121-236 9696 Fax 0121-236 9699
33 Wine Street, Bristol BS1 2BQ
0117-9264306 Fax 0117-9294515
9 Princess Street, Manchester M60 8AS
0161-834 7201 Fax 0161-833 0634
16 Arthur Street, Belfast BT1 4GD
01232-238451 Fax 01232-235401
71 Lothian Road, Edinburgh EH3 9AZ
0131-228 4181 Fax 0131-229 2734
HMSO Oriel Bookshop,
The Friary, Cardiff CF1 4AA
01222-395548 Fax 01222-384347

HMSO's Accredited Agents
(see Yellow Pages)

And through good booksellers